KU-661-735

The Government of
GREAT BRITAIN

The Government of
GREAT BRITAIN

THIRD EDITION

Graeme C. Moodie

UNIVERSITY OF YORK

METHUEN & CO. LTD
11 NEW FETTER LANE   LONDON EC4

First published in Great Britain
(U.S.A. second edition) 1964
Reprinted twice
SBN 416 23150 0

First published as a University Paperback 1964
Reprinted four times
SBN 416 68580 3

Third edition 1971
SBN 416 61010 2 Hardback
SBN 416 61020 x Paperback

© *1971 Thomas Y. Crowell Company, Inc*

This title is available in both hard and paperback editions. The paperback edition is sold subject to the condition that it shall not, by way of trade or otherwise be lent, re-sold, hired out or otherwise circulated without the publisher's prior consent in any form of binding or cover other than that in which it is published and without a similar condition including this condition being imposed on the subsequent purchaser.

Printed Offset Litho and bound in Great Britain by Cox & Wyman Ltd, Fakenham, Norfolk

EDITOR'S FOREWORD

In our time the study of comparative government constitutes one of many fields or specialties in political science. But it is worth recalling that the most distinguished political scientists of the ancient world would have had difficulty recognizing the present-day distinction between the study of comparative government and study in other subject areas of the discipline. Think of Plato, for example, whose works abound in references to the political systems of his own and earlier days. Or consider Aristotle, whose *Politics* and related writings were based on an examination of more than one hundred constitutions. Twenty centuries after Aristotle the comparative emphasis continued to be strong in the work of Montesquieu and Rousseau, among others. In the nineteenth century the comparative tradition entered a period of decline, but there are signs that the merits of comparative political analysis are once again gaining recognition. At many colleges and universities, the introductory course in political science is no longer focused exclusively on American government. The comparative approach—in politics, in law, in administration—is becoming increasingly important in the political science curriculum.

This book, one of a series, is designed to reflect that approach without, however, marking a sharp departure from the substance and method of most comparative government courses. Thus most of the books in the series deal with one national government. Several volumes, however, deal with more than one government, and the approach of the entire series is distinctly comparative in at least two senses. In the first place, almost all of the books include material descriptive of other political systems, especially that of the United States. In addition, the books follow a common outline, so far as possible, that is designed to promote comparative treatment. Of course, there is nothing to keep the instructor or student from treating a particular governmental system in isolation, if he chooses to do so. On the other hand, his approach to political institutions and functions can be as comparative as he wishes.

A further advantage of this series is that each volume has been written by a distinguished scholar and authority in the field; each author is personally and professionally familiar with the political system he treats. Finally, the separate books make it possible for the instructor to design his course in accordance with his own interest or the interests of his students. One book may be substituted for another and any book may be put aside for one semester without affecting the others. The books, in short, unlike most one-volume texts, give the instructor maximum freedom in organizing his course. This freedom will be virtually unlimited as the forthcoming titles in this series complete a survey of representative governments of the world.

But to return to Aristotle once again, it remains true that the best judges of the feast are not the cooks but the guests. I have tried to indicate why, in my view, the recipe for the series is a good one. Let all those who teach comparative government, and all those who take courses in that field, proceed to judge the books for themselves.

ARNOLD A. ROGOW

PREFACE

This book is not another conducted tour around the intricacies of British constitutional law nor another tourist's guide to the picturesque political legacies of a glorious past. It is, however, another introduction to British government and politics. Some explanation should therefore be offered of why it has been written and of the ways in which I hope it does more (or less) than merely duplicate the work of others.

To begin with, it has been written as part of a series of books on different countries so organized as to lend themselves particularly to comparative study. But it is also meant to be a self-contained introduction to government and politics in Britain.

As such its guiding principle has been to try to put forward—so far as is possible in a restricted space—the information necessary to understand what British politics is about as well as how the system works. For this reason more attention has been given to the economic and social context than is customary in textbooks on the British constitution. This is not, therefore, merely an account of formal institutions and constitutional rules, but a book about the organization and functioning of government in British society.

Of necessity it includes an account of the structure of government, but it is an account that attempts to depict something of the dynamics of its construction as well as its form. Considerable attention is paid to the role of ordinary members of Parliament, the nature of party discipline, and the actual operation of the rules about ministerial responsibility. In some respects, the treatment given to these topics also departs from the traditional story.

I hope that this book will be found useful in introductory courses of different kinds. It is, obviously, a configurative study, yet one intended to play a part in comparative government. Its framework is largely institutional, but I have tried not to neglect approaches centered on decision-taking or on theories of group interaction. It is, however, very definitely an *introduction* to its subject and is therefore not directly usable in purely functional comparative analyses (although I hope nothing here will have to be unlearned by anyone who might wish to proceed to that level of sophistication). For the same reason I have tried to give the maximum amount of information compatible with readability and, the final chapter excepted, to limit evaluation and the more speculative kind of interpretation to the minimum compatible with an understanding of the system.

A brief account must inevitably amount to a personal interpretation that reflects the opinions, interests, and prejudices of its author. The reader should therefore be given some advance indication of my preconceptions. Broadly speaking, they are radical and libertarian. I was a Labour candidate at the 1959 general election in what is still a fairly safe Conservative constituency.

For their help in eliminating at least some of the errors and obscurities of the original draft, I wish to thank Professor D. D. Raphael of Glasgow University and Dr. Geoffrey Marshall, Fellow of the Queen's College, Oxford, who read the entire manuscript, and Dr. Alfred Brown, Mr. Farquhar Gillanders, and Dr. Gustav Jahoda, all of Glasgow University, who read parts of it. For those shortcomings that remain, as well as for the general interpretation and approach, I must accept full responsibility.

My principal debt of gratitude, however, is to my family, and especially to my wife. But for their affectionate encouragement and forbearance it is doubtful whether I could have found the time or the peace necessary to write this book. To them, therefore, I dedicate it.

G.C.M.
GLASGOW, SCOTLAND
JUNE 1961

PREFACE TO THE THIRD EDITION

In the nine years since the last edition of this book many changes have taken place in British government—even apart from the influence of a Labour government of 1964–70. In addition, much new research has been published, especially about the behavior of voters and the other major political actors. I have tried to do justice to both kinds of development within the limits imposed by space and by the fact that this is still intended to be an introductory book. The revisions of detail and, in places, of interpretation, have therefore been extensive. Some entire chapters and parts of most chapters, have been completely rewritten, while the basic information has been updated, so far as is possible, to the Conservative party's return to power in June 1970.

The balance and focus of the book have not been changed. They still reflect the author's view of the primary concern of the empirical study of politics. It is to understand who decides what, how it is decided, what constraints are imposed on the decision-maker, and what particular set(s) of circumstances must be present for a decision to be made. Even (or particularly) to begin to gain such an understanding it is essential to know the basic, formal structures and processes of government. But it is also essential not to stop there: one must try to locate those structures and processes in their social, economic, and cultural context. The difficult and really interesting problem for the student of politics is to see how these two sets of factors interact (which is why one must eschew dogmatic allegiance to either an "old-fashioned" institutional or an "avant-garde" behavioral approach). I hope, all the same, that the book may be of some use to those with different perspectives and that it contains sufficient "hard" information for the reader to be able to criticize the author's own judgments and interpretations.

I wish to record my gratitude to the authors and publishers concerned for permission to adapt material from D. E. Butler and A. King, *The British General Election of 1966* (London: Macmillan, 1966), pp. 208–9, for the tables on pp. 140 and 141 of this text, and R. K. Kelsall, *Report on an Inquiry into Applications for Admission to Universities* (London: Association of Universities of the British Commonwealth for the Committee of Vice-Chancellors and Principals of the Universities of the United Kingdom, 1957), p. 10, for the table on p. 51 of this text.

I also wish to thank my colleagues at the University of York for giving me a period of leave in which I could (among other things) prepare this new edition, and the publishers for the translation, where it was needed, from English into American.

G.C.M.
YORK, ENGLAND
JULY 1970

CONTENTS

xi

1

Background

The continuity of its constitutional tradition is a distinctive feature of British political life.[1] English history over the past thousand years has often been bloody and violent, but it has been singularly lacking in drastic and lasting constitutional upheavals. England has not been successfully invaded and occupied by a foreign power since the Norman Conquest in 1066, nor has its form of government been changed by warlike means since the mid-seventeenth century. Moreover, these events introduced no lasting constitutional breaks and dramatic fresh beginnings comparable to those associated with the French, Russian, or even American revolutions. The direct ancestry of today's monarchy, ministers, Houses of Parliament, and judicial system can therefore be traced back as far as medieval, if not (as was once taught) Anglo-Saxon, England. Nevertheless, none of these institutions have become frozen in "Anglo-Saxon," or "stained-glass," attitudes. On the contrary: such continuity is possible only for a system that is consistently adaptable. Admittedly, much of Britain's constitutional law is antique, perhaps even antiquated, but the political and constitutional powers, status, and relationships of the major institutions of government have been and still are subject to continuous development and change.

[1] The tradition itself, however, is primarily English rather than British, as the Irish, Scottish, and Welsh components of the United Kingdom have contributed little, constitutionally speaking, to the present system of government. See Note at the end of the chapter.

One result of this process is that the task of describing the British system of government presents certain peculiar difficulties. There is no one constitutional document corresponding to the American Constitution that can provide the student with a reliable outline in the form of a central corpus of constitutional rules. Acts of Parliament, of course, contain important constitutional rules in some areas. Judicial decisions help complete the picture, but to nothing like the extent that Supreme Court decisions do in the United States. Like a three-color reproduction from which one of the colors has been left out by the printer, any picture of British government remains grossly misleading if it does not include the nonlegal rules of the constitution. These binding "usages," as they are normally labeled in the United States, are referred to in Britain as the "conventions" of the constitution. There may be no simple or decisive way in which to determine the precise content of the conventions or how exactly they apply to particular situations. Yet they form a more extensive and fundamental part of the British constitution than, for example, the conventions of the American Constitution. This means that any description of the British political system, particularly a brief one, will inevitably be a personal interpretation in respect both to the choice of rules to be included and to the way in which they are stated.[2]

Another result of the process of change and continuity is that it is impossible to introduce British government without saying something about its history. It is equally impossible to survey the whole of that history here. Instead, it is proposed merely to pick out certain themes and events that seem particularly important for understanding the modern scene.

The death of Queen Elizabeth I in 1603 may arbitrarily be viewed as a watershed in British history. It marked the end of the so-called despotism of the Tudor dynasty, which began with the accession of Henry VII in 1485. The hundred-year rule of the Tudors comprised a high point of monarchical power. Before

[2] For a more comprehensive treatment of this and other difficulties involved in describing the British constitution, see G. Marshall and G. C. Moodie, *Some Problems of the Constitution,* 4th ed. (London: Hutchinson, 1967), especially Chapters 1 and 2.

them, the principal theme of constitutional history is perhaps the development of the power of the central administration as represented by the monarch and his servants. The Tudors were followed immediately by almost a century of constitutional struggle and unrest. Thereafter, it may be said, the story is of the way in which the powers of the crown were brought increasingly under the control of other elements within the constitution. With Parliament and the courts acting as the spearheads in the struggle, the task was accomplished not so much by limiting or abolishing those powers as by transferring the right to exercise them from the person of the monarch to the collectivity of the cabinet. Today, indeed, "the crown" normally denotes the cabinet and other ministers drawn from the leaders of the political party or parties that control a majority of seats in the popularly elected chamber of Parliament, the House of Commons. The cabinet itself, it might be added, is an entity almost entirely unknown to the law.

In the reigns of the Tudor monarchs, too, may be seen both the flowering of the medieval system of government and the secure foundations of much of the modern. The actual instruments of Tudor rule existed before them, if used less competently and under different circumstances. The distinguishing feature of their "despotism" lay in the energy and efficiency with which they pursued their aims rather than in any radical constitutional innovation. Yet changing conditions and the nature of their purposes helped create the bases for the successful resistance to and final defeat of greater (and less wise) royal pretensions under the Stuarts in the seventeenth century.

Government was financed basically by revenues obtained from the extensive properties owned by the crown, by customs duties, and by judicial fines. The Tudors made sure that these sufficed for all normal purposes by good management of their own estates and of the nation's affairs. They ran both private and public affairs through their own servants and advisers, but the household and public servants came increasingly to be distinguished from each other. The latter, moreover, soon became the instruments of the Tudors' own executive will. The king's council, the principal center of royal decision-making in all fields of government, came to consist of men chosen for their ability and loyalty to the throne rather than of the powerful, landed nobility. In its nucleus, the holders of the great offices of state, may be seen the direct ancestors of modern ministers and cabinet.

Royal rule was maintained largely through the judges appointed by the crown to the central common-law courts and to the regional assize courts. One of their most important duties was to supervise the work of the unpaid justices of the peace, who were then, as they remained into the nineteenth century, the principal figures in local administration. The energetic and efficient use of these institutions made it clear that "government is the king's business" and that no opposition would be allowed to flourish, whether from peasants protesting violently against economic conditions, aristocrats and pretenders plotting to seize the throne, or from Catholics at home and abroad. The peasants were revolting against the impoverishment that resulted from the private enclosure of common land, the beginnings of capital accumulation required to finance expanding commerce, and inflation. The aristocratic plots were largely the aftermath of a century of conflict between contending magnates, centering on the rival ambitions of the great houses of York and Lancaster. This "War of the Roses" [3] had, however, weakened and discredited the noble families concerned, allowing the Tudors to confine their governmental role largely to membership of the House of Lords (the Upper House of Parliament). The Tudors thus finally established the supremacy of the crown over one of its traditional rivals for power, the great aristocratic landowners. The landed magnates continued to exert preponderant influence upon government for another two centuries and more, but no longer as king-makers, and they had increasingly to share their influence with others.

The other great power of medieval times was the Church. The Tudor breach with the Papacy under Henry VIII leading to the confiscation of church property and the establishment, in place of the old Catholic Church, of the reformed Church of England

[3] So called because of the white and red roses that were the emblems of York and Lancaster respectively.

(of which the monarch is still the temporal head), led to a continuous threat of Catholic conspiracy and invasion. But it marked the supremacy of the crown in ecclesiastical as well as lay matters. It was these measures—the actions necessary to suppress the consequent unrest and the wide discretion exercised by the king's council—that earned the Tudors the title of "despots."

Tudor power, great though it was or became, was yet bridled. It was comparable neither with that of modern despotisms nor even, at least in its aims and procedures, with that of other contemporary European monarchs. It is significant, for example, that the same period saw the development of greater security of tenure for the royal judges and the growing prestige and independence of the legal profession as a whole, both of which were vitally important in the later struggles against royal power. Nor was the crown, even by itself, considered to be above and beyond the law. The law was supreme. And within the legal system, supremacy lay with statute law, which was made by the king in Parliament. Although the supremacy of statute law antedates the Tudors, the power of Parliament continued to grow during their "despotism."

Technically Parliament means the coming together of crown, lords (both lay and ecclesiastical), and Commons; any resulting legislation is enacted, in the words of the established formula, "by the King's most Excellent Majesty, by and with the advice and consent of the Lords Spiritual and Temporal, and Commons, in this present Parliament assembled, and by the authority of the same." More popularly, however, Parliament is taken to mean only the two Houses of Parliament. It is thus that the word is used when one talks of the increasing influence of Parliament under the Tudors. Such references call particular attention to the increasing importance of the Commons, that is, of the local communities (commonalities) that were represented in Parliament by two knights elected from each shire and two burgesses elected from each borough. It must also be remembered that the landed magnates were forced more and more to exercise their power through the Upper House rather than directly through the crown.

Parliaments were summoned and dismissed by the monarch

only when he felt it desirable or necessary. Most commonly and most fundamentally it was the royal need for more money that prompted a summons. (Since the fourteenth century new financial burdens had come to be imposed on the people only with the assent of their representatives in Parliament.) The attempts of the Commons to secure royal "redress of grievances" as a condition of its assent to new taxation constituted its earliest assertions of political influence. Given prudent management of the crown's independent sources of revenue, it was nevertheless only in times of war or other emergency that recourse to Parliament was necessary in order to obtain supply (i.e., agreement to supply the financial needs of the crown). By the time of the later Tudors, however, the Commons was acquiring another basis of influence as the crown sought its support in struggles against rival social forces. The members of the Lower House, or the communities that they represented, gradually became a vital element in the national struggle for political power.

The Tudors recognized the potential strength available to them in the support of the landed gentry and urban merchants who, for religious and economic reasons, had become more politically conscious. These local community leaders were more and more drawn into central and local administration (in the council and as justices of the peace); and the Tudors were careful to obtain their assent, granted through their representatives of Parliament, to the statutes that authorized such major changes as those involved in the expropriation and reform of the Church. Indeed, the whole Tudor system may be said to have become increasingly dependent upon these ever more prosperous and influential sections of the nation. For although the crown continued to monopolize the initiative in government and to exercise extensive discretion and power, it could do so only in ways broadly acceptable to the Commons. The so-called Tudor despotism was in fact a balance of power, not a one-way system of command. It is memorable that the Tudors were among the most popular of British monarchs with the majority of their subjects, as they still are today in historical legend. In Britain the most popular monarchs and governments are almost always those that represent a comparable blend of strong and decisive leadership with concern for popular wishes; among these wishes, frequently, is one simply for a government that governs.[4]

This balance did not survive the Tudors. It was upset by a combination of factors, among them the increasing prosperity of the new landed and commercial interests, the religious attitudes of the Stuart monarchs and their claim to rule by divine right, and the personalities of the leading figures of the age. The result was the most turbulent period in British constitutional history. We are not concerned here with the details of the seventeenth-century disputes in which one king was beheaded and another abdicated; in which there were experiments in royal rule without Parliament and parliamentary rule without a monarch; in which, for a time, England was subject first to civil war and then to military dictatorship. These controversies, however, slowly (after 1660) gave birth to a new constitutional settlement, the nature of which must be described.

The principal constitutional, as opposed to purely religious, developments were marked and consolidated by the Convention Parliament's invitation to William and Mary of Orange to succeed to the throne in 1689, the enactment of the Bill of Rights in the same year, and the Act of Settlement of 1701. With the addition of the Act of Union, 1707, whereby the joining of the crowns of England and Scotland (1603) became a full political union with the creation of the new legal entity of Great Britain, the legal basis of the modern constitution is virtually complete. The Revolution Settlement, as it is usually called, is remarkable for its moderation and its concern with immediate practical problems rather than with declarations of resounding principle or doctrine. The English Bill of Rights, for example, is comparable, not to the first ten amendments to the American Constitution, but to the second and lesser known part of the Declaration of Independence, in which ringing statements about "inalienable rights" give way to a list of very concrete and specific grievances against the British crown. Like the Declaration of Independence, the English Bill

---

[4] Although never to the exclusion of other considerations.

of Rights talks in terms of the restoration of ancient rights rather than of legal innovations. In effect, it simply gave legal expression to one interpretation of past practice by prohibiting the crown's use of certain means whereby the Stuarts had attempted to evade the influence of Parliament and the courts. The crown was thus forbidden to maintain a standing army, to suspend the laws, or to levy money by prerogative rather than parliamentary grant (to name what are probably the most important provisions). In conjunction with the invitation to William III and the Act of Settlement, however, the Bill of Rights established the principle that monarchs rule in virtue of Acts of Parliament, and ensured that, in the last resort, they must bow to the will of Parliament. The Act of Settlement also provided that monarchs may neither be nor marry members of the Roman Catholic Church, that judges should not be subject to dismissal at the royal pleasure, and that holders of offices of profit under the crown may not sit in the House of Commons (a provision that was honored mainly in the breach, and was modified by the Regency Act of 1705). In all other important respects the legal position of the crown remained and remains unchanged. The importance of the settlement lay more in what it made possible than in its immediate effects upon the working of the constitution.

Like the new American Constitution it was to influence, the eighteenth-century system of government in Britain was characterized by a partial separation of powers modified by mutual checks and balances. The independence of the judiciary was by then firmly established. Parliament had successfully asserted its right to a share in governmental authority, and was not to be challenged again as the principal forum for public political criticism and debate or as the center of legislative activity. Within Parliament, the special authority of the House of Commons in the field of public finance was generally recognized. In other respects the two Houses were substantially equal: the same broad interests were represented in both, they were linked by personal ties of kinship and patronage, and not until these bonds were weakened in the early nineteenth century could the general issue of superiority be raised and decided.

Executive responsibility, moreover, still rested with the monarch, as did the power to withhold assent to bills passed by Parliament. In the discharge of his duties the king was, of course, dependent upon his advisers—ministers whom he appointed and dismissed. Just as American presidents have varied in their relationships with their "cabinet," so did the kings take a greater or lesser degree of interest in the work of their ministers, depending both on the personality of the monarch and the ministerial talent available. That George III wielded a more constant and extensive power over policy than his two predecessors reflected differences in these respects rather than in constitutional doctrine. Monarchs certainly had to take account of political circumstances in their choice of advisers, as must all heads of government. In particular, because of the need for parliamentary cooperation in finance and legislation, they had to consider their ministers' ability to obtain that cooperation. This increasingly came to mean the ability of ministers to manage the House of Commons.

If the policies of a monarch and his ministers were broadly acceptable to the country there were several ways they could assure themselves of the necessary parliamentary support. Firstly, but of limited efficacy, was the appeal to party. The Tory and Whig parties, which had emerged from the constitutional and political struggles of the seventeenth century, still survived in a comparatively weak and loose form, probably divided by tradition and personality as much as by differences of policy and principle. From about 1714 onward, however, many, perhaps most members of Parliament owed uncertain allegiance to either party or to none at all. At the turn of the century the party system (if such it can be called) was weak enough to encourage the formation of ministries drawn from both parties, but strong enough to prevent the experiment from being successful. Thus, although most governments were thereafter formed of men from only one party (insofar as they were party men at all), party loyalty was not sufficient to ensure the support of a parliamentary majority.

Secondly, recourse had to be made to crown patronage, normally administered by the First Lord of the Treasury. (When he was in the House of Lords, much of the patronage power had to be administered by the chief minister in the Commons.) Pensions, honors, and appointments to sinecure or working positions, granted either to members of Parliament or to their friends, relatives, and dependents, played much the same role in British politics then as in American politics a century later, and for similar reasons. On the other hand, monarchs had more political freedom than most American presidents, at the same time as they distributed their benefits over a narrower social stratum. However, among the recipients of offices who continued to sit in the House of Commons were men who, to all intents, must be regarded as civil servants rather than politicians, and who accordingly supported the king's governments because they felt this to be their duty rather than because they were bribed into agreement.

Thirdly, the king and his ministers had to obtain the support of various "independents" who were neither party nor place men, however much some might have relied upon local interests or the backing of private patrons. Their acceptance of any ministry tended to depend on the economy and efficiency of administration and, given these, they could normally be counted upon not to oppose the crown, with which governmental leadership undoubtedly still lay.

Should these methods fail to achieve the necessary cooperation, one final remedy lay in the hands of the monarch: the dissolution of the House of Commons in order to secure a fresh majority. The necessary votes were obtained by appealing directly to the country for the support required to maintain the king's government and by the exercise of crown "influence" (the contemporary euphemism for Treasury funds and patronage) in the constituencies amenable to it.

In all respects but the last (whose importance is easily exaggerated), and excepting the presence in Parliament of officeholders under the crown, the broad picture bears obvious and significant resemblances to the American Constitution. Had ministers been kept out of Parliament or had the United States persevered with the early experiment of having members of the president's "cabinet" appear before Congress, and had the monarch become elective or the president continued to be elected indirectly in fact as well as in law, the similarities between the two systems of government might still be as striking as their differences. (The federal nature of the American union, to mention but one additional factor, would have ensured that differences remained great, although possibly relating more to the atmosphere than to the formal structure of central government.)

In fact, however, the two constitutions have moved further apart. Not least among the reasons for this has been the influence of the hereditary nature of the monarchy and of the parliamentary membership of its ministers upon the later development of the British system.

What happened, briefly, is this. The failure of George III's American policy, his subsequent periods of insanity, and the various personal shortcomings of his two immediate successors lessened respect for (without yet discrediting) royal leadership. At the same time the rising costs of government, growing concern for administrative competence, and increasing attacks upon the extent of royal "influence" in Parliament (which were not confined entirely to those who had been excluded from its benefits) led to a more extensive and systematic supervision of public finance, a gradual paring of royal patronage (beginning in 1782), and the exclusion of new categories of officeholder from Parliament. Given these developments and the traditional legal immunity of sovereigns, who could not easily be removed or made politically accountable, it was natural that the personal authority of the crown should diminish. It was equally natural that the chief beneficiaries should be the king's ministers, whose position was simultaneously being strengthened by other political changes.

The accelerating industrial revolution, the increasing application of capital and knowledge to agriculture as well as industry, and the attendant social dislocations were diversifying the major interests within the nation. The groups deriving the most immediate economic benefits therefrom found that wealth did not automatically admit them to existing social and political privileges. The most important legal barriers consisted of discriminations against Protestant as well as Catholic dissenters from the Established Church, and the traditional distribution of parliamentary constituencies that gave little or no weight to the new centers of industry and population.[5]

The interests of the new capitalists thus impelled them into political activity just as their wealth and economic influence provided them with the means to do so. Their grievances and attitudes were increasingly reflected by the Whigs, who were almost continuously out of office in the late eighteenth and early nineteenth centuries. Thus new life was injected into national politics and a corresponding intensification of the party political struggle resulted. Inevitably, too, the growth of rationalism and radical social criticism, though never so great in Britain as in France, operated in the same direction. One of the principal constitutional effects of this was to forge new links between the various ministers. A common loyalty to their party tended to replace individual loyalties to the king. (It then became the custom to refer to the ministers collectively, or at least to the most important ones, as "the cabinet.") Similar links developed between the cabinet and at least a substantial body of their supporters in Parliament; in the relations of these two groups the older techniques of "management" were henceforth to play a much less conspicuous part.

The upshot of all these changes was, on the one hand, that it became more difficult to secure parliamentary cooperation with the executive by means of royal patronage and influence and, on the other, that it became less necessary to do so as the party came to provide an alternative source of political organization and initiative. In terms of the day-to-day working of the constitution, the most obvious change was that the king had less discretion in his choice of ministers because a Parliament organized

[5] The new urban industrial centers had grown up largely outside the boundaries of the ancient boroughs, many of which, by this time, returned members to the House of Commons who represented few voters and, in effect, only the interests of some large landowner or of the most lavish spender. These were termed "rotten boroughs."

on increasingly rigid party lines allowed him less room to maneuver. From this, in turn, resulted a diminution in royal influence over any particular set of ministers. If there is, or appears to be, but one group of ministers that can secure the support of Parliament, it is clearly in a strong position vis-à-vis any monarch who might be disposed to reject its advice.

Another part of the process was the development of a ministerial leader. The unofficial title and position of first, or prime, minister had been given to Robert Walpole in the first half of the eighteenth century. He had acquired them as a result of his own preeminence and the relative indifference to government of the first two Georges, but, by the end of the century, both title and position became customary as a result of the changed relationships between monarch and party. An enlarged electorate, acknowledgment of the sovereign authority of the people represented in and by the House of Commons, and the development of the nationally organized two-party system were all that were required for the monarch to become almost entirely nonpolitical through the transfer of his ruling power to the prime minister and cabinet. (Were the party system in the United States to permit Congress to assert and exercise continuing leadership as the embodiment of a majority electoral decision, then by the purposeful use of its powers of investigation, ratification, legislation, and finance, it could effect a similar transfer of executive power to a cabinet responsible to it and a similar political neutralizing of the president. Given such a change in the party system, the probability of which is not here being endorsed, the very few constitutional amendments that *might* be necessary would probably be secured with little difficulty.)

The developments about which we have been speaking were consummated during the nineteenth century,[6] especially by the

---

[6] The process was not completed until much later. Women voted for the first time in 1918, but only if they were thirty years of age or older. Not until the 1929 election could adult women vote on the same basis as men, and not until the election of 1950 was the system of "one man (or woman), one vote" and only one vote, fully adopted.

series of statutes that progressively extended the franchise to the majority of the adult population. The first of these statutes, the Reform Act of 1832, is now acknowledged to be one of the major landmarks of British history. Its most important provisions were to abolish the majority of the "rotten" boroughs, to reduce the representation given to many areas whose size and significance no longer justified their traditional number of seats, and to redistribute the seats concerned to some of the new and populous areas, particularly London and the northern industrial cities. The Reform Act also modified the property qualification for voting. Probably the two most significant results were to enfranchise the middle classes in the boroughs and to give the vote to the rural tenant-at-will who paid a certain minimum rent in the counties. These tenants-at-will were a group whose complete insecurity of tenure made them peculiarly susceptible to pressure from their landlords.[7] In all, the electorate was increased by about two hundred thousand, to a total of about six hundred thousand.

The significance of the Reform Act did not repose solely in its provisions, important though it was to have reduced the massive predominance of the landed interests. Its title, "an Act to amend the representation of the people," admitted a departure in principle from the old exclusive preoccupation with interests and communities, and thus anticipated the later and more radical adoption of number as the chief criterion for representation. The bill's passage both resulted from and stimulated a further consolidation of the party system in the House of Commons, just as it recognized that House's superiority over the House of Lords. (The Lords' opposition to the Act had been overcome only when the king was persuaded to threaten the creation of sufficient new peers to provide a majority for the government.) Above all, perhaps, it and the circumstances in which it was passed intensified those forces that were limiting the monarch's discretion by strengthening the House of Commons and the ministers in which it placed its confidence. Conversely, after 1832 it was made clear that it was upon the confidence of the Commons and not of the

[7] The secret ballot was not introduced until 1872.

monarch that the cabinet depended for its authority and its existence.

If the first and vital breach was made in 1832, the most extensive reforms were the product of later legislation. By the Reform Act of 1867 minor changes in the counties enlarged the rural electorate from over five hundred thousand to nearly eight hundred thousand, while the substantial enfranchisement of the workers in the boroughs resulted in an electorate there of nearly one and a quarter million—though the failure to redistribute seats adequately still gave a preponderant voice in Parliament to the representatives of the counties and small towns. Not until 1885 was this defect largely eliminated. The Redistribution of Seats Act of that year, combined with the extension of the vote to the rural worker in 1884, also finally served to reduce the share in government of the aristocratic landed interests to its proper size. These interests were also the chief sufferers from the introduction of secret voting in 1872, and from the succession of Acts that fixed upper limits to electoral expenditure in the constituencies and that declared many of the traditional ways of winning votes and influencing people to be corrupt.

With the Reform Acts, whose work was finally systematized and completed by the Representation of the People Acts of 1918, 1928, and 1948, it may be said that the modern constitution was born. It was through them that first the controllers and then the operators of Britain's modern industrial society were permitted a voice in the formal system of government. It was to organize this new mass electorate that, from 1867 onward, the political parties developed their extra-parliamentary structure. The impact of these new groups, demanding and then acquiring the right to vote and social emancipation, led to the transformation of the old Tory and Whig parties into the Conservative and Liberal ones, based more on principle than on mere personality and "influence," [8] and, in this century, to the rise of the Labour party. It was in answer to the demands of the new voters that the govern-

[8] The names first appeared around 1830, but the transformation mentioned here was gradual and remained partial until the 1860s.

ment was forced to intervene in ever wider areas of the national life—initially, perhaps, to remove "hindrances to the enjoyment of the good life" [9] represented by antiquated regulations and prohibitions (e.g., religious discriminations), and subsequently (e.g., by establishing and promoting minimum standards of public health and hygiene) in more positive fashion. Finally, it was largely because of the strains imposed by these new activities that the apparatus of administration, both central and local, was reformed and the last vestiges of patronage removed from the permanent public service.

The British constitution is thus a continuously changing blend of the ancient and modern. One of its strengths has been that for the most part it has permitted governments to wield the power necessary to govern effectively without allowing them to rule for long in an arbitrary and irresponsible fashion, disregarding the wishes at least of the more powerful and articulate sections of the governed. Another source of strength has been that, on the one hand, no rigid constitutional or political orthodoxy has been able to ossify the institutions of government and, on the other hand, partly for this reason, it has not been necessary totally and swiftly to reorganize them at the cost of destroying established habits of thought, behavior, and sentiment. Although the British system of government is rarely free from criticism, and is occasionally the subject of acute controversy, its basic form commands wide support today.

Many labels may be attached to the system as it now is. No single one of the most common labels tells the whole story, but between them they provide a reasonably accurate short description, as follows:

1. *Constitutional Monarchy.* The queen is still the head of state, and by law is the head of government as well. She plays an important role socially and symbolically, but for the most part

[9] The phrase is taken from T. H. Green, the late-nineteenth-century political theorist. See his *Lectures on the Principles of Political Obligation* (1895). See also A. V. Dicey, "The Debt of Collectivism to Benthamism," in his *Law and Opinion in England in the Nineteenth Century,* first published in 1905, Lecture IX.

the conventions of the constitution prescribe a purely formal part in the conduct of government. Much is still done in the queen's name, and many acts of government still require her participation, but with a few important exceptions she performs these functions only upon the advice (which she must follow) of Her Majesty's Government, that is to say, of the prime minister and his ministerial colleagues, and in accordance with the wishes of Parliament.

2. Cabinet Government. Broadly speaking, it is the cabinet, as the inheritor of the powers of the crown, that governs, in the sense that it directs the administration and determines national policy in the legislative as in all other fields. But it may be said to govern "by and with the advice and consent" of the Commons and, to a very minor extent, the Lords "in . . . Parliament assembled, and by the authority of the same." In the cabinet one finds the modern embodiment of a fusion of governmental powers which, more than the eighteenth-century separation, has generally characterized British government.

3. Responsible Government. Cabinets are composed of the leaders of the party (usually) or parties that form a majority in the House of Commons as a result of the previous general election. Dependent for its existence upon the support of this majority, the cabinet is therefore responsible (accountable) to the electorate through the House of Commons, before whom it must be prepared to defend its actions and its record.

4. Party Government. Since 1945 there has existed, to all intents, a two-party system (Conservative and Labour). Both main parties are, compared to American ones, relatively cohesive and homogeneous in terms of policy and principle.[10] The parties organize the House of Commons, provide governments, act as the force that generally assures those governments of parliamentary support, and serve as indispensable links between the government and the governed.

[10] Although the Labour party, after 1951 and again after the election of October 1959, has often appeared to be intent on falsifying this generalization. In both parties, of course, the homogeneity is often overstated.

5. Parliamentary Government. The supremacy of Parliament is frequently cited as one of the fundamental principles of the constitution.[11] It holds true today in the sense that an Act of Parliament is superior to all other forms of law and that there are no legal limits upon the legislative power of Parliament (meaning, in this context, the crown-in-Parliament) in constitutional as well as in "ordinary" matters. In practice perhaps the most important aspect is that no government with the support of Parliament behind it will find itself unable to carry through its policy simply because of *legal* obstacles. British government is parliamentary also in the sense that Parliament, and principally the House of Commons, remains the foremost arena for political debate and for criticism of the government.

6. Democratic Government. British government is democratic at least in the sense that the House of Commons is elected on a basis of universal adult suffrage, that the ultimate decision between alternative governments and policies lies with the electorate, and that the process of discussion and opinion formation is extensive and substantially free from political interference or censorship.

To these structural descriptions might be added two others that relate to the political system as a whole.

7. Pluralism. There are many legitimate actors on the political stage. Different governmental organs, political parties, pressure groups, and· other less formal and organized groups may and usually do play some part in political life. It is, as we will argue later, a structured pluralism, however, and not a perfect political market.

8. Deferential. The attitude of the general public toward the government and toward political leaders may be labeled "deferential" in the sense that popular criticism and participation are tempered by a degree of trust that both eases the conduct of gov-

---

[11] It receives its best-known modern statement in A. V. Dicey, *Introduction to the Study of the Law of the Constitution,* 10th ed., E. C. S. Wade, ed. (London: Macmillan, 1960), the first edition of which appeared in 1885. The principle is reiterated in most modern British texts and will be discussed more fully in Chapter 5.

ernment and, it may be supposed, reflects a degree of satisfaction with its past conduct.[12]

To analyze all the conditions necessary for the continuing and free working of the system would require a lengthy treatise. It is clear, however, that among these conditions are the following: the evolution of the system along with the social forces that it must express and contain; its success in coping with the emergencies of war and economic crisis, as well as with what one continues to regard as normal conditions; a degree of social and political homogeneity in the country as a whole sufficient to encompass dispute without totally undermining toleration of dissent; and a general political temper that encourages forbearance (or possibly indolence) in the use of, and opposition to, power and privilege of all kinds.

NOTE: SCOTLAND, IRELAND, AND WALES

Scotland was an independent kingdom until 1707. In 1603, however, there took place a union of crowns when James VI of Scotland succeeded to the English throne as James I of England. (He was the first of the Stuarts.) By the Act of Union of 1707 the two countries united to form the new country of *Great Britain.* By this Act Scotland retained its own established Presbyterian church and much of its own legal system, but gave up its own parliament and, instead, sent members to the one at Westminster. Today Scotland has its own minister, the secretary of state for Scotland, who is always a member of the cabinet, assisted by a minister of state and three undersecretaries. He is in charge of four departments located in Edinburgh and exclusively concerned with Scottish affairs. (They are the Home, Education, Health, and Agriculture departments.) This administrative revo-

---

[12] On the attitude of the British see in particular E. A. Nordlinger, *The Working Class Tories* (London: MacGibbon & Kee, 1967), who modifies and advances the approach adopted in G. Almond and S. Verba, *The Civic Culture* (Princeton: Princeton University Press, 1963). See also F. Parkin, *Middle Class Radicalism* (Manchester: Manchester University Press, 1968), Chapter 3.

lution took place partly for reasons of convenience and partly in response to the ever-present national consciousness of the Scots.

The larger part of Ireland is completely independent, although its citizens enjoy full rights of British citizenship, including voting, when resident in the United Kingdom. The smaller part, Northern Ireland (sometimes referred to as Ulster), is subject to the British crown and government. With Britain it forms the *United Kingdom*. It sends representatives to Parliament in London, but also has its own cabinet and parliament in Stormont. Its constitution was designed as part of a federal Irish constitution enacted in 1920, but when that constitution was rejected in Southern Ireland, the Ulster government remained. Its constitutional relations with the United Kingdom government are not federal but devolutionary, since the United Kingdom Parliament possesses the right to pass any legislation it wishes for Northern Ireland, including an Act to abolish the Stormont government. In practice, however, this is unlikely to happen. The local political and party situation is quite unlike that prevailing in Britain, as it is centered upon a religious conflict that is exacerbated by social divisions and its association with Ulster's relations with the rest of Ireland, for which reason it is not discussed in this book.

Wales was conquered and constitutionally absorbed by England in the thirteenth century. In 1961 some 26 percent of the population were Welsh-speaking, almost all of whom also spoke English. Despite the appointment of a Minister for Welsh Affairs in 1957, Wales must still be considered as an integral part of the English system of law and administration.

2

Society and People

In this chapter an attempt is made to provide a picture of British society today. The information set out is selected in the belief that it is particularly relevant to an understanding of the *political* life of the country. The portrayal is therefore very limited. It will necessarily be incomplete as well as reflect to some extent the author's personal estimate of what is politically most significant.

GEOGRAPHY

That Britain is an island kingdom "anchored" off the coast of the European continent is perhaps the single most important, as it is the best-known, geographical factor. Even in World War II the surrounding waters served as a highly effective defense against invasion, if no longer against bombardment. The continuity of constitutional development that has already been noted clearly owes much to the immunity thus conferred. Significantly, it has also been possible to dispense with a large permanent garrison at home—large standing armies and free government being at best uneasy bedfellows. The sea has probably helped to insulate Britain against the most disruptive effects of European political and ideological forces. Above all, the existence of such a clearly defined territorial boundary, combined with the absence of any corresponding barriers to internal communications, has facilitated the relatively early growth and development of national self-consciousness.

On the other hand, Britain is not so far removed from the European mainland (some twenty miles at the nearest point) as to be entirely isolated from it or able to ignore the possibility of invasion. Britain cannot, therefore, afford to stand aloof from European politics. And, in fact, it is impossible to divorce the study of British from European history. It is equally impossible, however, to study British history with reference only to domestic and European affairs. If the sea to some extent has separated the British from their nearest neighbors, it has played as great a part in their history by joining them to all parts of the world readily accessible to water-borne transport. From the sixteenth century on, therefore, the British have devoted many of their energies to overseas exploration, colonization, and trade. Britain's position as an influence in world politics, and indeed its existence as a relatively wealthy industrial community has depended and still depends on the maintenance (in some form) of its overseas connections.

The area of the United Kingdom is 94,499 square miles, but its population at the time of the 1961 census was over fifty-two million. The density of population is thus among the highest in the world; it is 557 people per square mile, and for England alone, it is 863 (in Japan it is 587; in the United States, 54).[1] On the other hand, the country possesses few of the natural resources necessary for its own survival. The once ample coal supplies are dwindling (and increasingly difficult to extract) and not even the development of nuclear power stations since the 1950s or the discovery in the 1960s of substantial fields of natural gas under the North Sea are likely to provide all the fuel required. There are virtually no other raw materials, and domestic agriculture in 1968–69 provided only about half the food consumed.

[1] Translating the British figures into American terms, it is as though (1950 census figures) one-third of the entire American population were to live in the state of Oregon, or if eight times the population of Texas were to live in one-third of its area. Even so, large areas of Britain are still very sparsely populated, particularly in Scotland where the population density is a mere 170.

POPULATION

The rate of increase in the population was at its greatest between about 1750 and 1900. The total was still in the region of seven million in 1750, but it quadrupled in the next hundred years, and reached forty million early in the twentieth century. Before then it was kept low by a high death rate, which was reduced rapidly as the industrial revolution and the increase in knowledge proceeded, and since then it has been slowed down by a rapidly falling birth rate, which has shown signs of recovery only during and since World War II.

The estimated population in 1967 was about 53,500,000,[2] with the following age distribution:

Age group	Number
0–14	12,550,000
15–24	7,880,000
25–44	13,240,000
45–64	13,250,000
65 and over	6,650,000

At present, therefore, there is a "bulge" at and below school age, but otherwise Britain has an aging population. At the beginning of the century less than one in fifteen had reached retirement age of sixty-five; by 1957 just under one in eight had, and by 1980, it has been estimated, the figure will approach one in six. Apart from the efforts of both major political parties to demonstrate their interests in the financial position of old-age pensioners (and for this there may well be reasons other than mere vote-catching), the size and age-distribution of the population have not yet had any noticeable impact on politics. Some political interest has been taken, however, in other aspects of Britain's population.

Religious divisions have played an important part in British history, and to this day continue as a permanent undercurrent.

[2] This figure is for the home population only.

Membership of the principal denominations (in Great Britain) is as follows:

Established Church of England (Episcopalian)	27,658,000*
Other Episcopalian	210,000
Established Church of Scotland (Presbyterian)	1,234,000
Other Presbyterian	70,000
Methodist	620,000
Baptist Unions	295,000
Congregationalist	198,000
Roman Catholic	7,982,000†

* Baptized membership as distinct from regular communicants. The latter apparently number about 10 million.
† Including children.
SOURCE: D. Butler and J. Freeman, *British Political Facts 1900–1968,* 3d ed. (London: Macmillan, 1969), pp. 296–301.

Such sample surveys as have been carried out suggest that attendance figures are appreciably smaller, and average about 10 percent of the total population on ordinary Sundays. The political influence of the churches appears to be dwindling as attendance drops and as the churches seek a "new significance" rather than power. True, on certain social and moral questions the churches are important pressure groups, and political leaders continue to act and speak publicly in a manner befitting an officially Christian country, but no religious community or organization can still claim to be a "power in the land" outside Northern Ireland, and even there the established Church leaders have had difficulty in calming their followers in the face of a bigotry whose roots are not exclusively theological.[3]

The Roman Catholic Church is commonly believed to exercise a wider influence on the votes of its members. Particularly in those urban areas where there is a sizable Catholic population,

[3] In Northern Ireland the main denominations are Episcopalian (345,000), Presbyterian (413,000), and Roman Catholic (498,000). The Catholics, who are largely of the working class, are also inclined to favor a political union with Eire.

many active politicians believe the Church to be an important factor even within the political party (or parties) to which, largely for other reasons, its members belong. These beliefs have not been publicly substantiated—nor need they be; the beliefs themselves may suffice to influence political behavior.

In any case, it is certain that in parts of cities like Glasgow and Liverpool it may be a political advantage to possess an Irish name or be a known Catholic, just as in other areas it is, or has been, advantageous to take a prominent part in the affairs of another denomination. But, in general, public religious observance, except possibly in predominantly Catholic areas and parts of Scotland or Wales, no longer seems essential to a political career, nor do the relations between the various religious groups constitute a major political issue outside Ireland.

Ethnically the British population is relatively homogeneous —at least for most political purposes. This does not mean that it is, by any standard, racially or ethnically "pure." The Norman Conquest served only to add one more strain to an already mixed heritage of Celts, Angles, Saxons, Jutes, and the rest. Even to call this mixture "Anglo-Saxon" is to endorse a serious misconception. Since the time of the Normans there have been many additions, particularly from Europe. The 1961 census, for example, reported the presence of 447,000 aliens, of whom 337,000 were from other European countries and 80,000 from the United States. These figures do not include Commonwealth immigrants of whom, in the same year, there were over 596,000. On the other hand, the net movement of population throughout this century has been outward, particularly to the older Commonwealth countries and to the United States. In the early 1960s this led to some concern about an alleged "brain drain" of scientists and others, but less so than did the purely domestic migrations from the north of England, Scotland, and Wales to the increasingly congested but economically buoyant Midland and south-east. It is to these latter areas, too, that the bulk of the colored immigrants have been drawn in search of employment and opportunity.

Despite the national net loss of population, therefore, the influx of immigrants from India, Pakistan, and the West Indies (at a rate of well over 50,000 per annum between 1953 and 1965) has made immigration—by which is usually meant in fact "colored immigration" [4]—a new political issue. Established opinion continues to be antidiscriminatory, official talk is of the difficulties in housing and in looking after new immigrants, but the tighter controls on entry introduced by the Commonwealth Immigrants Act of 1962 (passed by the Conservatives over Labour opposition) and reenforced by Labour legislation in 1968, in practice bear most heavily upon the aspirations of Asians, Africans, and West Indians. Foreshadowed by a riot in the Notting Hill area of London in 1958, trumpeted by Labour's unexpected loss of two constituencies in 1964, apparently over its attitude on race, and continually reemphasized by the popular response to alarmist and dramatic speeches by certain members of Parliament from areas with significant colored minorities,[5] race relations seem to have become a lasting factor in British political life.

As yet the issues are social and moral, rather than overtly political—avowed "racist" candidates have yet to poll well, except as the standard-bearer of a major party—but this situation may not survive any sharp economic slump, and race is already important in certain localities. The race question has thus far led to two political innovations of some significance. The first is that the United Kingdom has finally dropped its policy of treating all Commonwealth citizens on a par with its own, although once they are legally admitted to the country, the principle still holds. The other is the attempt to establish and maintain nondiscriminatory standards by government action: the Race Relations Acts of

[4] The vocabulary of skin color is most unsatisfactory. "White," a color, is an inaccurate label for people of predominantly European extraction whose color is white only when they are very ill or dead. At other times "pink," "pale," or at best "off-white" are the more correct epithets. However, to talk of "colored" and "white" people is now standard, and since adequate substitutes do not exist, we have to make use of these terms here for the sake of intelligibility.

[5] Chief among them being former Conservative minister Enoch Powell, who is member for a Midlands constituency, Wolverhampton.

1965 and 1968 make discrimination and incitement to racial hatred illegal and provide a combination of penalties and conciliation machinery to uphold these prohibitions in the public domain.

Given that the colored population of over 1 million (in 1968) is growing and is concentrated in a few areas, and that housing and other social resources continue to be relatively scarce, there is little ground for believing that the widespread attitudes of severe or moderate intolerance will vanish quickly.[6] It is important, nonetheless, that these attitudes exist alongside the egalitarian conviction of others and that they have not become entrenched in domestic legislation or official behavior. The politically most important divisions within the British population continue to be based on occupation and class rather than on race and religion. They will be discussed in the next two sections.

THE ECONOMY

Throughout the greater part of the nineteenth century Britain could justifiably claim to be "the workshop of the world." Its early start in the industrial race, abundant domestic supplies of cheap fuel (coal), and its many established trading links throughout the world enabled it to become, and for many years remain, the leading manufacturing nation. It is still one of the wealthiest, measured by per capita income.[7] But it must be compared with other Western European countries rather than with such a wealthy

---

[6] This is despite the sharp cut in immigration to 36,000 by 1967 from a peak of well over 60,000 in 1965. On the question of "race" see, for example, Paul Foot, *Immigration and Race in British Politics* (Harmondsworth: Penguin Books, 1965), E. S. B. Rose and others, *Colour and Citizenship* (London: Oxford University Press, 1969), and *Colour and Immigration in the United Kingdom 1969* (London: Institute of Race Relations, 1969).

[7] Estimated by the Organization for Economic Cooperation and Development (OECD) to be $1,980 in 1967, as compared with $4,040 in the United States, $2,190 in France, and $320 in Turkey.

giant as the United States.[8] Since its industrial heyday in the nine-teenth century, however, it has suffered not only from competition as other countries industrialized, but also from a slackening in its own rate of growth. Between the wars this was partially concealed by the fruits of its investment overseas (over £4,000 million in 1939).[9] Although British assets abroad have now increased beyond this level despite the fact that about half were sold to pay for supplies during World War II, the resulting income has not sufficed to prevent recurrent crises in the balance of payments—indeed the rate of investment overseas may have helped to produce them. The economy continues to expand, but more slowly than in other developed countries, and Britain's share in an expanding world trade has fallen throughout most of the postwar period. One indication of this is that the index of industrial production in Britain only moved from 84 to 112 between 1956 and 1966, whereas in West Germany, it moved from 67 to 118, in France from 68 to 117, and in the United States from 80 to 125.[10] That the British index has moved so slowly is in large part attributable to such factors as a continuing lack of investment and poor management in many industries or firms. Thus as long ago as the 1930s Mr. Rostas estimated [11] that factory productivity in Germany was 11 percent greater and in the United States 125 percent greater than in Britain, while between 1953 and 1959 gross fixed investment increased only by 32 percent in Britain as against 70 percent in West Germany, 49 percent in France, and 55 percent for the European Economic Community (EEC) as a whole.

International trade is the basis for Britain's industrial produc-

---

[8] For example, Britain produced not much over 23,000,000 tons of steel in 1966, as compared with over 120,000,000 in the United States; while the gross national product in 1967 was $109,250,000,000 ($803,-910,000,000 in the United States).

[9] The equivalent of $16,000,000,000 at the then prevailing rate of exchange.

[10] 1963 = 100 in all cases. See OECD, *Main Economic Indicators 1957–1966* (Paris, 1968), pp. 487–516.

[11] "Industrial Production, Productivity and Distribution in Britain, Germany and the United States, 1935–37," *Economic Journal* (April 1943), pp. 39–54.

tion and its standard of living alike. In 1961 the main constituents of that trade were as follows:

Section		Imports	Exports
0 and 1	Food, drink, tobacco, and live animals	1,765,300,000	330,600,000
2	Basic materials	950,500,000	146,000,000
3 and 4	Fuels, lubricants, etc.	794,000,000	134,500,000
5	Chemicals	329,400,000	492,800,000
6, 7, and 8	Manufactured goods	2,515,600,000	3,777,700,000
9	Post parcels, etc.	86,700,000	144,200,000
	TOTAL	£6,441,500,000	£5,025,800,000

Shipping, interest on investments, insurance and banking earnings, and the tourist trade are normally counted upon to bridge the gap between imports and exports, but since 1945 aid and loans from abroad have been indispensable means of overcoming recurrent crises. Sections 0–5, it will be noted, contribute well over half the total imports and contain what may be called the main "survival" items. The volume of exports has expanded quickly, the index having risen from 85 in 1956 to 112 in 1966—but the corresponding figures for West Germany are 54 and 135, and for France, 54 and 125 [12] and Britain's share of the world total has declined from 8.8 percent in 1961 to 7.01 percent in 1968.[13] Much of British foreign policy is explicable in these terms alone. An additional gloss on foreign policy is provided by figures showing the direction of Britain's overseas trade. The most striking development is the lessening importance of the Commonwealth, whose share of British trade dropped from about 40 percent in 1961 to little over 20 percent in 1968, a change only partially attributable to the withdrawal of South Africa and the economic sanctions on Rhodesia. By 1968 Britain traded almost as much with the EEC countries, the principal partner being the United States (over 10 percent) and the other European Free Trade As-

[12] OECD, op. cit., pp. 487–516. The base year for the index is 1963.
[13] The world total here excludes China and the Soviet Union. The proportions are calculated from figures in Whitaker's *Almanack 1970*, p. 600.

sociation (EFTA) members (about 14 percent).[14] In other words, the great bulk of trade is in industrial products with other developed countries in the west.

The importance of manufacturing in the economy is also demonstrated by the occupational distribution of the population. In 1969 the total labor force was about 25,250,000. The following table gives the main occupational divisions and the change in numbers compared with 1954 and 1962 in order to indicate the trends. Note that manufacturing, distribution, and services account for the vast majority of people, with less than 2 percent engaged in agriculture and forestry.

British politics are therefore those of an advanced industrial society vitally affected by its relations with other countries. They are also primarily the politics of an urban society. Some 80 percent of the population can be classified as urban, and only about 20 percent as rural. Furthermore about 40 percent of the population live in seven major population centers, one of which, Greater London, contains almost one-fifth of the total population of Britain. This is not to say that farmers and the agricultural community generally are neglected by governments, nor that they have no political voice of importance. In fact, the interplay of the large number of constituencies that contain *some* agricultural electors, the need to obtain the farmers' cooperation in increasing agricultural production since 1939, and the effectiveness of the National Farmers' Union in presenting its case to successive governments has ensured that the interests of farmers have been well taken care of. But the principal political issues and the fundamental cleavage between the parties rest upon the divisions felt most acutely among the urban and industrial population. Fundamentally, the contest between the two major parties in large measure reflects the conflict of interest between organized capital (prop-

---

[14] The EEC members are France, West Germany, Italy, Belgium, the Netherlands, and Luxembourg. EFTA consists of Austria, Denmark, Norway, Portugal, Sweden, Switzerland, and the United Kingdom who formed the Association in 1960; Finland has been associated with it since 1961.

PRINCIPAL OCCUPATIONS OF THE BRITISH PEOPLE IN 1969

	NUMBERS	CHANGES	
		Since 1954	*Since 1962*
Agriculture, forestry, and fishing	413,000	−600,000	−477,000
Mining and quarrying	448,000	−428,000	−272,000
Construction	1,444,000	−280,000	−137,000
Food, drink, and tobacco	812,000 ⎫		
Paper, painting, and publishing	634,000 ⎪		
Other manufacturing and processing	7,201,000 ⎬ +510,000		−305,000
engineering, electrical, and shipbuilding	2,478,000 ⎪		
vehicles	824,000 ⎭		
Gas, electricity, and water	395,000	+ 19,000	+ 9,000
Transport and communications	1,584,000	−108,000	− 88,000
Distribution, hotels, and catering	3,345,000	+543,000	+ 31,000
Professional, financial, scientific, and miscellaneous services	4,883,000	+846,000	−200,000
Central government service	584,000	+ 1,000	+ 68,000
Local government service	818,000	+ 90,000	+ 61,000
Armed forces (including women)	390,000	−440,000	− 62,000
Unemployed	540,000	+260,000	+124,000

SOURCE: Adapted from Whitaker's *Almanack 1970,* p. 611, where the total labor force is given as 25,258,000. The changes given are measured from the totals printed in earlier editions of this book; the definitions of the occupations have been modified, but the broad picture is unaffected by this.

erty) and organized labor. It is now necessary, therefore, to look at the industrial organization of the society.

Each enlargement of the public sector of the economy has provoked controversy, but it has been bitter only with respect to the iron and steel industry and the 1950 proposals to take over sugar and life insurance, these being the only industries to be clearly profitable at the time. As a result, the latter proposals were dropped and legislation passed denationalizing steel in 1957 and renationalizing it in 1965. By 1969, in addition to such service organizations as the British Broadcasting Corporation and hospitals (as part of the National Health Service), the nationalized sector of the economy included principally, the Bank of England (the central bank for the financial system), the production and basic distribution of energy (gas, coal, electricity, and atomic energy), transport (railways, civil aviation, and some road haulage), communications (telephones, cables, radio, and television), and the main steel plants. Between them these industries owned net fixed assets of some £16,000 million, annually invested as much as all private manufacturing industry (£1,700 million), employed about 8 percent of the labor force, and contributed some 11 percent of the gross domestic product.[15] To the extent that they are more amenable than private industry to direct government control [16] they clearly provide important points of access and leverage for government control of the economy as a whole, but they do not dominate the economy nor even set the pace industrially. On the contrary, they work in an economic context of predominantly private ownership and control, and their board membership is largely composed of private directors and managers who have grown up in private industry. Britain may have a "mixed" economy, but the public sector does not yet provide a basis for any political group or attitudes distinguishable from those found in private industry.

The private sector, as in the United States and other advanced capitalist countries, is characterized by the coexistence of a small number of giant concerns with a host of small and medium-sized enterprises, the divorce between personal ownership and mana-

---

[15] The figures are fom Jeremy Bray, *Decisions in Government* (London: Gollancz, 1970), p. 130.

[16] The constitutional position is outlined in the Notes to Chapter 5, pp. 151–52.

gerial control, and the development of links—through interlocking directorates, trade associations, mutual shareholdings and the like—especially between the larger units. As early as 1935, a later classic study has shown that in thirty-three trades over 70 percent of the work force were employed by the three largest units, and that in such key sectors as chemicals and engineering the corresponding figure was 40 percent.[17] These were minimum figures, given the strict definitions adopted. Twenty years later, according to the National Institute of Social and Economic Research, the quarter million company accounts issued in 1953–54 revealed that the 50 largest companies took 19 percent of all the profits; the 100 largest, 25 percent; and the 512 largest nearly 40 percent. Among the 512 largest, moreover, the largest 100 held over two-thirds of the assets. The Board of Trade has issued figures for 1963 that cover some 2,000 companies, the shares of which are quoted on United Kingdom stock exchanges and whose net assets amounted to £16,517 million (banking, insurance, and financial concerns not included). Of these the 121 biggest, with net assets of at least £25 million, accounted for 60 percent of that total, while the 31 biggest, with net assets of at least £100 million, owned some 34 percent of the net assets.[18] A later study calculated that in 1968–69, the 50 largest industrial companies accounted for over half the total turnover and profits of the 500 largest.[19] In the 1960s particularly, and even before the process received selective encouragement from the Labour Government, the business (and at times front) pages of the newspapers constantly reported fresh mergers and takeovers in such widely separated areas as newspapers, real estate, motor vehicles, computers, electrical engineering, and life insurance—to name only those that have attracted the greatest publicity.

No statistics about ownership of assets, numbers employed,

[17] See H. Leak and A. Maizels, "The Structure of British Industry," *Journal of the Royal Statistical Society,* CVIII (1945), pp. 142–207.

[18] Board of Trade, *Company Assets, Income and Finance in 1963* (London: HMSO, 1965).

[19] A special report in *The Times,* November 3, 1969, quoting from the fifth annual edition of *The Times 500* (London, 1969).

proportion of output, or any other comparable measure of productive concentration give a complete picture of the structure of industry. The relations between the legally separate and formally autonomous units must also be taken into account. In Britain the most significant aspects of these relations are the extensive network of interlocking directorates between the major industrial, banking, and insurance companies on the one hand and, on the other, the proliferation of trade associations which, in their turn, are interlinked through membership of other associations for such purposes as relations with the public and, above all, with government.

Politically, the most important of these "peak" associations appears to be the Confederation of British Industries (CBI). Its members, consisting both of individual firms and of trade associations, cover at least 75 percent of the productive capacity of the country, and its direction is drawn largely from the bigger industrial, banking, and insurance companies. On all major questions of economic and social policy the CBI may expect to be consulted by the government directly or through the many advisory committees on which it has permanent representation. On questions primarily affecting but one industry, the appropriate trade association rather than, or as well as, the CBI will normally be the official spokesman.

World War II and the attempts of the immediately postwar Labour government to plan the economy stimulated both the formation and the enlargement of these associations—for administrators it is much easier to deal with one body than with all the members of a trade or industry separately—with the result that there are now few (if any) important sections of the economy not covered by a trade association. Much of the work of the associations is concerned with technical problems of common interest, collective bargaining with trade unions, and public relations, as well as dealing with the government. But one cannot ignore their effect upon prices and output. It is clear that many of them either formulate and embody agreements of a monopolistic, or cartel-like nature or pave the way for them. The controllers of the private sector of the economy are also linked through such bodies as the British Institute of Management and the Institute of Directors, which are directly connected with each other and the CBI. It is thus impossible to form any impression of the British economy other than that it is directly controlled by an oligarchy.[20] The same people are also to be found on the boards of the nationalized industries.

It is becoming fashionable, particularly in official Labour party publications, to emphasize the fact that the control of large modern companies is increasingly being divorced from ownership. Against this it is sometimes pointed out that, in fact, substantial shareholdings still exist. Professor Sargant Florence found, for example, that in eighty-five large firms with over £3 million paid-up capital, the typical one had between ten and twenty thousand shareholders, but that about twenty of them (individuals and/or other companies) owned nearly one-third of the voting shares. He also concluded that it is possible for such a small group, with as little as 20 percent of the voting shares, to establish "oligarchic minority owners' control." [21] However, it is not very important to determine whether control rests with a majority or minority of owners, or even with nonshareholding directors—at least, not for our present purposes. The essential point is that those who control the private economy are directly accountable at best to a small number of people whose outlook on broad policy questions is likely to be akin to their own,[22] and at worst, only to themselves. It does not follow, of course, that they need pay no attention at all to the interests or opinions of anyone else. Most obviously, they cannot afford to ignore the social and political context (including the possibility of direct governmental action)

[20] It has been suggested that the key members could all meet together in a fairly small motion-picture theater. It is not being asserted that they act on all political issues as a homogeneous group, nor even that in any way they form a single organized or self-conscious group. See the further discussion in Chapter 11.

[21] P. Sargant Florence, *The Logic of British and American Industry* (London: Routledge and Kegan Paul, 1953).

[22] The total number of adult shareholders appears not to exceed 2,000,000, 90 percent of whom have very small holdings indeed and play no part whatsoever in the management of their property.

in which they must survive and carry on their business, but over which they themselves exercise some influence, partly (but by no means solely) through the Conservative party.

The principal countervailing force is probably the trade-union movement. In 1967 the Ministry of Labour recorded a total trade-union membership of over 9,900,000, but this figure includes several bodies not normally considered to be trade unions. The Trades Union Congress (TUC) represents affiliated unions with a membership of only about 8,200,000. The correct figure probably lies somewhere between these two totals. Although, in the same year, total trade union membership only included about 40 percent of the labor force, it extended to well over 75 percent in certain industries and was generally high in manufacturing where most basic wage rates are covered by nationwide collective agreements between management and unions. In 1967 there were 555 unions (1,024 in 1939), of which 160 were affiliated to the TUC, the only large one not affiliated being the National Union of Teachers. The ten largest affiliated unions, those with over 200,000 members, accounted for almost two-thirds of the total affiliated membership (62.7 percent, with nearly 5.5 million members). Among the unions may be found examples of craft, industrial, and general unions as well as federations of many separate ones. But organization by trade, skill, or type of work is more typical than organization by industry. It is this fact that may account for some of the thorniest problems in industrial relations.

It is not possible to measure the power and status of unions precisely, although they are now firmly established features of British society. Like their counterparts among associations of employers, they, either individually or through the TUC, are represented on numerous government advisory committees, and will be consulted on many major issues of social and economic policy. However, trade-union representatives have rarely been found on government-sponsored committees fulfilling a direct controlling or administrative function affecting prices, output, or investment in an industry. Trade unionists are found on the boards of nationalized industries, but in smaller numbers than, for example, men who continue to be directors of private companies. One reason for this has, of course, been the reluctance of the unions to become too closely associated with the management of these industries, lest it interfere with their freedom to negotiate on wages and conditions of work. On the other hand, through their intimate connection with the Labour party, they are able to supplement their direct economic influence with some measure of political power.

As a natural corollary of the organization of the economy, there exists a considerable inequality of income and wealth, although the impact of the former is appreciably modified by taxation. The figures can best be left to speak for themselves. In 1968 the distribution of incomes before and after direct taxes had been paid was roughly as follows, counting the incomes of man and wife as one, and of juveniles separately:

DISTRIBUTION OF INCOME BEFORE AND AFTER DIRECT TAXES

	BEFORE TAXATION		AFTER TAXATION	
Range (*in Pounds*)	*Numbers*	*Total income* (*in Pounds*)	*Numbers*	*Total income* (*in Pounds*)
50– 499	7,294,000	2,351,000,000	8,244,000	2,865,000,000
500– 999	9,136,000	6,726,000,000	10,240,000	7,674,000,000
1,000–1,999	9,510,000	12,972,000,000	8,298,000	10,922,000,000
2,000–4,999	1,668,000	4,430,000,000	954,000	2,478,000,000
5,000 and over*	192,000	1,700,000,000	64,000	406,000,000

* This includes 42,000 incomes over £10,000 before taxes, totaling £700,000,-000; after taxes there were under 2,000 such incomes totaling £63,000,000. SOURCE: Figures adapted from *Whitaker's Almanac 1970*, p. 613.

The redistributive effect of the principal means of direct taxation is obvious. Comparisons with the prewar situation are complicated by changes in the value of money, but it is clear that incomes are less unequal now than they were in 1938, both before and after taxes. Thus it has been estimated that in 1938 some 88 percent of incomes were below £250, as against 60 to 65 percent under the equivalent income of £950 in 1968. At the upper end of the scale, the 2,000 highest incomes in 1938 averaged

£43,500, of which a third was retained after taxes, and in 1956 they averaged £35,000, of which little over a sixth was retained (no allowance being made here for changes in the value of money).

Comparing personal incomes before taxes in 1938 and in 1955, it has been shown that the share of total income accruing to the first hundred thousand dropped from 11.7 percent to 5.3 percent; to the first half-million dropped from 21.5 percent to 12.3 percent; to the first million dropped from 27.8 percent to 17.4 percent; and to the first five million from 51.6 percent to 42.6 percent. Taking account of the price level, it appears that the top groups also had appreciable drops in real income (by about a half in the case of the first hundred thousand) while every group from the second million downward has secured a rise in real income before taxes. Another index of change is provided by the share of personal incomes accounted for by different types of income. Between 1938 and 1956 the share of personal incomes paid out in the form of wages and salaries rose from 56 percent to 65 pereent, for example, while rent, dividends, and interest fell from 22 percent to 11 percent.

Despite the redistribution of incomes that has taken place—principally as a result of taxation and inflation—inequality is still obvious and extensive. It should be emphasized, however, that inequality in spending power (standard of living) is only roughly measured by income figures alone. They take no account of "income" derived from capital gains, expense allowances to business executives and others (for automobiles, meals, and in some cases houses and education), or the spending of capital, which play an increasing and, in London's West End for example, very noticeable part in modern Britain. Nor do they take account of the different kind of addition represented by expenditure on consumers' durable goods under installment-plan schemes, the total indebtedness for which increased from £369 million in 1957 to almost £1,400 million in 1965, after which it declined slightly as a result of government action.

Fewer figures are available for the distribution of property, and they are less precise, but it is possible to indicate the general pattern. Using tax statistics published by the Board of Inland Revenue it has, for example, been calculated that, in the early sixties, one-quarter of personal wealth was owned by the richest 0.5 percent of the population and over one-half by the top 2.5 percent.[23] In 1965–66, according to another study, only 4 million taxpayers (of a total of nearly 22 million) had any income from investments and 500,000 of these owned 60 percent of the total net investment income of over £1,800 million. At the richest end of the range, moreover, there were 37,490 taxpayers with investment portfolios worth, on average, at least £250,000.[24] In 1936–38, however, the richest 1 percent had owned 56 percent of all personal wealth; there has therefore been some reduction in inequality in the thirty years covered by these figures.

To the extent that money brings political power and social prestige, then power and prestige are very unequally distributed. Fortunately for the survival of democratic government in Britain the power of the purse is not unlimited either socially or politically.

SOCIAL STRUCTURE

OCCUPATION AND SOCIAL CLASS

It is a matter of common experience among visitors and residents that the British people are divided by a complex system of social stratification of which they are highly conscious. In addition to the separation imposed by differences of occupation and income common to most societies, they are further kept apart by differences in accent, appearance, and manner to an extent rarely found in, say, the United States.[25] The system, moreover, is national in the sense that there is, broadly, one system rather than a series of

---

[23] See S. Britten, "Tax Wealth Not Gains," *The Observer,* April 8, 1962.

[24] See Oliver Stutchberry, *The Case for Capital Taxes* (London: Fabian Society, 1968), p. 5, and the general argument throughout. It remains to be seen how far the picture will be altered by the increased capital gains tax introduced in 1965 and the attempts made in 1969 to tighten the inheritance taxes.

[25] At certain periods it is probable that in Boston, Massachusetts, and the Deep South comparable social conditions prevailed.

local or regional ones; indeed, to possess a "regional" accent may suffice to bar an individual from full acceptance at the highest level and, generally speaking, the thicker any such accent is, the lower in the scale will a person be placed. The result is that, for many people, an awareness of their status colors their whole approach to life—though by no means necessarily committing them actively to waging a political class war. On the other hand, the enforced mixing and sharing imposed by national participation in World War II led to a temporary breakdown in class feeling which, when it received comment at all, was welcomed by almost everyone known to the author.

Giving an objective picture of the class structure is not made any easier by the prevalence of class consciousness. Different people attach different meanings to the concept of "class," and different pictures emerge according to the criteria of "class-membership" adopted. The official census, for example, groups the population into five social classes and seventeen socio-economic groups, but G. D. H. Cole and others have criticized the bases on which these classifications rest. The British Market Research Bureau, on behalf of the Hulton Readership Survey, has produced a fivefold classification based on the appearance, speech, occupation, type of house, and residential district of the subjects interviewed. The resulting categories are named the well-to-do, middle class, lower middle class, working class (some 60 percent of the total), and poor. Yet again, a detailed investigation carried out by the London School of Economics has found substantial agreement among its subjects about the status ranking of occupations and a general belief that the population should be divided simply into upper, middle, and working classes, although agreement did not extend to the precise boundaries and nature of each class. The reported conclusions of this study still provide the most useful and concrete introduction to class in Britain.[26]

The London study is primarily concerned with occupational mobility as at least one dimension of social mobility. For this

[26] See D. V. Glass, ed., *Social Mobility in Britain* (London: Routledge and Kegan Paul, 1954).

purpose occupations have been grouped, by the investigators and after confirmation by a survey, into seven categories, as follows:

Category	Percentage of employed men in Britain (approx.)
1. Professional and higher administrative	3
2. Managerial and executive	4.5
3. Upper inspectorial, supervisory, and other nonmanual workers	10
4. Lower inspectorial, supervisory, and other nonmanual workers	12.5
5. Skilled manual workers and routine nonmanual	41
6. Semiskilled manual workers	16.5
7. Unskilled	12.5

The confirmatory survey revealed remarkable agreement upon the status ranking of particular occupations and upon the general reliability of this sevenfold classification, although the gaps in status between the categories are nowhere very large.

On the basis of a sample of almost ten thousand adults throughout Britain, a measure of mobility between the generations was then obtained. In crude figures, it was found that the proportion of adults who, in 1949, had reached the same occupational status as that last possessed by their fathers averaged 35.1 percent, but that the proportions varied among the categories. Thus it ranged from 47.3 percent for category 5 and 38.8 percent for category 1, to 21.2 percent for category 4 and 18.8 percent for category 3. This is somewhat misleading in that it takes no account of changes in population and the number of available positions in each category. Accordingly, Professor David Glass and his associates compiled indices of association that take these into account and measure the departure from a purely random association between the status of father and son; the higher the figure, the greater the degree of intergeneration stability, with unity representing "perfect mobility." It was then found that categories 1 and 2 showed a high degree of stability, with indices of 13.158 and 5.865 respectively, while category 5 was in fact highly mobile, with an index of

1.157. On the other hand, in all categories, and whether movement was up or down, a person's status rarely moved far from his father's.

A more restricted survey disclosed that the vast majority in all categories felt that opportunities for social advancement were much wider for their children than themselves, primarily because of improved educational opportunities—although in the main survey there was no significant change in the indices of association for different age groups, a discrepancy that might be explained by the fact that the younger men are still moving upward. Most important for social stability, the smaller survey also showed that, for the most part, parents had ambitions for their children that were in line with the general pattern of mobility, the upper categories having a professional career as the target and the lowest ones, a category 5 career. Not measured by the London study, but overwhelmingly borne out by personal testimony, is the fact that the gap between the highest and lowest categories has narrowed appreciably in the past sixty years, however wide it still may be in terms of living standards, sickness and death rate, consumption patterns, or leisure interests, to mention some of the main criteria.

Occupational categories are not, however, identical with class at all points. The smaller survey carried out by Glass and his associates, for example, showed that members of categories 1 and 2 saw themselves as middle class, as did members of categories 3 and 4, while categories 5, 6, and 7 saw themselves as working class; but one-third of categories 3 and 4 (plus routine nonmanual workers) labeled themselves working class, while about one-quarter of categories 5, 6, and 7 placed themselves in the middle class. The deviant groups were concentrated, so to speak, at the margin: among routine white-collar workers and skilled manual workers. Women as a group tend to upgrade themselves, while the sons of manual workers tend to see themselves as working class, whatever their occupations. (It appears that the reasons for these "deviations" did not consist of snobbery, inverted or otherwise, but of images of the classes concerned, which were in some ways unique: the "deviants" would have placed other members of their occupational category in the same class as themselves to a very large extent.) Moreover, the same survey indicated considerable divergencies in the definitions of the various classes put forward by different groups and individuals: for example, categories 1 and 2 tended to define "upper class" in terms of family or "breeding" (a metaphor commonly used in discussions of the aristocracy or upper class, and apparently drawn from the royal sport of horse racing, but rarely pursued further), a definition applicable to a minute section of the population, whereas the lower categories tended to define it in terms of income, to equate it roughly with "the rich," and thus to include within its boundaries most, but not all, members of categories 1 and 2.

Occupational ranking is not identical, either, with income or wealth, since it apparently takes account of the type of income (salary, fees, commission, or wages, for example), the source of income (government service or shopkeeping, for example), and education as well as monetary reward.[27] The last of these, education, should really be thought of as a distinct criterion of social status, along with money and occupation. Not only do many consider it an essential part of a class image, but it is clearly an important determinant, and result, of income and occupation.

EDUCATION AND SOCIAL CLASS

Although many well-known schools were founded in the sixteenth century and before, it was not until the nineteenth century that even a rudimentary primary education was available for any substantial portion of the population (the first government grants to private, mainly church-run, schools being made in 1833), and not until 1870 that legislation was passed compelling school attendance up to the age of twelve.[28] Acts of Parliament in 1902 and

[27] Even this is not intended to be a comprehensive list of the criteria whereby people evaluate the status of various occupations.
[28] These statements, and most of this section, apply only to England and Wales. Scotland's system and history differ in some important respects. However, because less than 10 percent of the British people live in Scotland, and therefore it is the English system that is most important politically, it will be safe and convenient largely to ignore the Scottish one. Since 1870, moreover, the differences have tended to lessen.

1918 placed state education under the control of the larger local government authorities and extended its scope into the field of secondary education, while compelling school attendance or other full-time instruction between the ages of five and fourteen. No other major change took place before World War II.

In order to appreciate the educational background of the present adult population, it is necessary to say something about the general shape of the prewar system. In 1931 some 80 percent of the population between the ages of eleven and fourteen attended state elementary schools, some of which provided, in their senior classes, more advanced education of an academic or scientific nature. The number of these classes, and of separate state secondary schools, increased during the thirties while, in the more senior schools, some provision was being made for children staying on after the school-leaving age of fourteen. But it cannot be said that any adequate system of secondary education existed for most of the school population. Quite outside the state system there existed, and continue to exist, the private, sometimes called "independent," schools. These included some pioneering progressive schools and many schools possibly better classified as money-making rather than educational establishments, but the most important were the grammar schools[29] and the "public schools" in the field of secondary education, and those primary ones, known as preparatory schools, designed to prepare pupils for entry to the public schools at the age of twelve or thirteen.

The grammar schools generally provided a high standard of education up to the age of about eighteen, mainly but not exclusively in general arts subjects. Their name derived from the fact that the earliest ones taught Latin grammar. Most of them drew their pupils, who attended during the day only, from their own local area, and supported themselves from the fees paid by their pupils and from endowments. Today the name is applied to many other schools—under local authority as well as private management—which provide an academic education. The public schools are mainly boarding schools, draw their pupils from a regional or

[29] Most grammar schools have been absorbed into the state system whereas the rest are "direct grant" schools (see below).

national area, and also support themselves from endowments and fees (which must be high to pay for board as well as tuition). They are thus exclusive as well as private. The name "public school" is a nineteenth-century creation. It refers to the fact that, unlike many of the private schools that then existed, they are run by a board of governors who have no personal financial stake in the schools but who serve as trustees, while the schools themselves are designed to be no more than self-supporting financially. They have all tended to stress the development of the body and "character" through organized sports, collective loyalty, and the acceptance of responsibility—an emphasis that at best has bred self-assurance and the capacity to make decisions but at worst has bred arrogant class-conformism. The best public schools, however, have used their relatively high teacher-pupil ratio and well-qualified staff to provide an excellent academic education. They continue to fulfill the social functions of training future administrators—in government, business, and the armed services, if no longer in the colonies—and of socializing the children of new recruits to the upper echelons of society. As a result of all these factors the demand for their product continues and their endowments still grow, while neither of the two commissions set up by the Labour Governments of 1945 and 1964 has suggested acceptable methods of integrating the independent schools within the national system.

Not everyone would agree that the type of character and social outlook encouraged in public-school children is ideal either for society or for the individuals concerned. There can be no argument, however, about the place of the public schools and, to a lesser degree, the grammar schools in the social structure. In short, the higher the status of the father, the greater the child's chance of attending a grammar or public school, and to have attended one or the other is an invaluable passport to high occupational status, directly or by means of further study at a university. Two examples of the influence of schooling upon career will have to suffice. J. F. S. Ross has estimated that in the interwar years, the House of Commons on average obtained 56 percent of its members from public schools, 21.5 percent from other independent secondary schools, 22.5 percent from the state elementary schools, and that one member in five had been at one or the other of two public schools, Eton and Harrow, with annual outputs of about 250 and 120 boys respectively.[30] Of the top five levels in the civil service, those normally carrying a significant degree of authority, over one-third in 1939 had been to a boarding school, under one-fifth to a state secondary school, and the others to various other kinds of fee-paying secondary school.[31] To buy education at a public or other independent school has thus been an important means of transmitting high social status to one's children. Conversely, gaining entrance into a grammar school or public school, where scholarships, savings, or luck permitted, was and is an almost certain way of moving up in the status scale. At best, however, "education as such appears to modify, but not to destroy, the characteristic association between the social status of father and son." [32]

The Education Act of 1944, passed by the wartime coalition government, was designed to equalize educational opportunity. It remains the legislative basis for today's educational system, the salient features of which may now be described. In England and Wales about 5 percent of all schoolchildren, including the vast majority of those at public schools, remain totally independent of the national system, although local authorities may, and very occasionally do, pay fees for a boy or girl in their area to attend such a school. Within the state maintained system there are the so-called county schools wholly maintained by the local authority; the voluntary schools provided by some other body (mainly churches) but wholly or partly maintained by the local authority; and the direct-grant schools, which receive a grant from the Ministry of Education and are subject to inspection, but

---

[30] In his *Parliamentary Representation,* 2d ed. (London: Eyre and Spottiswoode, 1948), pp. 41–52. The definition of a public school is vague, and the one adopted by Ross may be too wide; but it would apply to schools attended by less than 3 percent of the population.

[31] R. K. Kelsall, *Higher Civil Servants in Britain* (London: Routledge and Kegan Paul, 1955), pp. 118–34. For more recent figures, see page 51, and Chapters 5 and 6.

[32] D. V. Glass, op. cit., p. 307.

which are outside the control of the local authority. The last category, mainly consisting of secondary schools, must provide up to 50 percent of their places to the local authority, but in total cater to only 1.5 percent of all schoolchildren, as opposed to well over 90 percent in the county schools.

One of the main principles of the 1944 Act was to introduce a sharp break between primary and secondary education at the age of eleven and over. On the basis of intelligence and aptitude tests, often supplemented by reports from primary-school teachers, children were allocated to one of three types of secondary school some time between their eleventh and twelfth birthdays. The three types were the grammar schools, providing a more or less academic education designed to equip children for further education or the higher white-collar occupations; the secondary modern schools, whose "main role," according to a special article in the Manchester *Guardian* for July 28, 1959, ". . . is to staff the lower echelons of Britain's vast industrial machine—particularly with unskilled and semi-skilled workers," and the secondary technical schools (the smallest category) providing training in various industrial, agricultural, and commercial subjects.[33] The grammar school, however, is the highroad to subsequent prestige and material reward. Only there, for example, will the majority of pupils take the examinations for the General Certificate of Education (GCE). These are conducted under the auspices of the Ministry of Education, but administered by examination boards consisting largely of university teachers. GCE results serve as the most important basis for admission to a university and the award of grants for further education, as well as for acceptance in numerous skilled and white-collar occupations.

Since the 1944 Act was implemented, two politically important changes have taken place within the state system. The first is the decision to stop using the strict selection process to determine which children go to which type of secondary school. Selection quickly came under fire, mainly from the Labour party but also

[33] There are, in addition, various special schools for children with various kinds of mental or physical handicap, both at the primary and secondary level.

from enough Conservative supporters to induce their party not to oppose its modification directly.[34] The selection process itself seemed fallible; the numbers of places in each category of school differed too widely between the different local authority areas for justice even to appear to be done, and an increasing body of evidence suggested that to select was in part to make a self-fulfilling prophecy, the secondary modern school being regarded as inferior by teachers, parents, and children. To modify the process was not enough to calm anxiety completely. The demand therefore arose for the introduction of comprehensive, all-ability secondary schools akin to American high schools, both for educational reasons and in the name of social equality. In 1970 all local authorities were obliged to propose schemes for transforming secondary education along comprehensive lines.[35] Consequently, the numbers of children attending comprehensive schools grew from 7,988 in 1950 to 604,428 in 1968 and, it has been estimated, to over 1 million in 1970. According to official 1968 Department of Education and Science (DES) returns, children were divided between the different categories of state secondary school as follows:

	Number	Percent of Total
Secondary modern	1,367,367	(47.2)
Grammar	655,702	(22.7)
Comprehensive	604,428	(20.9)
Technical	62,021	(2.1)
All other*	205,869	(7.1)
	2,895,387	(100.0)

* Mainly special schools for children with various kinds of mental or physical disability.

The second important change is the immense growth in the costs of public education, for which one of the chief causes has been the unforeseen increase in the number of children staying

[34] See D. Butler and A. King, *The General Election of 1966* (London: Macmillan, 1966), p. 93.
[35] The new Conservative government has removed the obligation, but the trend is likely to continue.

on at school beyond the minimum statutory leaving age of fifteen (to be raised to sixteen in the 1970s). Thus, whereas in 1950, 70 percent of the relevant age group left school as soon as they could, in 1968 only 31 percent of a larger total did so. Significantly for higher education, moreover, the number staying on until the age of eighteen increased from 2.1 percent of the age group in 1950 to 5.8 percent—a trend that (in 1970) is expected to continue. In 1969–70 public expenditure on all forms of education rose to over £2,200 million and, for the first time in British history, exceeded the budget for defense.

It is difficult to estimate the precise effects of the 1944 Act upon social mobility. It is clear, however, that equality of educational opportunity has not yet been achieved. The independent fee-paying schools remain largely unaffected and, indeed, are reported to have longer waiting lists for entry than ever before. Within the state system itself, moreover, the children of parents from the higher occupational levels not only appear to stand a better chance of attending a grammar school, but, once admitted, fare better and stay on past the minimum leaving age longer than do children of, say, manual workers.[36] Conversely, and to this extent the system helps to perpetuate and not merely reflect the class structure, there is a significant increase in median income the higher the age at which people finish their education—although the difference is greatest among the older age groups in the population.[37]

However, there are signs that the difference is now lessening. In any event, the extent to which the remedy for the differences

[36] Thus, according to investigation of a 10 percent sample, 35 percent of those entering grammar schools in 1946, and over 50 percent of those staying on after fifteen were children of people in census categories 1 and 2, as opposed to about 21 percent and 15 percent from categories 4 and 5 (Central Advisory Council for Education *Report on Early Leaving,* 1954). See also D. V. Glass, op. cit., pp. 291–307.

[37] See Mark Abrams, "Rewards of Education," *New Society,* July 9, 1964, p. 26, where he reports the result of his sample survey study of the relationship between income and education. Amongst those aged 45–64, the median income of male heads of households who continued their education to age nineteen or beyond was three times that of those who had left school at fifteen or earlier.

within the state system lies in further educational reform is probably slight. Insofar as one is here presented with non-hereditary factors, like the incentive to study or the facilities to do so at home, the remedy must consist of more radical and more generalized types of social action that deal directly with the bases of social stratification. The degree of inequality is well summarized in the table on page 51.

To complete the picture it may be noted that only about a quarter of all United Kingdom entrants to British universities are the children of manual workers and that the numbers entering vary considerably according to the type of secondary school from which they came. Thus, while 7.8 percent of all boys leaving secondary school in 1967 entered a university, the proportion of boys who did so from secondary modern schools was less than 1 percent as opposed to 4.1 percent from comprehensive, 25.2 percent from state grammar schools, 27.1 percent from those independent schools that had sought and obtained official recognition as efficient, and 37.6 percent from direct grant schools. The proportions of grammar school pupils and children of manual workers who entered Oxford and Cambridge are beneath the national average for all universities.[38] On the whole, university education appears to be less important for social mobility than school education, although it may be decisive for some individuals (for example, the very few university entrants from a secondary modern school).[39] The numbers involved may be comparatively small. University education nevertheless does provide a possible means of promotion into the professional middle class or beyond, even for children from much lower in the social scale: for those affected, it may have dramatic results.

In the academic year 1969–70, there were forty-four universities in Britain of which only six were founded before 1800 (four of them in Scotland) and of which over half were founded or

---

[38] Kelsall, op. cit., pp. 32–34 and 37. The figures include children educated in Scotland, grouped in the rough equivalent categories of schools. According to a table in *The OECD Observer,* vol. 47 (1970), p. 43, however, a higher proportion of British university students were of working-class origin in 1960 than in any other OECD country.

[39] D. V. Glass, op. cit., pp. 291–307.

CHILDREN'S SCHOOL RECORDS CLASSIFIED BY FATHER'S OCCUPATION
IN PERCENT

	NONMANUAL		ALL MANUAL		SKILLED MANUAL ONLY	
	Male %	Fe-male	Male %	Fe-male	Male %	Fe-male
Grade I in selection test for secondary school	33.5	36.1	66.5	63.9	45.3	43.9
Category A in maintained grammar school record	52.6	62.1	47.5	37.9	38.8	32.8
Admitted* to British universities from maintained grammar schools, 1955–56	63.5	74.5	36.5	25.5	30.3	21.9
Admitted* to British universities from all secondary schools, 1955–56	74.0	81.4	26.0	18.6	21.7	16.1

* United Kingdom students with permanent addresses in England.
SOURCE: Adapted, by permission, from R. K. Kelsall, *Report on an Inquiry into Applications for Admission to Universities* (London: Association of Universities of the British Commonwealth, for the Committee of Vice-Chancellors and Principals of the Universities of the United Kingdom, 1957), p. 10.

achieved university status after 1945. They are all self-governing, coeducational, and private in the sense that they are neither owned nor managed by the central or local governments. On the other hand, universities may be established only by a Royal Charter, which is awarded on the recommendation of the University Grants Committee (UGC)[40] and the Department of Education and Science (DES) if the government is prepared to make the necessary resources available. They are in fact financed by government grants to the extent of over 70 percent of their normal revenue and they look to the government also as a (in some cases, the) principal source of money for capital expenditure. The steady growth in the annual total of grants for both purposes, which reached

[40] For further information about the UGC, see Chapter 6.

£250 million in 1969, resulted, in 1967, in the decision to open university accounts to inspection by the Public Accounts Committee of the House of Commons, assisted by the comptroller and auditor general and his staff.[41]

In October 1969 almost 220,000 students (including 38,000 postgraduates) were enrolled in these universities. About 140,000 of them received grants from their local authority which, in many cases, amounted to the full cost of fees and maintenance. (With few exceptions, all who are admitted by a university will receive a grant whose amount usually depends on parental income.) Grants to students at universities and other institutions of higher education cost the government almost £100 million in 1969.

Despite the fact that the number of universities has almost quadrupled since 1939, Britain's student population still constitutes one of the lowest in the industrialized western world at about 8 percent of the relevant age group.[42] This bald comparison is misleading, however. The proportion of students admitted who eventually graduate is, at over 85 percent, exceptionally high (in the United States it is in the region of 50 percent). However, if one merely considers the universities, one is seriously underestimating the number of people in higher education. In various colleges —art, technical, teacher training, and commercial—another 200,000 full-time students (October 1969) were studying a variety of courses leading to qualifications of university degree standard. By the end of 1970 many of the colleges will amalgamate into thirty polytechnics whose concentration will be on advanced work for degrees awarded by the Council for National Academic Awards (established in 1964) or similar qualifications. The polytechnics will, in effect, constitute a system of state universities under direct supervision of the DES and local authorities, but will be granted substantial academic autonomy, and will be

[41] See Chapter 5. Because of this extension of government interest, and the closer degree of guidance adopted by the UGC in the sixties, a proposal was floated in 1969 to establish a new university that would be independent of government financial support.

[42] DES press notice, November 25, 1969.

distinguished from the older universities by, at least initially, a greater emphasis on teaching (as distinct from research) and on the more practical and applied aspects of the various disciplines.[43] Taking all forms of higher education together, it is clear that first-year students amounted to something like one-quarter of the eighteen- to nineteen-year-old age group by 1968.[44] These numbers are expected to increase, and possibly to double by 1980, even excluding the unpredictable number who, through radio, television, correspondence, and local courses, will enroll in the Open University—which is scheduled to begin classes in 1971 and is designed to make higher education readily available to virtually anyone capable of benefiting from it. Other kinds of further—i.e., post-secondary school—education, full and part time, cater to another one and three-quarter million in the major government-aided institutions alone. How to finance or render less expensive the continuing expansion will therefore be a principal policy consideration for the 1970s.

Graduation from a university (or polytechnic for that matter) is obviously an important determinant of occupational status, although, as we have seen, admission is itself greatly influenced by a person's secondary education. Among the universities, moreover, the traditional preeminence of Oxford and Cambridge has not been noticeably undermined. Having for centuries been the only universities in England and Wales, and possessing further advantages in their residential and collegiate nature, they attract a large number of the ablest members of each generation. This is both a cause and a result of their reputation for providing the best available university education (the extent to which the reputation is justified is irrelevant here) and is also closely related, again both as cause and effect, to the disproportionate number of Oxford and Cambridge graduates in the higher levels of busi-

---

[43] This bifurcation of higher education between the universities and the polytechnics is commonly known as the "Binary system."

[44] In which year, according to the DES, 21.4 percent of the group took up new government grants to enter higher education in England and Wales.

ness, government, and the civil service, as well as university teaching, to name only the most important examples. Thus, to amplify this statement in the political sphere, on the average from 1918 through 1951, 32 percent of members of Parliament had been to either Oxford or Cambridge (56.5 percent had not attended any university); of the 185 persons who had been cabinet ministers from 1916 to 1955, 87 had been at Oxford or Cambridge; and, in 1967, of the graduates in the highest class of home civil servants (the Administrative Class, three-quarters of whom possessed a degree), 64 percent were from Oxford or Cambridge.[45] It is worth noting that graduates from Oxford and Cambridge in 1938–39 made up 22 percent of all those graduating, and that this figure had dropped well below 15 percent by 1965.

These educational developments since World War II, although largely to be explained in terms of the demands for skill generated by the economy, must exercise an important long-term influence on the distribution of opportunity—even if the effect is only, as pessimistic egalitarians fear, to help the lower middle class and, possibly, to enlarge its membership. Meantime, however, it continues to reflect, and in some degree to maintain, the inequalities of status, prestige, and influence in British society. Thus, a social survey of the civil service concludes, with reference to its highest ranks, that the "chances of a successful career are enhanced by 'superior' social origins, a privileged school background, and a university education at Oxford or Cambridge. These three variables are also correlated with each other . . . [but] university attendance seems to be the crucial predictor of chances of reaching the upper grades of the administrative class." [46] To a lesser but still significant extent, the conclusion applies to most other major social institutions. Despite unequal access, however, education

[45] Figures from J. F. S. Ross, *Elections and Electors* (London: Eyre and Spottiswoode, 1955), p. 419; W. L. Guttman, *The British Political Elite* (London: MacGibbon and Kee, 1963), p. 106; and a memorandum submitted to the Committee on the Civil Service by A. H. Halsey and I. M. Crewe, *The Civil Service, Vol. 3 (1): Social Survey of the Civil Service* (London: HMSO, 1969), p. 27.

[46] Halsey and Crewe, op. cit., p. 89. It should be added that the Civil Service Department is trying to attract more recruits from other universities.

modifies the influence of wealth and inherited status and complicates the social structure with elements of "meritocracy."

POLITICS AND THE SOCIAL STRUCTURE

Education, occupation, and income thus appear to be the primary determinants of social status. Particularly at the peak of the social scale, however, an individual is liable to classification in terms of his ancestry and not only on the strength of his achievements. The existence and prestige of the monarchy probably provide a partial explanation for the continuing vitality of this older idea of a hereditary aristocracy whose claim to social preeminence does not rest upon, although it is closely associated with, the monetary and occupational badges distinctive to modern industrial societies. This small "upper class" is not an exclusive caste. Intermarriage and other ties link it closely with other highly placed groups. It is not by any means to be identified with the possessors of titles, not even with the peerage: many lords, as well as knights, must be classified as middle class and, in a few cases, working class, while many acknowledged members of the upper class do not themselves bear any title.

It is easy, perhaps, to criticize the notion that heredity confers social status directly. On the other hand, no account of the rise of socialism in Britain can ignore the role of the aristocracy as the concrete embodiment of a classification system alternative to that of purely economic and financial success. Socialist criticism of social differences must surely have been facilitated by aristocratic resistance to the social ambitions of industrial and commercial leaders as well as by the challenge the latter presented to the older system. British society has not yet been permeated by the capitalist or industrial ethos to the same extent as American. Today it is the coming together of the aristocracies of birth and wealth at the top levels, rather than the distinctions between them, which is most apparent to the outside observer. The educational system, the incursions of the aristocracy into business (necessitated by taxation and the declining profitability of landowning), and external pressure from political radicalism have probably been the most important factors making for upper-class "togetherness." Throughout history, however, the British aristocracy has shown itself, when compared with many of its continental European counterparts, to be remarkably adaptable and receptive to new blood.

Given the significant degree of occupational immobility and its relation to the educational system and the distribution of income, and given also the degree of class consciousness present in British society, it is inevitable that class and status should be essential elements in the political life of the country. In the next chapter we shall see the close connection that exists between class and allegiance to the Conservative and Labour parties. Equally important, however, is the influence of class upon the relations between some of the principal wielders of power and influence within the community.

One effect of the social structure we have described is to create a wide network of personal links among many of the top decision-makers in government, the civil service, the armed forces, the Established Church of England, and certain sections of the economy. Inevitably, something of the sort is to be found in any society. People of wealth and influence naturally come together socially as well as in the course of business. But in Britain, not only do the "top people" acquire social ties through membership of the same clubs or patronage of the same hotels and resorts; many of them already share a common background of public school, Oxford or Cambridge, or even of ancestry.

The associations with government (i.e., with ministers and members of Parliament) are particularly notable under Conservative party rule, when kinship, business, and educational background combine to produce an extensive and intricate web of relationships throughout the political, financial, and social worlds.[47] The importance of this web, it may be suggested, lies in its nature as an informal system of access to some of the key decision-mak-

---

[47] For a study of some aspects thereof, see the study by T. Lupton and C. Shirley Wilson, the results of which were published in the *Manchester School,* January 1959, and which is reprinted in R. Rose, ed., *Policy-Making in Britain* (London: Macmillan, 1969), pp. 5–25.

ing areas, and the encouragement it gives to an equally informal system of decision-making and mutual consultation "between friends," sometimes referred to as the "old boy network." [48] From it the Labour party is largely excluded.

Undeniably, informal discussions and negotiations are indispensable adjuncts to any system of government. It is also undeniable, however, that relying upon them very extensively may raise grave difficulties for all concerned when a non-Conservative government is in office, and at any time may lead to irresponsibility, excessive secrecy, a failure to consider relevant information or opinion, and the frustration of the democratic process. On the other hand, it may also lead to flexibility, speedy decisions, and, for those involved, a high degree of confidence in the decision-making process.

The foregoing picture of a ruling elite, or interconnected set of elites, lacks sufficient perspective and may be misleading if it is not qualified. The immobility at the top levels is by no means total: people from a wide range of social origins are to be found in all the key groups mentioned. The educational reforms of 1944 may, and probably will, in time lead to greater mobility into the top positions. These points affect only the personal composition of the ruling groups, however; they do not affect the groups' position in society, and may not radically affect the behavior of the groups. More important is the fact that the top decision-makers are by no means united on all issues. Clearly the interests of key people in such occupations as the civil service, banking, and insurance will frequently be in sharp conflict with each other.[49]

---

[48] The *Report of the Tribunal appointed to Inquire into Allegations of Improper Disclosure of Information relating to the Raising of the Bank Rate* (London: HMSO, Cmnd. 350 of January 1958), and its *Proceedings and Evidence,* provide a revealing and unique account of its operation.

[49] Lupton and Wilson, loc. cit., "suggest that 'top decision-makers' as well as being linked by kinship, business interests, and similar background, are also divided by competing, even conflicting, interests. Indeed kinship itself, in certain circumstances, may act as a divisive as well as a uniting force."

Nevertheless, it is probably safe to assume substantial agreement upon the desirability of maintaining the conditions—social, political, and economic—that permit these people to exercise their influence and pursue their interests in the accustomed fashion. (Disagreement exists about the precise nature of these conditions, and about the way in which the "top people" can best ensure the continuance of their power in the face of uncontrollable changes in circumstances. Such disagreements should not be confused, although they often are, with arguments about *whether* the present ruling groups are entitled to their positions of special power. It is equally important not to confuse arguments about the personal composition of ruling groups with ones about the desirability or otherwise of fostering any small ruling groups at all. The "progressive" character of the Conservative party since its defeat at the 1945 general election, in the author's judgment, relates only to the personal composition of the ruling groups and to the methods of maintaining their position; on the more fundamental questions the Conservative outlook is little different from what it has been in earlier years.)

The most important and obvious qualification that must be made to an "elitist" picture of British society is provided by the representative system and the existence of political parties that provide a direct challenge to the power of the established decision-makers in society. The Liberal party, until World War I, and thereafter the Labour party, have not only been channels whereby excluded groups have achieved a share in government and an acknowledgment of their right to do so, but, by their very existence and programs, they have made it necessary for all parties and groups to exercise their power in ways more acceptable to the people as a whole.

The distribution of power in society has placed severe limitations upon what any reform government can achieve by democratic methods, and at no time in this century can it be said that either the Liberal or Labour parties have successfully sustained a direct radical attack on the power of the ruling groups. On the other hand, they have made it possible for manual workers to attain government offices that would have seemed unthinkable fifty years ago, and they have been influential in bringing about at least the sense of wider opportunity to which we have already referred, as well as a wide extension of the material badges of status and recognized worth. It is the impact of political democracy and liberal ideals upon an oligarchical society, and vice versa, which give much of the tone and style to British politics.

3

The Political Public

The election of a new House of Commons must by law be held no later than five years after the previous one. It may, however, be postponed with the consent of the House of Lords. This provision has only been invoked during the two world wars. On the other hand, there is no need for a government to wait five years before advising the monarch to dissolve Parliament and order the election of a new one, and it rarely does. There were, for example, thirteen elections in the fifty years following the 1918 one—and this includes a period of ten years, 1935–45, in which no election was held.[1]

There is only one election of members of the House of Commons, but the choice of prime minister and the cabinet is immediately dependent upon its outcome, as the government consists of the leaders of the party or coalition of parties winning a majority of seats in the House.

THE ELECTORAL SYSTEM

For electoral purposes Britain is divided into 618 constituencies,[2] each returning one member to the House of Commons, and each consisting of an average of 57,000 electors. As a concession to nationalist feelings, the size of a constituency is smaller in Scot-

[1] For further discussion about the power to dissolve the House of Commons see Chapter 4.
[2] There are twelve more in Northern Ireland, with an electorate in 1966 of about 922,000.

land and Wales. It also tends to be smaller in the more rural constituencies than in urban ones, not in order to give a greater voice
to the country voter, but to prevent areas from becoming unman-
ageable. Since 1944 the task of defining the constituencies has
been entrusted to permanent boundary commissions, which apply
certain general rules agreed upon by the major parties and embodied in Acts of Parliament, and which are appointed by the
government, although they are independent of political control in
their operations. By an Act of 1958 the commissions must review
constituency boundaries every ten to fifteen years. Their recommendations are generally, if not necessarily, accepted by the cabinet and Parliament.[3]

Universal adult suffrage is the rule,[4] each qualified person having one vote in the area in which he or she resides. The local
registration officer, a senior local-government official, is responsible in each area for compiling the annual register of voters. Those
who move their place of residence between registers, if they give
sufficient notice and satisfy certain other very minor conditions,
may vote by post in their former constituency, as may invalids
and others prevented by the nature of their employment from
polling in person. Only a person whose name is on the register
may vote, and it is an offense to vote in more than one constituency. A few people may be disfranchised through omissions when
the register was compiled or through failing to apply for a postal
vote, and in some constituencies where there have been large
movements of people, this may be important. But the great majority of the adult population find themselves automatically entitled to vote near their homes at each election. Voting machines
are not used, votes being cast by marking the official ballot papers
with pen or pencil. The papers are numbered, so that allegations

[3] However, the recommendations have not always been accepted cheer-
fully. See P. G. Richards, *Honourable Members* (London: Faber,
1959), pp. 44–49; and G. Marshall and G. C. Moodie, *Some Problems
of the Constitution,* 4th ed. (London: Hutchinson, 1967), pp. 96–101.
In 1969 they were rejected by the government despite strong objec-
tions to its decision.

[4] In January 1970, eighteen years replaced twenty-one as the legal age of
majority.

of fraud or irregularity may be checked if necessary. Only under those circumstances would the secrecy of the vote be violated in any way, and even then the way in which individual legitimate votes were cast would not be made public. The counting of the votes is carried out manually by the returning officer and his assistants, who are also usually local-government officials, in the presence of the candidates and their representatives. The candidate who secures the largest number of votes is elected, regardless of whether or not it amounts to an absolute majority of all the votes cast. Where there are three or more candidates standing in a constituency, it is thus possible to be returned to Parliament with well under 50 percent of the votes.

One result of this "first past the post" system, taken in conjunction with the different sizes of constituency, is that the number of seats won by a party in the House of Commons is never in exact proportion to the number of votes won in the country. If one takes the ten elections fought since women secured the vote on the same conditions as men, namely those from 1929 through 1966, we find the following notable "injustices" (as critics of the system would put it): only in 1931 and 1935 did the government with a parliamentary majority also win 50 percent or more of the total number of popular votes. In 1929 and 1951 the party with the largest number of popular votes did not even win the most parliamentary seats (the sufferers being, respectively, Conservative and Labour) but, on the other hand, only in 1929 did no party secure an absolute majority of seats in the House of Commons. The Liberal party, in this period, has been consistently underrepresented—for example, in 1929 it gained over one-fifth of the votes but less than one-tenth of the seats, and in 1950, almost one-tenth of the votes but only about one-seventieth of the seats. The experience of the Labour party might also suggest a need to reform the system: it won about one-twelfth of the seats with nearly one-third of the votes in 1931; almost two-thirds of the seats with 48 percent of the votes in 1945, and then, in 1951, a hundred fewer seats with a slightly increased share of the vote.

In fact, however, neither the Conservative nor Labour party

favors electoral reform today, and the consensus of academic opinion supports them in this.[5] The system is not purely capricious. Usually, the tiny overall majorities of six and two in 1950 and 1964 being notable exceptions, it ensures that an adequate working majority is given to that one party that gains the largest share of the votes or, as in 1929 and 1951, to that one of the two biggest parties whose popularity is on the increase; for any given swing in votes it is possible to predict, within reasonable limits, the resulting change in parliamentary strength. It is thus substantially fair as between the two major parties. The winning party, moreover, can normally be counted upon to pay as much attention, in the conduct of government, to its popular as to its parliamentary support.

It is the lesser parties that suffer most, but not necessarily mortally. If the support for a minor party is geographically concentrated, as was the case with the Irish Nationalists before World War I, rather than diffused thinly and evenly over the whole country, as has been the case with the Liberals more recently, a party will probably win *at least* its fair share of seats. But even in the case of the Liberals, it is difficult to believe that the electoral system has done more than hasten a decline brought about by internal disunity and the party's failure to retain or capture the support of any major socioeconomic interest. The supplanting of the Liberals by Labour as the other main party itself demonstrates that the system puts no insuperable barrier in the way of a newer party, provided only that its potential appeal is strong enough and wide enough.

For these reasons, reinforced by the traditional preference for strong governments, which calls for governments with cohesive majorities behind them in the House of Commons, the electoral system is generally acceptable to the British people. It is supported largely because it works reasonably well in terms of a

[5] See, in particular, D. E. Butler, *The British Electoral System Since 1918* (London: Oxford University Press, 1963); the case for reform is well argued in J. F. S. Ross, *Elections and Electors* (London: Eyre and Spottiswoode, 1955), and E. Lakeman and J. S. Lambert, *Voting in Democracies*, 2d ed. (London: Faber, 1955).

two-party system, and may even help to maintain a two-party system—just as, in turn, it is maintained by the two major parties and criticized only (since they became a minor party) by the Liberals.

THE PARTY SYSTEM

It is not literally true to say that Britain has a two-party system. Besides the two major parties, Conservative and Labour, some thirty parties put up candidates at the general election of 1966 and/or at by-elections in the following three years, and fifteen parties did so at the 1970 general election. Of these, the most significant is the Liberal party, which has never contested fewer than one hundred seats in a postwar election. Moreover, splits in existing parties (such as those affecting the Liberals in 1886 and 1932), or the rise of new organizations (like the Irish Nationalists in the nineteenth century and the Labour party in the twentieth), may at any time add to the number of parties.

It is substantially correct, nevertheless, to talk of a two-party system in the sense that this appears to be the parliamentary norm and that, whenever it is departed from, it tends to reestablish itself. Historically it was in the interests of the crown and its chief advisers to try to unify their supporters, an attempt that encouraged a similar unification among their parliamentary opponents if they were to be successful. Once established, such polarizing tendencies are in some degree self-perpetuating. The desire to defeat its former comrades may impel a break-away group to adhere closely to the other major party, from which, in time, it becomes barely distinguishable. Thus the Liberal Unionists and later the Liberal Nationalists have been absorbed by the Conservative party in all but name.[6]

[6] In Scotland the Conservatives, who had little support there before being joined by the Liberal Unionists, are called Unionists officially, as are their allies from Northern Ireland (Ulster Unionists). The Liberal Nationals maintain a degree of organizational independence in Parliament and elsewhere—but to the outsider this is their only distinctive feature.

The desire to remain one of the two chief contenders for office makes the established parties anxious to prove third parties unnecessary by embracing their policies so far as their own principles and supporters will allow. A third party will probably have difficulty in maintaining a "balance of power" role in Parliament. It is liable to find that only one of the major parties is sympathetic to its aims, in which case it either becomes increasingly dependent upon that party, or is forced into unconstitutional action, as happened eventually to the Irish Nationalists. Alternatively, if it is in a position to determine which of the two other parties shall form a government, it is not only subjected to internal division about which party to support, but it is also liable to become increasingly unpopular with the electors for confusing the issue, blurring the lines of responsibility, or for making the "wrong" choice of government. The Liberal party almost certainly suffered in this way after it had first supported, and then later withdrawn its support from the minority Labour governments of 1924 and 1929–31. On top of all this, the ascendancy of the two major parties is ensured by the electoral system and, since the end of the war, by the electorate's manifest dislike for any diversion from what it apparently regards as the main issue, namely the decision as to whether there should be a Conservative or Labour government in the succeeding Parliament.[7] We may therefore concentrate on these two parties in discussing party organization.

The leaders of the Conservative and Labour parties in the House of Commons are either past, present, or potential prime ministers. The other leading figures in each party will be past, present, or potential members of a government. Whether in office or in opposition, therefore, the parliamentary party leadership is normally the most powerful single group within each party. Its position is bolstered, too, by the tradition of "collective respon-

[7] Since 1945 no genuinely independent candidate has won a seat in a general election. In the House of Commons elected in 1966 only the Speaker, one Northern Ireland M.P., and twelve Liberals were independent of the two major parties. By the end of 1969 they had been joined by two "defectors" and four new members, including the Scottish and Welsh nationalist victors of two by-elections.

sibility" when in office,[8] according to which all the members of a government must be prepared publicly to defend the complete record of the government or resign. That is, they must present a united front to the public. To lend conviction to its claim to be the alternative government, the opposition party must show that it, too, is capable of promoting a correspondingly cohesive team. Politically, unity almost always brings strength. The strength of this leadership has steadily increased and its power is rarely threatened. But the leadership must nevertheless use its power in ways that do not disrupt its party—and this is not always easy.

The leader of each party is selected by his colleagues in Parliament. In the Labour party the members of Parliament choose their leader by ballot; but after his initial election a leader has only once been opposed, in 1960. The balloting is repeated annually when Labour is in opposition. The deputy leader and the other members of the parliamentary committee are also chosen by annual ballot when in opposition, although it is becoming clear that a Labour prime minister would not feel bound to appoint every member of the committee to an important ministerial post, despite the practice of referring to them collectively as the "shadow cabinet."

Up to and including the selection of Sir Alec Douglas-Home to succeed Harold Macmillan in 1963, the Conservatives chose their leader by a process of informal consultation and recommendation by their elder statesmen. The final decision, however, rested with the monarch (acting upon advice) and subsequently, with a party meeting; when in opposition the decision of the party meeting was not formally ratified until the new leader had been appointed prime minister. The 1963 election, coinciding with the annual party conference and taking place when no man commanded a clear preponderance of support, became so chaotic that it led to something approaching a public brawl before Sir Alec was nominated by Mr. Macmillan.[9] Partly further to remove the monarch from the risk of such involvement, and partly because for a day

[8] See Chapter 4.
[9] See the journalistic account in A. Howard and R. West, *The Making of a Prime Minister* (London: Cape, 1965).

there remained some doubt as to whether Home could persuade certain key figures to serve in his cabinet, an elaborate system of formal balloting was introduced and was used early in 1965 to select Sir Alec's successor. A Conservative leader, once chosen, appoints his cabinet or "shadow cabinet," as well as the heads of the party organization, without further formal constraint. But, as in the Labour party, the leader must heed the wishes of his supporters in all he does.

Significant historical and ideological differences also exist between the parties in the constitutional relationship of their leader with the annual party conference. The Conservative party in Parliament antedates its national organization, and any attempts to give the latter a greater than ancillary status have failed. The Labour party, on the other hand, was established in 1900 jointly by trade unions and Socialist organizations as their parliamentary spokesman.[10] The constitution of the party still embodies this conception to the extent, for example, that the annual conference is stated to be the supreme policy-making body, whose decisions must be implemented by the other party organs, including, it might be thought, a Labour cabinet. The practical need for day-to-day policy decisions in Parliament and the centripetal influence of the cabinet system have undermined this original intention, but have not been able to free Labour leaders from a heavier and more difficult task of "managing" their conference than faces the Conservatives. By and large they have succeeded: but only so long as the leadership is fairly united and can maintain sufficient support among the largest trade unions.

In Labour conferences all organizations represented wield a block vote—i.e., they cast, in one block, as many votes as they have members affiliated with the Labour party, without regard to the divisions of opinion within the organization. The decisive voting power then rests with the unions, which accounted in 1967 for over 5,500,000 out of a total of 6,300,000 party members, and particularly with the seven largest unions, which, when they are all in agreement, command a majority.

[10] It was originally called the Labour Representation Committee. It did not adopt the name of the Labour party until 1906.

Successive Labour governments have made it plain that they are not the servants of the conference or its National Executive Committee (which includes some of the parliamentary leadership). Nevertheless, the traditional ideology of the party confers a legitimacy upon conference decisions such that they are not disregarded lightly or without the need to offer a strong justification. Hugh Gaitskell, supported by most Labour members of Parliament, successfully fought the 1960 decision "committing" the party to a policy of unilateral nuclear disarmament, but it is far from certain that he would have continued as leader or been able to maintain an even formally united party had he not secured a reversal of the decision in 1961. Normally, therefore, the leaders take great care—through their representatives on the National Executive Committee, constant consultation and negotiation with union leaders, more informal means of influencing the agenda and proceedings of the conference, and by seeking neither to do nor propose anything that the conference is certain to reject—to avoid a fundamental confrontation. Although drama and friction are endemic features of the process, the leaders lead.[11] The party has prided itself, however, on the public way in which its major decisions are reached, and its equally public acknowledgment of its political and financial dependence upon the trade-union movement.[12] Conversely, it attacks the Conservative party for its failure to disclose the sources of its income, or to acknowledge its widely believed dependence on the business world in respect to both policy and finance.

In both parties, then, the leaders emerge from the parliamentary conflict, and are immediately (but not wholly) dependent

[11] For conflicting accounts of the situation see R. T. McKenzie, *British Political Parties,* 2d ed. (London: Heinemann, 1963); S. H. Beer, *Modern British Politics* (London: Faber, 1965); and a study of the Labour party by Lewis A. Minkin (forthcoming).

[12] The unions normally contribute over two-thirds of the party's national funds, the rest coming mainly from individual subscriptions and donations. This two-thirds does not include contributions to the local party organizations in each constituency. See Martin Harrison's *Trade Unions and the Labour Party since 1945* (London: Allen and Unwin, 1960).

for their position upon their parliamentary colleagues. They must also be acceptable to the business and trade-union sources of finance. And by no means least, they must be acceptable to the party militants, i.e., the actual rank-and-file members. Their support is necessary not only because of their participation in the conferences, for all that it may be secured or alienated there (in which fact, perhaps, lies the main significance of conference). It is necessary rather because of the other bases of rank-and-file influence: they constitute the indispensable, and almost entirely voluntary corps of helpers who do the actual work of the parties in the constituencies; and they select the party candidates for all elections. These local party workers are enticed into the party to some extent by its policies and personnel. Once in, however, their attitudes and their morale will influence both—primarily through their contacts with and importance to the successful party candidates. And once in, they are subject to little control from the central party organization and leaders. In effect, central control consists only of the power to refuse to recognize a candidate or constituency organization as authorized users of the party label, and to expel, or refuse to sanction the local expulsion of, individual party members. The power rarely needs to be used, and then mainly in the Labour party (subject to ratification by its conference), but it is an indispensable weapon in the hands of any party jealous for its reputation and anxious to maintain a noticeable degree of political homogeneity.

Both parties thus contain hard cores, in terms of interests and members, from whom they draw their finances and their workers, and who limit as well as inspire party policy. It is one of the tasks of their leaders to reconcile the inevitable conflicts within the party cores, and then to reconcile the interests and attitudes of the cores with those of the electorate at large. Success in this task is neither easy nor inevitable. But it is recognized to be the duty primarily of the parliamentary leaders to accomplish it, and in both parties the basic difficulties are similar. The important differences between the parties lie more in the tone and atmosphere of the intraparty struggle than in the constitutional provisions. The Conservatives are apparently prepared to allow more discretion to the leader, while being no less prepared to change him; and Labour members appear to demand more consideration from their leader, while being no more prepared to change him.

The most important feature of the party system is, of course, that it provides and supports governments. It is this, as has been suggested, that largely determines the location of power and initiative within the parties. It is also, with their work in organizing, mobilizing, and educating the voters, the parties' great justification. The parties' role of providing and supporting government is most evident in the House of Commons, where they provide the leaders from whom governments are formed, and then, in the case of the majority party, vote loyally and regularly in support of government policy. Most distinctively and effectively, however, it is the very fact of there being only two major parties which, in conjunction with the electoral system, normally assures a government of a fairly stable and coherent majority large enough to facilitate the conduct of business and to free the cabinet from continuous preoccupation with the purely tactical problems of maintaining that majority.

The two-party system ensures, also, that at any given moment there exists both a government and a clear alternative government.[13] The government is thus constantly reminded of its mortality and the need to justify its actions; the opposing party is thus constrained, not only to criticize and oppose in the hope of supplanting the government, but to do so in a responsible manner fitting to a party that may itself have to contend, as the next government, with the same problems; and the electorate is thus presented continuously with a concrete choice—the government or the alternative government—which encourages their sense of responsibility, as well as giving them the final power of decision. The party system, in other words, normally ensures both organized support for and organized opposition to the government of the day. The importance of this confrontation and interplay receives formal recognition in the official title of Her Majesty's Opposition for the alternative party, and a state salary for its leader.

[13] That is, it ensures this result to the extent that any institution can do so.

The parties are able to sustain this organized confrontation only to the extent that they are united in the support of their leaders and policies and so, at least on all major questions, can rely upon their members to vote solidly together. The requisite degree of party voting in the House of Commons is not simply a product of central "discipline," but rather of party loyalty, of the constitutional relations between the cabinet and its majority, and of a significant degree of agreement on the distinctive principles for which each party stands.[14]

There is, as there must be in any viable democratic system, considerable common ground between the programs of the two parties, and a near-identity of approach among the most moderate members of each. Nevertheless, the parties are divided by conflicts of doctrine. The Conservative party is imbued with the principles of respect for existing authority and tradition, Burkean reform, individual self-help, and partly consequentially, private enterprise. The Labour party, on the other hand, stands for a greater degree of equality, social reform, collective action, and public control of economic activity (if necessary through public ownership) as the means toward an ultimate and variously defined goal of social democracy. These principles in part provide criteria for party membership, and in part reflect the aims and desires of the party members and the interests that form the party cores. In neither party are the principles kept entirely pure and unsullied by electoral or other practical considerations—although the Conservatives have the advantage that their principles lend some endorsement to such empirical adjustments, whereas Labour's principles are less readily accommodating. But it is impossible to understand either party without appreciating the importance of its doctrinal tensions and commitments, which may exacerbate as well as assuage the other conflicts within its ranks.

VOTING

The British elector votes for the party rather than the man. Indeed, it is often asserted that the personality of the candidate is not

[14] For further discussion, see pp. 112–23.

likely to attract or repel more than five hundred votes. This is probably too small a figure in some cases, but at best the candidate's individual qualifications are much less influential than his party label.

In part, this is the natural result of the fact that the basic electoral issue is the party composition of the government during the succeeding parliament. Since the House of Commons may be referred to as the "electoral college" for the prime minister, the voter will necessarily be vitally interested in the parliamentary voting intentions of each candidate. Since the prime minister is normally a party leader, chosen because of his party support, the voter must pay great attention to party labels. More than that: any nonparty or minor party candidate is at a considerable electoral disadvantage simply by virtue of the fact that his intentions are unclear (or unreliable) or that he will not be in a position to influence the choice of prime minister.[15] Of course, unlike the members of the Electoral College for an American president, M.P.s are not only electors. They are also the continuing members of a representative assembly with other important duties. For this reason the qualifications of each candidate are given some attention by a portion of the electorate and, in part consequentially, by the party that nominates him.

Candidates, being primarily party standard-bearers, are all expected to give public support to their parties' policies. This means that the same basic issues and arguments, by and large, are presented in each constituency. Since, as we have seen, Britain is a fairly homogeneous society, with centralized governmental and economic systems, it is not surprising that remarkably uniform swings of opinion throughout the country have been distinctive features of recent elections. General elections are thus truly national events—with a national decision reached on national issues.[16] Only when the fate of a government is not involved, that

---

[15] If he were, he would be a member of a majority group (actually or potentially), and voted for on that ground.

[16] Another aspect of the national character of elections is the absence of any "locality rule" about the residence of candidates. Most M.P.s will have stood for more than one constituency in the course of a long

is to say, at isolated by-elections, do the voters appear ready to give support to minor parties or to pay much heed to purely local and personal matters. Not even at by-elections, however, does one encounter radical departures from national voting habits.

A second part of the explanation for the electors' concentration on party labels is that by voting for a party the demands of the voters most effectively obtain a response in government. A recent comprehensive survey of British voting habits suggests, for example, that the Labour victory in 1964 was in some degree related to the feeling that a greater proportion of national resources should be devoted to social services, a proposition that was clearly echoed only in Labour's program.[17]

Probably the most important explanation, however, is that the parties create order in the political universe for the average relatively disinterested and politically uninformed citizen. A 1955 survey in a Bristol constituency found, for example, that many voters were incapable of correctly attributing simple and much publicized policy proposals to the parties that propounded them. Significantly, the extent to which respondents agreed or disagreed with the same proposals was materially affected by whether or not the statement was identified for them in party terms; conversely, whether or not individuals correctly identified particular statements as emanating from their own party depended on whether they agreed with the party's position on the issue in question.[18] This revealing study, in conjunction with Butler and Stokes finding that over 90 percent of their sample were prepared to admit to a degree of party commitment,[19] clearly indicates that the political parties are major political reference groups. Voting at general elections thus reflects the decision-making role of the

career, and rarely will an established parliamentary figure be allowed to remain for long out of the Commons, should he be defeated, before being returned from a safer constituency or, as a last resort, being given a peerage.

[17] D. Butler and D. Stokes, *Political Change in Britain: Forces Shaping Electoral Choice* (London: Macmillan, 1969), pp. 343–49.

[18] R. S. Milne and H. C. Mackenzie, *Marginal Seat* (London: Hansard Society, 1958), pp. 121–26.

[19] Butler and Stokes, op. cit., p. 206.

election, the demands of the electorate on government, and, through identification with a party, public support for at least one aspect of the governmental system.

If the prevalence of party voting is the most important single characteristic of the British electorate, the second most important is the high correlation between party allegiance and social class. It has been estimated that class voting in Britain is probably more marked than in any other Western style democracy.[20] Studies of British voting uniformly reveal that as one moves down the class ladder the percentage of people voting Conservative decreases, while the percentage of people voting Labour increases.[21]

The relationship receives striking illustration in the recent investigation by Butler and Stokes. They use a six-category scale based on occupations that ranges from the higher managerial and professional people down to unskilled manual workers. With each step down the proportion of respondents who identify themselves with the Labour Party increases—but not evenly. There is a big shift in the proportion at the boundary between manual and nonmanual workers. But, and this is particularly notable, the biggest "jump" comes between those nonmanual workers whose job contains a supervisory element and those whose job does not. Combining the categories into a two-class division, they obtain an excellent "snapshot" of the principal cleavage in British politics. Thus, if one takes the three top groups together—higher managerial, lower managerial, and other nonmanual "supervisory" employees—their votes divide roughly into 80 percent Conservative and 20 percent Labour, while the three lower groups together—subordinate nonmanual, and both skilled and unskilled manual —divide roughly into 68 percent Labour and 32 percent Conservative.

The same relationship holds between subjective class rating and

[20] R. R. Alford, *Party and Society: The Anglo-American Democracies* (New York: Rand McNally, 1963; London: Murray, 1964).

[21] In addition to the studies already cited, see J. Bonham, *The Middle Class Vote* (London: Faber, 1954); M. Benney and others, *How People Vote* (London: Routledge and Kegan Paul, 1956); and A. H. Birch, *Small Town Politics* (London: Oxford University Press, 1959).

party identifications. Butler and Stokes report that of those who see themselves as middle class, 79 percent see themselves as Conservatives and 21 percent as being pro-Labour, while of those who class themselves as workers, 72 percent see themselves as pro-Labour and 28 percent as Conservatives.[22]

The correlation between class and party voting is both high and significant, but the relationship it reflects is far from simple. For one thing, a minority in every class and occupational category supports what might be called the "other party." The precise extent of class and party identification, furthermore, is affected by such factors as parental influence, social mobility, religion, income and way of life, and the areas in which people live. And, granted that "the behaviour of the electorate (in the 1960s) was shaped by generalised attitudes and beliefs about the parties far more than by any specific policy issues," [23] nevertheless party record, issues, and policies can also affect the way or the extent to which electors translate their party self-image into voting behavior. Not even the connection between party allegiance and actual voting is hard and fast; in the period 1964–66, for example, as many as one-third of the electorate seem to have switched either between the two major parties, one of them and a third, or voting and not voting.[24]

As significant as the facts of party voting and its class basis, is the fact that these relationships are not socially and politically disruptive. A survey carried out among urban working-class males showed, it is true, that some 50 percent of respondents liked nothing about the other party and about 58 percent disliked nothing about their own party. But these figures also mean that about one-half of the respondents liked something about the other party and that over one-third disliked something about their own party.[25]

It is possible, to take another example, to classify voters as

[22] Butler and Stokes, op. cit., pp. 76 and 106.

[23] Ibid., p. 359.

[24] Loc. cit., passim.

[25] E. A. Nordlinger, *The Working Class Tories* (London: MacGibbon and Kee, 1967), pp. 155–59.

either deferential or instrumental, depending on whether they support a party because it (or its leaders) is thought to possess superior social qualifications for the exercise of authority or because it is believed to be more effective in "delivering the goods." Recent studies have not confirmed the hypothesis that deferential voting is the prerogative of the "anomalous" working-class Conservative. On the contrary, they show both that deferential voting is on the decline and that some deferential voters support Labour, just as some workers support the Conservative party on instrumental grounds.[26] The obvious conclusion to be drawn is that the cleavages among the electorate do not invariably coincide or reinforce one another. That is, partly because of the adaptability of the parties, the distribution of both basic attitudes and opinions on the issues is much more diverse within each party and much more similar between the parties than the crude figures of party and class voting might suggest. Although voters are extremely loyal to their own class, family, coworkers, and party, this evidence suggests that their loyalties are not unconditional.

This conclusion is relevant, not only to arguments about the stability and calm of British political life, but also to the system's flexibility. For it follows that parties continually have to earn the allegiance of their supporters, that the possibility of a landslide result at a subsequent election, comparable to those of 1906, 1931, or 1945 can never be ruled out, and that some of the stability of British voting habits[27] is explicable, not solely in terms of the irrational commitments of the voter, but also in terms of the continuing adaptation of the parties and their programs to changing conditions and attitudes.

It would seem that the result of a general election is mainly the product of the electoral system itself, and of the influence of such long-term factors as the death of existing voters and the coming-

[26] See Nordlinger, op. cit., and R. T. McKenzie and A. Silver, *Angels in Marble: Working Class Conservatives in Urban England* (London: Heinemann, 1968).

[27] For example, in 1955 in one Bristol constituency, about two-thirds of those interviewed had not changed their vote over the four elections of 1945, 1950, 1951, and 1955; see Milne and Mackenzie, op. cit., pp. 76–77.

of-age of new ones on the basic allegiances of the voters. But the most intense and public aspect of an election is the campaign immediately preceding it. Campaigns, it seems, can affect the balance of votes between the parties by up to 2 percent.[28] Given that even after the Conservative victory of 1970 a national swing of less than 3 percent would suffice to put Labour back in office, it follows that the campaign itself cannot be ignored in any account of voting behavior.

The primary purpose of the campaign, however, is to activate a party's loyal supporters by meetings, local canvassing and, in particular, by a national campaign that uses television, radio, and the daily press. The important local aims of the campaign are to maintain or increase morale, to enable the candidate or M.P. to get to know his own constituency, and (as it were) to enable the candidate to plug into the informal local network of gossip and information, whose effect cannot easily be measured but cannot be denied. The precise nature of the British campaign, compared with those in the United States, is shaped by three distinctive features. The first is that until 1970 British ballot papers printed only the names of the candidates, not their party affiliation. A primary purpose of the campaign in each constituency has therefore been to establish the connection between name and party in the minds of the electors. A second distinctive feature is that there are much stricter legal limitations on the amount of money that may be spent on behalf of any particular British candidate. In 1964, for example, the effect of these limitations was that the total expenditure in all the constituencies was a mere £1.25 million, and that, on average, Conservative candidates spent a mere £766 per constituency and Labour candidates £746. The final distinction is that there are no legal limits on what can be spent nationally on behalf of a party, as opposed to expenditure by or for a named individual in a particular constituency. Thus, in the same election, Transport House spent about £600,000, in addition to some £300,000 that had been spent on advertising in the period from May 1963 to September 1964. These figures, however, should be contrasted with the Conservatives' advertising expenditure of

[28] Butler and Stokes, op. cit., pp. 430–31.

over £1 million, the 1964 campaign against nationalization that is believed to have cost the Steel Industry approximately £1.25 million, and the £250,000 spent by Aims of Industry on general propaganda in favor of private enterprise.[29] There is no evidence, however, that the political benefits bore any direct relationship to the amount of money spent.

It should not be concluded from this very brief survey of some of the forces at work in a British election that the process is basically irrational, despite the ambiguous role of policies and issues. This is no place to examine at length the question of voting rationality;[30] it must suffice to point out that among the factors that seem to influence long-term allegiance is that of experience, by which is meant the personal experience of each voter and that of his relatives, friends, acquaintances, and coworkers; that election results seem to bear some relationship to the general impression of competence given by the existing government;[31] and that, to quote from Butler and Stokes again, "individual political issues, especially those defined in terms of the goals that matter to a wide section of the public, can have substantial impact as they reach the ordinary voter through the channels of political communication." [32]

MEDIA OF COMMUNICATION

The British electorate, like those of other countries, is remarkably ignorant of many things the politically sophisticated regard as ele-

[29] These figures are taken from Richard Rose, *Influencing Voters* (London: Faber, 1967).

[30] It is, however, a central theme of G. C. Moodie and G. Studdert-Kennedy, *Opinions, Publics and Pressure Groups* (London: Allen and Unwin, 1970). See also, the discussions in Milne and Mackenzie, op. cit., pp. 188–99, and P. G. J. Pulzer's excellent survey, *Political Representation and Elections: Parties and Voting in Great Britain* (London: Allen and Unwin, 1968), pp. 127–31.

[31] "*Existing* government" because a dissolution of Parliament is not accompanied by the government's resignation. The government that advises the holding of the election continues in office at least until the results are known.

[32] Butler and Stokes, op. cit., p. 214.

mentary. Significantly, "the identity of the party 'in power' is one of the few facts that are almost universally known." [33] But some did not know that Harold Macmillan was prime minister in 1963, when he had held that office for seven years, and an earlier study found that 20 percent could not name even one party leader (the corresponding figure in the United States was 16 percent).[34] And this in the country which publishes more books per head of the population, and buys more newspapers, than any other in the world.[35] Nevertheless it is not mere irony to talk of the media of communication: any parliamentary candidate who expects to survive question time at one of his public meetings by trusting to public ignorance will certainly be stopped short by encountering a surprising amount of knowledge. For this he should "blame" the press and television.

THE PRESS

In addition to about one hundred daily and Sunday papers, of which a fifth are published in London, there are over a thousand weekly or biweekly local or provincial papers. Of the total, eight daily (all morning papers) and seven Sunday papers have national circulations. The smallness of the country and the existence of well-developed transport services from the principal printing centers of London and Manchester make it possible for a morning paper to be distributed on a national scale, and there is now only a minority of households not reached by at least one national paper, each with an average readership of three or more people per copy. The accompanying table gives the details of the national papers, including ownership, circulation, and "mortality," during the sixties. To the list given there should, perhaps, be added the one paper with an explicitly party connection: the *Morning Star,*

---

[33] Butler and Stokes, op. cit., p. 29.
[34] See Butler and Stokes, op. cit., p. 26, and C. Almond and S. Verba, *The Civic Culture* (Princeton: Princeton University Press, 1963), p. 96.
[35] In 1968 over 21,000 books were published; over 600 daily newspapers are commonly sold for every 1,000 inhabitants.

edited and published for the Communist party, with a circulation of around 65,000.

The national character of the press means that although there are relatively few newspapers, the population has a meaningful choice between them. This choice seems to be exercised largely on partisan grounds, in the sense that, whether or not they are conscious of a paper's political leanings, the bulk of each paper's readership shares its partisan views and rarely changes its newspaper-reading habits.[36]

Another effect of the large national market is that a paper can afford to, in fact must, specialize its appeal—and not only in a political way. In the words of the Report of the 1949 Royal Commission on the Press,[37] the consequence is that "the gap between the best of the quality papers and the general run of the popular Press is too wide, and the number of papers of an intermediate type is too small." Since that time the gap has remained wide in terms of the serious coverage of national and international affairs, the space devoted to sex, crime, and sensation, and the care with which fact and opinion are kept separate (not that the separation is as strict in any British newspaper as in the leading quality newspapers in the United States or certain western European countries). And the gap has widened in the sense that the pressure of rising costs has hit the intermediate papers hardest while the quality papers and the most popular ones have increased their circulation, if not their financial strength.[38] However, the verdict is still applicable.

The quality newspapers write for an audience who demand reliable and full information, combined with intelligent comment, on a wide range of serious topics. This audience is limited in number, but over the nation as a whole it is large enough to sustain several first-rate papers. The rest cater to a mass audience whose range of interests seems to be fundamentally limited to essentially

[36] See Butler and Stokes, op. cit., Chapter 10, especially pp. 229–39.
[37] Cmd. 7700 of 1949, §678.
[38] National Board for Prices and Incomes, Report No. 141, *Costs and Revenue of National Newspapers* (HMSO, Cmnd. 477 of 1970).

NATIONAL NEWSPAPERS 1958–68[1]

			Circulation[4]	
Dailies	*Politics*[2]	*Owner*[3]	*1958*	*1968*
The Guardian†	Ind. Rad.	Scott Trust	178,692	280,877
Daily Telegraph†	Cons.	Berry Family	1,133,585	1,407,328
The Times†	Ind. Cons.	Lord Thompson group[5]	248,248	401,314
Daily Express	Cons.	Lord Beaverbrook	4,040,572	3,852,613
Daily Mail	Cons.	Northcliffe group	2,150,988 ⎫	2,095,474
(*News Chronicle*)[6]	Lib.	Daily News Trust	1,267,341 ⎭	——
*Daily Mirror**	Ind.	International Publishing Corporation (IPC)	4,526,453	5,034,236
*Daily Sketch**	Cons.	Northcliffe group	1,223,948	914,946
⎧ *Sun** [7]	Ind.	News Ltd. (R. Murdoch)	—— ⎫	1,065,972
⎩ (*Daily Herald*)[7]	Lab.	Odham's Press; IPC in 1961	1,523,334 ⎭	——
Sundays				
Observer†	Ind. Rad.	Trust	638,074	902,647
Sunday Telegraph†	Cons.	Berry family	682,693[8]	750,751
Sunday Times†	Ind.	Lord Thompson	795,192	1,460,994
News of the World	Ind.	News of the World, Ltd., 1969	6,767,348 ⎫	6,191,142
(*Empire News*)[9]	Cons.	Lord Thompson	2,161,230 ⎭	——
The People	Ind.	IPC	4,899,748	5,532,959
(*Reynolds News*)[10]	Lab. & Co-op	Co-op Press, Ltd.	367,574	——

NATIONAL NEWSPAPERS 1958–1968 (cont.)

Sundays	Politics[2]	Owner[3]	Circulation[4] 1958	1968
Sunday Express	Cons.	Lord Beaverbrook	3,397,913	4,237,545
(Sunday Dispatch)[11]	Cons.	Northcliffe group	1,834,857	——
(Sunday Graphic)[12]	Cons.	Lord Thompson	1,185,787	——
Sunday Mirror*	Ind.	IPC	5,378,242	5,137,531

[1] Dagger indicates a quality newspaper; Asterisk indicates a tabloid. [2] Political labels affixed by the author, not necessarily by the paper. [3] Ownership given as in December 1969. [4] Circulation figures taken from the *Newspaper Press Directory*, 1959 and 1969. [5] Taken over from the Astor family in 1966. [6] Sold to and absorbed in the *Daily Mail*, 1960. [7] The *Daily Herald* had its name changed to the *Sun* by IPC as one of a number of changes, another being the removal of TUC supervision, designed to turn a loss into a profit. Late in 1969 the *Sun* was sold to R. Murdoch who turned it into a tabloid. [8] This figure is for 1962, the first full year of the *Sunday Telegraph*'s publication. [9] The *Empire News* was sold to and absorbed by the *News of the World* in 1960. [10] *Reynolds News* was closed down in 1967 because it was losing both money and circulation. [11] The *Sunday Dispatch* was sold to and absorbed by the *Sunday Express* in 1961. [12] The *Sunday Graphic* was closed down in 1960 because it was losing both money and circulation.

local, personal, or domestic matters within their own experience, or to other matters treated in analogous terms. The "human-interest" story, the deflation of political disputes into purely personal rivalries, the "features," are perhaps the inevitable result of writing nationally for a market more attuned to local gossip, yet deprived thereof by modern impersonal urban life, and hungry for some human link with, some interpreter of, the wider and more potent social context. The survival of the local press, albeit under increasing economic difficulties, attests to the impossibility of catering to all genuine local interests on a national scale, just as the apparent need for stories of sex and sensation may attest to the shallow and unsatisfying quality of synthetic "human interest." [39] The national character of the market is thus partly responsible for the existence both of some of the best and of some of the worst newspapers in the Western world.

The Royal Commission could find no evidence of outside pressure from any source or of a deliberate policy of distortion, but only of a willingness (or need) to "give the public what the public will buy," and a failure sufficiently to resist the temptation to lower standards in the interests of commercial success. It proposed the establishment of a General Council of the Press, composed mainly of newspaper people but with some lay members and a paid lay chairman, "to safeguard the freedom of the press" and "to encourage the growth of the sense of public responsibility and public service amongst all engaged in the profession of journalism." [40] Nor has it been able to deal with the one major potential threat to the freedom of the press, the renewed movement toward concentration of ownership.

It was mainly because of public concern over this last problem that a new Royal Commission was set up in 1961. The report issued in 1962 [41] echoed this concern and asserted a public interest in the matter, but without proposing (any more than did its predecessor) any change in the rights or pattern of ownership and control. The press lacks the political influence it was once thought to have. For one thing, it is the most partisan and the most sophisticated who pay the most attention to the press. In 1964, for example, although two-thirds of the electorate followed the campaign in the press, only 28 percent said it was the most important medium; but, according to a 1962 survey of a sample of M.P.s and candidates, the press was the main source of information for over 70 percent of the latter. By way of contrast, none of the leadership group cited television, as opposed to 65 percent of the

[39] On the question of modern trends in "popular" culture, see Richard Hoggart, *The Uses of Literacy* (London: Chatto and Windus, 1957), where the point is made that those who claim to cater to popular taste may in fact be seriously underrating (and corrupting) their readers.

[40] *Report*, 676–84.

[41] Cmnd. 1811 of 1962.

voters' sample who said it was the most important medium.[42] The main currents of opinion also cut across partisan newspaper readership groups. The most recent and detailed study concluded that the press "has some role in changing the relative strength of the parties in the short run as well as in forming and conserving more enduring allegiance." [43] But as we have seen, the readers of the press feel that it is still not as important a medium as television.

RADIO AND TELEVISION

From its inception sound broadcasting has been subject to social regulations. Since 1926 it has been the monopoly of the state-owned, but not government-run, British Broadcasting Corporation, and been financed entirely out of the sale of licenses for receiving sets (in effect a form of earmarked tax).[44] Until 1954 television was also exclusively its preserve. The administrative control of the BBC lies with a director-general, appointed by and responsible to a board of governors. The governors are appointed and paid by the government for limited terms of office, but once appointed, are independent of the government in almost all respects. They are selected from people who have reached some distinction in public life other than, and usually exclusive of, party politics. Broadcasting was placed under the control of a public corporation to prevent its misuse by private interests and not to confer additional persuasive power upon the government of the day. Its political independence has, indeed, been a matter of constant public concern and, at least in peacetime, rarely if ever encroached upon. It was nevertheless by playing on fears of political exploitation of television, judiciously mixed with complaints about lack of choice and of the BBC's alleged "stuffiness" that an energetic lobby succeeded in ending the television monopoly and in having commer-

---

[42] See Butler and Stokes, op. cit., p. 220, and a study by Dr. I. Budge cited in A. Barker and M. Rush, *The Member of Parliament and His Information* (London: Allen and Unwin, 1970), p. 42.

[43] Butler and Stokes, op. cit., p. 244.

[44] The overseas services of the BBC are, however, financed out of general taxation. As a result they operate under government supervision.

cial television introduced in 1954.[45] To appease the opposition, however, control of this second network was vested in another public corporation, the Independent Television Authority. The ITA owns the transmitting stations, being financed by payments from the companies that contract to provide programs in the different regions. The ITA is also charged, by law, with ensuring the observance of certain standards of performance. For the most part the companies have been formed by people already established in the popular entertainment and newspaper worlds. They are financed by the sale of time to advertisers who do not, however, thereby acquire any *direct* control over the programs. The companies' choice of programs must nevertheless be influenced by the need to attract the widest viewing public with which to entice the advertisers into the maximum expenditure. A Royal Commission report in 1962 [46] led to the BBC's being authorized to provide a second television channel, a decision neither to permit a second commercial TV channel nor the introduction of commercial radio, and to a tightening of the ITA's control over the program companies.

Until the 1964 election this structure, and an unduly strict interpretation of the legal requirement of political (i.e., partisan) impartiality, tended to confine election coverage to the official party broadcasts. These broadcasts are free to the parties who agree on the apportionment of time, roughly based on the number of candidates put up by each party. But, perhaps because the initial fears of this new medium had been calmed by experience, since 1964 the producers of programs have been increasingly independent and prepared for controversy.

By 1964 some 90 percent of households possessed TV receivers and, as we have already seen, electors rated it highly as a source of campaign information. An intensive study of viewers in two

---

[45] See H. H. Wilson, *Pressure Group: The Campaign for Commercial Television* (London: Secker and Warburg, 1961).

[46] *Report on the Future of Sound Radio and Independent Television*, Cmnd. 1753 of 1962. It contains valuable analyses of the place of the media in a democratic society that are of more than purely British relevance.

Yorkshire constituencies suggested that exposure to TV is a significant factor in modern British politics—but primarily as an influence on the level of information, the assessment of leaders, and the intensity with which precampaign attitudes and opinions are held. But in 1964 it was also found that those with the weaker levels of interest were the most persuadable, and that the Liberal party gained a great deal of its enlarged vote (compared with the 1959 election) directly from the impact of its larger number of TV broadcasts, an increase which did not, however, come exclusively from the less interested and informed.[47] In a close election, therefore, the impact of TV could be decisive—but the same verdict could be made, with the same validity, of the press, or a party leader, or many other factors. Election results are the product of too many ingredients for it to be rational to single out any one as the most important or the most sinister.

Apart from the press and broadcasting, it must be remembered that a conglomeration of periodicals, books, and informal channels cater to almost any level of any interest. None of these, furthermore, exist solely to give information to the public and to influence or mould public thought. They also serve the vital functions of expressing public opinion and of articulating public discontent. The press in particular performs an indispensable service in these respects, with newspapers representing as well as catering to the interests and attitudes of their readers. Thus, at opposite poles, the *Daily Mirror* for years was anxiously and avidly read by politicians who believed that it spoke for the under-thirty age group, and the *Times* continues to provide, in its correspondence column, something of a national forum for discussing everything from national policy to bird behavior: and, if the *Times* does not now have the preeminence and the semi-official status it had, for example, in the nineteen thirties, it is still the first outlet for those at all within the social pale who wish to call attention to some national "scandal" or "disgrace," or to comment on some event of

[47] J. G. Blumler and D. McQuail, *Television in Politics: Its Uses and Influence* (London: Faber, 1968). This book is full of findings of general interest to students of voting as well as findings relevant primarily to the subject of its title.

national interest. All the quality national papers now perform a comparable service, as do the leading political periodicals. It is probably safe to say that no strong current of opinion or discontent can long exist without reflection in the press or on the air—although the more far-reaching or unorthodox criticisms of society are, the longer they will probably have to wait and the more support they will have to receive before they will be given adequate attention.

In favor of the existing media is the fact that the best of them at least operate to keep the prevailing climate of opinion generally friendly to the expert and the learned. It is not sensible to expect nor, possibly, to desire that everyone be expert, least of all in political affairs. Social health demands only that there exist some people knowledgeable and interested enough effectively to stimulate and criticize the government and those in positions of power generally, and that these people be cut off neither from the rest of society nor from the information they require. It cannot be said that, by these criteria, British society is sick. It remains to be seen whether, in the future, the expansion in secondary and university education will be of the right kind and affect enough people to counterbalance the trivializing influence exerted by the less worthy kinds of journalism and mere entertainment. This, however, is by no means an exclusively British problem.

4

Cabinet Government

The essential features of the modern British system of cabinet government may be stated briefly. The monarch selects as prime minister a man who can command the support of a majority of members of the House of Commons. Normally only one man can do so—the leader of the party that has won the greatest number of seats at the previous general election. The prime minister then appoints (more technically, advises the monarch to appoint) his colleagues to the cabinet and other ministerial positions. He and his colleagues together constitute Her Majesty's Government and on most occasions wield Her Majesty's governmental powers. As such their powers may be summarized as comprising:

a) the final determination of policy to be submitted to Parliament;

b) the supreme control of the national executive in accordance with the policy *endorsed* by Parliament; and

c) the continuous coordination and delimitation of the activities of the several Departments of State.[1]

1919. In the original the word italicized above was "prescribed."

On coming to office the prime minister has about one hundred ministerial positions to fill from the ranks of his supporters in both Houses of Parliament. The majority of those appointed will be members of the Commons, but some must be members of

[1] The *Report* of the Haldane Committee on the Machinery of Government.

the Lords, and all must be or become members of one or the other.[2] Up to fifty of them will be ministers. Thirty will be heads of the various administrative departments and offices. The rest will be either nondepartmental ministers, such as the Lord Privy Seal, or Ministers of State. Neither of these are in charge of departments, but the latter are attached to large and important ones and are usually given some special responsibility; one of the Ministers of State in the Foreign Office is specially concerned with the work of the United Nations. In addition, all the main departments will have one or more parliamentary secretaries or undersecretaries[3] to assist the ministers in, particularly, the parliamentary aspects of their duties. The most important members of the administration, however, are those senior ministers who are included in the cabinet, the inner group of some twenty people, meeting regularly under the chairmanship of the prime minister and sharing constitutional responsibility for all conduct of government. The heads of the most important departments are always included, but the precise boundary of cabinet membership is a matter entirely for the discretion of each individual prime minister.[4]

Whenever people talk of "the government" in Britain, they are referring primarily to the prime minister and his colleagues in the cabinet. This has been the practice only since the mid-nineteenth

[2] Either by winning a by-election or being made a peer. During World War II a few men became ministers without any previous parliamentary experience, the most notable being Ernest Bevin, but this is rare, and even more rarely successful, in ordinary circumstances. By the Ministers of the Crown Act, 1964, no more than ninety-one members of the government may be in the Commons.

[3] The difference in nomenclature is of historic importance only. The older ministerial positions have descended from, and retain the title of, the Secretaries of State who were among the earliest full-time political servants of the crown. The later departments have almost all been placed under a minister, and their juniors are simply termed parliamentary secretaries, the "parliamentary" distinguishing them from the permanent civil-service ones.

[4] What is said here refers to normal peacetime practice. In both world wars, under Lloyd George and Winston Churchill respectively, special war cabinets were set up along somewhat different lines.

century. Before that "the government" meant " 'Government' by King, Lords and Commons." [5] In law, government is still carried on by these three ancient institutions, assisted, of course, by various servants of the crown, ministers among them. The existence of the prime minister and of cabinet ministers is legally acknowledged, in statutes standardizing their salaries and providing the prime minister with an official country residence, and in letters patent placing him ninth in the official order of social precedence. But neither from statute nor from common law can one obtain any idea of the vast powers of the cabinet and its head. It is by convention only that the cabinet has come to occupy its central position in the constitution, as it is also by convention that the doctrine of ministerial responsibility has come to determine its constitutional status and behavior. To this doctrine there are three main aspects. The first is the principle that the cabinet collectively, or some minister individually, shall be responsible for the great majority of the political or governmental acts of the monarch.

THE MONARCH AND
CABINET GOVERNMENT

Under English law the monarch can do no legal wrong (the principle that *rex non potest peccare*). It has, however, been possible to bring certain actions against the monarch's servants, including ministers and their antecedents, for acts in fact done by or at the request of the monarch. Ministerial responsibility, indeed, originally meant little if any more than that ministers were the people to be held legally responsible, if anyone could be, for the political decisions of the crown. One effect was to safeguard the monarchy, at least to some extent, from direct involvement in controversy and thus to protect its superior position. The principle was not, and could not have been, an effective defense against unconstitutional or nonconstitutional action. The turbulent events of the seventeenth century dramatically emphasized that inadequacy.

[5] Edward Freeman, *The Growth of the English Constitution from the Earliest Times*, 3d ed. (New York: Macmillan and Co., 1876), p. 124.

Thereafter the rise of liberal and, later, democratic ideas, the increased power of Parliament, and the accompanying need to devise peaceful constitutional means of changing government policy and personnel made it possible to preserve the monarchy only by steadily restricting its actual powers to govern. This has been achieved, in effect, by extending the doctrine of ministerial responsibility to mean that, in most areas of government, the monarch should exercise his or her powers only upon the advice of ministers supported by the House of Commons.

In the eighteenth century the monarch still exercised considerable influence on the selection of the advisers upon whom he had to depend: he could, in effect, pursue any policy for which he could find ministers prepared to accept responsibility, and by changing his ministers he could often secure a change in policy. To this end it was in order for the king to appoint ministers, dismiss them, dissolve or refuse to dissolve Parliament, and attempt to influence the outcome of the resulting elections so as to obtain a majority for *his* government. Even Queen Victoria (1837–1901) regarded it as an "affront" when Lord Melbourne's government was defeated at the polls in 1841. Today monarchs are not personally involved in elections—the choice nowadays being between the government and the *loyal* opposition—nor in any other aspect of the party struggle. The power to govern rests squarely with ministers, whose advice the monarch must normally accept, and who derive their authority to govern from election and not hereditary right.

Today more than ever, perhaps, "ministerial responsibility is the safe-guard of the monarchy. Without it the throne could not stand for long, amid the gusts of political conflict and the storm of political passion." [6] Yet it is argued by some that the queen may still, under certain circumstances, decide which advisers she shall heed. Undoubtedly the formal language of government implies this—but that language frequently misleads.

The doctrine of ministerial responsibility clearly does not and

[6] From a Memorandum to George V written by his private secretary, Lord Esher, in 1913. Quoted in Sir Ivor Jennings, *Cabinet Government,* 3d ed. (Cambridge: Cambridge University Press, 1959), p. 338.

cannot apply to the selection of a prime minister, although it is sometimes imagined that the retiring prime minister gives binding advice about his successor. In fact, he need not even be consulted, nor need his advice be taken. Simply because he is retiring, there is less security against mischievous advice, while there no longer exist any political penalties that can be inflicted upon him. This is, of course, particularly but not exclusively so if his successor must come from another party. To appoint a prime minister is therefore regarded as a personal prerogative (power) of the queen, for all that circumstances very rarely permit the use of any personal discretion. She must select someone who will be supported by a majority in the House of Commons, and normally there is but one man in a position to do so: the leader of the party with a majority of seats. Only when there is no such party (or when a coalition government must be formed for some other reason) or when the majority party has no chosen leader is there ever room for royal discretion—and not always then. In fact, only in 1931, when the National Government was formed under MacDonald, and in 1923 and 1957, when a Conservative government had to obtain a new prime minister before its own choice of successor had been made, has the monarch apparently made a real choice. Even in these cases, however, the monarch's choice in effect lay only between two men, and it appears, although not all observers agree on this point, that the monarch in fact did no more than ratify the decisions or preferences of the various party leaders concerned. Should similar situations arise in the future, moreover, there is ground for arguing that the monarch would more clearly leave the decision to the parties themselves. Some twenty times has a prime minister been selected in the first sixty years of this century; on all occasions except those mentioned the monarch's "choice" has been clearly dictated by the parties and their leaders.[7]

---

[7] As we saw in Chapter 3, the Conservative party changed its method of choosing its leader following Sir Alec Douglas-Home's selection in 1963. Even though it had been obvious that the queen had then acted on Mr. Macmillan's advice, her influence has been excluded from the Conservatives' new method of selection.

The monarch must avoid the suspicion of partisanship, lest the powers or even the existence of the monarchy become a political issue. So long as the present two-party system lasts, this is best ensured by allowing each party to choose its leader in its own way, and then automatically selecting the leader of the majority party as prime minister. Should a more fluid party system develop, then, like the president in the Third and Fourth French Republics, the monarch might have a more active part to play, although one still limited by the need to remain impartial.

The powers to dismiss a government and to force or refuse a dissolution of Parliament against the advice of an existing government are also sometimes listed among the monarch's personal prerogatives. Even prime ministers, for example, are careful to talk of "advising" or "requesting" a dissolution. However, it is difficult to see how these powers could be exercised in a two-party system without appearing obviously to favor one party as against the other. They cannot, therefore, seriously be considered as attributes of monarchy under normal circumstances. One exception must be noted, however. Should a prime minister who has been honestly and decisively defeated at an election request another immediate election or attempt to govern in the face of a majority in the House of Commons, then the monarch may well refuse the dissolution or dismiss the government. Only thus might it be possible once more to obtain a government backed by the authority of the electorate. It is also possible that, *with a multiparty system,* the monarch would on occasion be entitled to refuse a dissolution to a defeated government when another strong government could be formed without the need for a fresh election. Under such circumstances great care would still have to be taken to prevent an appearance of partiality, but it is only under a two-party system that to deny something to one party must inevitably appear to favor another. Furthermore, if there were a change in the number of parties, it is likely that there would also be a change in the behavior expected of and permitted to the monarch by politicians and the general public.[8]

[8] The precise powers of even constitutional monarchs depend closely on political circumstances and national custom. Thus, despite the exist-

If it be granted that, as it is often put, the British monarch reigns but does not rule, and that the general principle governing the queen's political role is that of public impartiality and private discretion, then it may be asked: What useful functions does the queen perform? Does she have any important powers at all?

She may personally attempt to influence the advice given to her, on the basis of the information about the government's deeds and intentions that she receives by right.[9] There is no evidence to suggest that her advice is now a major determinant of government policy. An able monarch who has reigned for many years could, however, acquire a more intimate and extensive knowledge of recent political history than any political figure, and might thus be in a position to give very valuable advice to any government. On occasion the monarch may usefully try to mediate between the parties, as George V tried to bring the Conservative and Liberal parties together over the Irish question on the eve of World War I. He failed, the basis for agreement being too weak. These, like the monarch's numerous formal functions—signatures, inspections, and receiving ambassadors—today could probably be as well performed by a nonhereditary and nonroyal head of state, as they are by governors-general and presidents in other parts of the Commonwealth. It does not follow, however, that it makes no difference to British politics that the head of state is in fact royal.

To abolish the monarchy would necessitate, among other things, far-reaching changes in the legal status of ministers and all other public servants who at present rank as servants of the crown, wielding its traditional and vaguely defined powers. To make these

---

ence of basically similar constitutional rules in the various contemporary European monarchies, there seem to be appreciable differences in the range of activities permitted to the sovereign in, say, Belgium, the Netherlands, and the United Kingdom.

[9] See W. Bagehot's famous statement that a constitutional monarch has "three rights—the right to be consulted, the right to encourage, the right to warn." *The English Constitution* (London: Oxford University Press, first published in 1867), Chapter 3. On the general point see F. Hardie, *The Political Influence of the British Monarchy 1868–1952* (London: Batsford, 1970).

changes would probably produce a corresponding change in the whole atmosphere of government that would not necessarily be for the better.[10] Socially it is likely that the introduction of republicanism would have some effect on the class system, in that hereditary positions in the social hierarchy might be undermined and the prestige of the House of Lords decreased. In and of itself, however, it is much less likely that republicanism would weaken social differences than it is that a more egalitarian society would lead to a less socially exclusive royal entourage. The monarchy, indeed, has proved itself very adaptable socially as well as politically to national developments and, on the whole, is now more affected by social changes than it is likely to determine them.[11]

The most obvious function of the monarchy is to provide color and pageantry in a society wherein neither otherwise predominates. Less worthily, but no less usefully, the royal family seems to provide vicarious splendor and spaciousness for many people whose personal lives are cramped and drab. If at times the members of the royal family seem forced into a glamorous role from some light opera, and at others simply to provide "bread and circuses," yet behind the publicity and occasional artificiality lies an important and genuine symbolic status. They symbolize the continuity of British society, provide a personal embodiment of the nation rather than "the state" (a word with a slightly foreign ring in British ears, and hence rarely used except in a pejorative sense), and are expected to represent the virtues of the British way of life. British history as taught in the schools is divided into dynasties

---

[10] It is not easy to be precise about this subject. One possible change, however, might be a more arrogant approach by governments who would no longer need to give public deference to a person with a stronger claim to embody, even if not actively to represent, the nation as a whole.

[11] Not even the most ardent royalist need share the evident worry of the Duke of Windsor about the fact that "the decline in the fortunes of the landed gentry has tended to leave the monarch and his court more or less marooned" (see his *The Crown and the People 1902–1953* [London: Cassell, 1953], p. 10), for there is every sign that the court and monarch are seeking a wider social basis, and no reason to doubt the possibility of success.

and reigns whose dates are the first to be learned, and whole periods are named after the ruling monarch. To identify with royalty is therefore easy, and to cheer a queen or princess a permissible outlet for national self-love.

It is extremely unlikely that any elected figure with a political past could attract the same emotional loyalty nowadays. What is even more to the point, for a political figure to do so would probably be dangerous. Indeed, it might be said that the greatest contribution made by the modern monarchy is that it attracts to itself some of the deepest nonrational feelings toward authority. It may thus help to preserve the political life of the country both from capricious withdrawals of support and from excessive yearnings for a "strong man." In itself monarchy may seem, at best, an anachronism in a modern democracy. Nevertheless, it is possible that, in Britain, cabinets owe more to the monarchy than their legal powers, and democracy, more than its institutional forms.[12]

THE PRIME MINISTER

If any single person today occupies a position of supreme governing power, it is the prime minister. He is principal adviser to the crown and thus also the principal inheritor of its powers. He is usually leader of the majority party as well as head of government. Above all, he it is who appoints the other members of his governmental team. Even if a prime minister retires for personal reasons that do not involve any change in the party situation, it is generally understood that every member of the administration places his office at the disposal of the incoming leader in order to give him a free hand in the construction of *his* government, as it will thenceforth be regarded. Similarly, the prime minister may at any

---

[12] Cf. the conclusion to F. I. Greenstein and others, "Queen and Prime Minister—the Child's Eye View," *New Society,* October 23, 1969. Some of these questions are pursued further in G. Marshall and G. C. Moodie, *Some Problems of the Constitution,* 4th ed. (London: Hutchinson, 1967), Chapter 3; see also G. C. Moodie, "The Crown and Parliament," *Parliamentary Affairs* (1957), and "The Crown and the Commonwealth," *Parliamentary Affairs* (1958).

time call upon any member to resign, or may move him to a new post, either to fill a chance vacancy or as part of a more extensive change in personnel (a so-called reshuffle).

Gladstone, the famous nineteenth-century Liberal leader, once said that the first duty of a new prime minister, when deliberating upon the appointments to be made, was "to reach for the butcher's knife." No prime minister, however, can be as free politically as he is constitutionally. He must have an eye not only for the effectiveness of his administration and its inner harmony, but also and above all to its ability to attract and hold the support of his party and the public. For this reason he cannot pass over the other leading figures in his party. There are always some others whom he must include in the cabinet because of the support they command, and not only, if at all, because of their administrative ability. It may be possible to pass over one or even two prominent party leaders, and it may be essential to ignore some of the claims of those who expect office, but the prime minister cannot, politically, ignore all of them even if he should wish to.

Nevertheless he continues to have the freedom to decide which particular post should go to each of his senior colleagues. His actual freedom will be greater, of course, when he comes to fill the less important posts. In general, it may be said, he is free to build as he wishes so long as the administration as a whole is reasonably representative of the principal political forces within the party and so long as he does not leave any sizable body of influential people outside the administration in a position to make trouble. It follows from this that his powers, certainly in peacetime, will be more restricted in a coalition than in the normal one-party government.

The prime minister's powers extend far beyond those to appoint and dismiss, crucial as they may be. His special status continues throughout his tenure of office. No one who has ever served on any committee can ignore the importance of the prime minister's position as chairman and his power to draw up the agenda. He is frequently the arbiter of disputes between ministers. Subject to cabinet ratification, he may make important decisions on his own and, by announcing them publicly in his capacity as chief spokesman for the government, make the ratification more likely. And, of course, upon his ability and energy depends the general efficiency and morale of the whole administration, a fact which is generally recognized, both by politicians and by the general public.

In part his powers derive simply from administrative necessity: someone must be chairman, prepare the agenda for meetings, supervise the general conduct of affairs, ensure that there is adequate preparation of business before the final decisions are taken, be prepared to take immediate action, on his own if necessary, and so on. A cabinet of twenty members is too large effectively to direct all the functions of modern government in formal conclave. Hence the need for committees and an inner council as well as for firm leadership from the prime minister.[13] There is little doubt that the efficiency of government is seriously impaired by weakness or indecision on the part of a prime minister. But considerations of efficiency alone rarely suffice to confer and sustain a position of power.

More fundamentally, he draws his strength from the twin sources of party and public support. As party leader he becomes both a focus for party loyalty and the chief party spokesman with the final voice in the presentation of party policy and the formulation of the election platform. It is in his capacity as party leader, too, that he acquires his frequently decisive influence upon the careers of his colleagues—an influence that is not confined to his period as prime minister.[14]

It is also because he is a party leader that he normally becomes prime minister and thus the most important national leader. As the latter, he is the automatic spokesman for the nation in international and domestic affairs, the person to whom people instinc-

[13] See below.

[14] Nor is it confined to the filling of ministerial posts. The patronage at the disposal of a prime minister extends, directly or through other ministers, to many other positions, including bishops in the Church of England, membership of innumerable committees and boards of all kinds, including the boards of nationalized industries, and, of course, inclusion in the honors lists (of peerages, knighthoods, and lesser ranks). See P. G. Richards, *Patronage in British Government* (London: Allen and Unwin, 1963).

tively turn in times of crisis or upon formal state occasions for an authoritative expression of policy and opinion. Above all, as national and party leader he is news and, more than any other politician, will benefit from that tendency to personalize ideas and organizations that characterizes modern society. For many, the prime minister *is* the party, *is* the government and, at times, may become the personification of the political nation, as Churchill symbolized and articulated the national resolve to continue the fight in 1940 and after.[15] With justice Sir Ivor Jennings has described the prime minister as "the keystone of the Constitution." [16]

Great as his powers may be, however, they are by no means unlimited. Political and constitutional necessity combine to ensure that, for the most part, the powers are wielded with respect for the wishes and interests of others. We are not, therefore, confronted with an example of irresponsible power used in defiance of public opinion. Quite apart from the controls exercised by the electorate and public over the activities of government in general, there are others operating within the framework of government upon the discretion of the prime minister in particular.

No powers are legally vested in the prime minister as such, but only in individual ministers or in the crown. Occasionally a prime minister will also take command of a department,[17] but normally his only other position is that of First Lord of the Treasury. This was at one time the most important ministerial position politically because it controlled the crown's powers of patronage, so important in managing the Commons, but it is now important pri-

---

[15] Only rarely is the nation sufficiently united politically for this last to be possible. It is the monarch, of course, who symbolizes the deeper and more lasting bases of national and social cohesion, the "way of life" rather than political cooperation. See the discussion of the monarchy, pp. 90–96.

[16] Jennings, op. cit., p. 173.

[17] Ramsay MacDonald was his own Foreign Secretary in 1924, Churchill his own Minister of Defence during the war and again in 1951, and Harold Wilson his own Minister for the Civil Service, from 1969 until his defeat in 1970. The responsibility for this post had previously been lodged in the Treasury. Apart from these examples, however, the practice is rare.

marily because it is the office usually filled by the prime minister.[18] It is as chief adviser to the crown that the prime minister exercises governing power. With this may be contrasted the position of the American president with whom the prime minister is more and more frequently compared, but in whom alone, by the letter of the Constitution, is vested responsibility for the executive power of the federal government. To a greater extent than a president, therefore, the prime minister is constitutionally constrained to work with and through others. These others must, in virtue of this fact alone, place some limit on the prime minister's power, and thus share the burden of responsibility—a fact that may assist him in carrying the load of office as much as it may frustrate his personal wishes.

The "ultimate deterrent" to the exercise of prime ministerial power, however, is the possibility of his colleagues combining to force his resignation by a "palace revolution." It was thus that Lloyd George became prime minister in 1917, as the culmination of mounting dissatisfaction inside the cabinet with the way in which Mr. Asquith had been conducting the war. Lloyd George in his turn was unseated in 1922 by a revolt among the rank-and-file M.P.s in the Conservative party, who thereby forced the party to leave the coalition that had continued after the end of the war. Lloyd George thus lost his majority in the House of Commons and had to resign. Similarly, the prime minister must carry his own party with him. Rarely can a prime minister triumph on an issue over which his party is relatively evenly and deeply split, as Sir Robert Peel did when repealing the Corn Laws in 1845.[19]

[18] For which reason it also carries with it a salary of £14,000 against the ordinary cabinet minister's £8,500. The general powers of those few prime ministers who have not been First Lord, however, have not been sensibly diminished.

[19] Peel carried through the bill he wished only, of course, because he was able to obtain a majority by the support of a sufficient number of members of other parties to supplement those of his own who remained loyal. But he ceased to be prime minister soon after. The action of Ramsay MacDonald in 1931, when he became prime minister of a coalition government composed almost entirely of Conservatives and Liberals and opposed by almost all his former Labour

The limits on the prime minister's powers are real, but they are essentially political in nature and to a large extent he is in a position to manipulate them. A "palace revolution" is possible only when there is agreement upon a successor and when that "successor" is willing to participate. A skillful prime minister can use his powers of appointment to encourage rivalries among his colleagues and to break as well as make reputations (for example, by assigning particularly difficult or unrewarding tasks to a minister). A prime minister, it seems, has to be a very clear liability to his party, and hence a threat to the tenure of office of almost all his colleagues, if the conditions for a successful revolt are to be satisfied. Thus for many years Mr. Macmillan survived the resignations or demotions, at one time or another, of the bulk of his senior colleagues as well as numerous political setbacks at by-elections and the collapse of central items of his program (particularly with respect to defense and foreign policy). Moreover, to the extent that he decides how particular decisions should be shaped—by *ad hoc* committees of ministers and civil servants, by informal gatherings of selected ministers, by cabinet committee, or in meetings of the whole cabinet[20]—he can do much to outmaneuver ministerial opposition on particular issues and ensure that he continues to rule for as long as he remains in office.

But, powerful as he may be, no particular prime minister is indispensable, irremovable, or omnipotent. Harold Wilson, widely believed to be a "strong" prime minister who successfully overcame more than one attempt to replace him, nevertheless had to give way over his proposals to reform trade union law when faced with opposition within the cabinet and amongst Labour M.P.s as well as from union leaders. A British prime minister depends on formal cabinet concurrence and on the continuing support, however obtained, of the other leading members of his party. Despite

---

party colleagues, provides another example of an occasion when a prime minister may successfully dispense with the support of his own party.

[20] See the discussion, below, of the uneven distribution of responsibility within the cabinet.

persuasive arguments to the contrary,[21] therefore, Britain does not have a system of presidential government.[22] The doctrine of collective responsibility is not yet a mere ritual.

COLLECTIVE RESPONSIBILITY

To say that a minister is "responsible" for some action may mean several different things. It may mean that he is the actual agent, the person deserving praise or blame therefor; in other words, the *author* of the action. Alternatively, it may mean no more than that he is *accountable* for the action in the sense that he is the proper person to be visited with the constitutional consequences or that he is the person under whose authority it was taken. In either case the responsibility may be legal or conventional. In fact, as we have seen, ministerial responsibility was originally primarily a legal concept. Moreover, even up to the eighteenth century ministers were accountable for their governmental acts through the judicial process of impeachment by the Commons before the House of Lords. Nowadays, however, impeachment is never resorted to and must be regarded as unnecessary as well as archaic, following upon the development of the newer conventions about ministerial responsibility. Using the word "responsibility" primarily, but not exclusively, in the sense of "accountability," it may be said that ministers both share in a collective responsibility for the general policies and record of the government and bear an individual responsibility for the actions and record of that portion of the administrative machine placed directly in their charge.

In accordance with these conventional rules about collective re-

---

[21] See J. P. Mackintosh, *The British Cabinet,* 2d ed. (London: Stevens, 1968), now the best single work on the subject, and R. H. S. Crossman's introduction to W. Bagehot, *The English Constitution* (London: Fontana, 1963). A. King, ed., *The British Prime Minister* (London: Macmillan, 1969), contains a useful selection of articles on this controversy.

[22] Nor, in the sense in which the phrase is sometimes used, i.e., to denote immense power, does the United States, if one is to believe Richard Neustadt in his *Presidential Power* (New York: John Wiley and Sons, 1960), and his contributions to A. King, ed., op. cit.

sponsibility, all members of the administration are expected to support its policies and its actions publicly, regardless of their private feelings on the matter. Should they for any reason no longer be prepared to do so, they must resign their offices (although not, usually, their seats in Parliament). Constitutionally, they cannot acquiesce in a decision and then, at some later stage when, for example, it becomes unpopular, claim that they were opposed to it and thus seek personally to escape the political penalties. In the words of Lord Melbourne, they must all "tell the same story." By the same token, it is impossible for the House of Commons to vote for the removal of a particular member of the government without also voting against the whole government, unless it is clear that the government is prepared to sacrifice that individual either as a scapegoat or because no collective responsibility is involved.[23] Just as, at an election, the voters must judge the government's record as a whole, so must they (and the House of Commons) judge the government as a whole. In short, the administration must stand or fall together. All its members must submit its policy to Parliament, must defend that policy, and, without exception, must resign or submit themselves to a general election if the House of Commons refuses to support it.

To say that the administration is collectively responsible in the sense of "accountable" is not, however, to say that they are all equally enthusiastic in their support of any particular decision. Within the government as well as outside it, the political choice facing an individual is rarely a simple one of *yes* or *no* to a single question. As with decisions about emigration, divorce, or a change of job, so with one about political allegiance: the choice is never (or hardly ever) between total satisfaction and total dissatisfaction. The principle of collective responsibility does not deny this, nor does it involve the pretense that no arguments or compromises ever take place among ministers. It requires only that the arguments be conducted in private. Significantly, the minutes of cabinet meetings, themselves confidential, record only the outlines of discussion and disagreement and refrain from naming the indi-

---

[23] See next section on Individual Ministerial Responsibility.

vidual members who put forward particular arguments. Nevertheless, it is usually possible to obtain a reasonably accurate idea of the general division of opinion on major issues, if not on more detailed ones, from political gossip (often based on some indiscretion), press reports (often based on political gossip), and above all, from the previous political record of the people concerned. This can be of great political and historic, if not constitutional, importance. Because of it, for example, widespread support could be given to Winston Churchill when he became prime minister in 1940, despite his having been a member of the immediately preceding Chamberlain government, whose conduct of the war had just been found wanting.

Collective responsibility does not mean that all members of the administration share equal authorship in that they play an equal part in the decision-making process. It has already been pointed out that the cabinet is the ultimate director of government policy. Other ministers usually attend cabinet meetings when the affairs of their departments are being considered, but this does not mean that they share the general powers of the cabinet. Less obviously, but as significant, there may exist an uneven division of responsibility (authorship) within the cabinet itself. For one thing, the cabinet nowadays makes extensive use of standing committees: on defense, legislation, home affairs, and the like, as well as *ad hoc* committees set up as circumstances require.[24] In many cabinets, moreover, there exists a small "inner council," to use Lloyd George's terminology, consisting of the prime minister and those of his colleagues whom he finds most sympathetic or stimulating, or whom he deems most important. Increasingly, however, prime ministers seem to work not so much with a single "inner council" as with a series of interlocking groups that are not necessarily even confined to members of the cabinet. Both efficiency and speed may benefit from this use of small and more or less specialist groups, but an even greater number of decisions are thus in effect made before appearing formally on a cabinet agenda. On other occasions, particularly in the realm of foreign policy, it is not unknown

[24] The details are rarely made public at the time, and not always afterward. But see the discussion in Mackintosh, op. cit., Chapter 13.

for a major decision to be made in this way, and not to be discussed in the cabinet until it is too late to reverse or modify it.[25] The special position of the prime minister not only represents a major form of inequality among cabinet members, but thus also leads to further inequalities.

It would be a mistake, nevertheless, to conclude that collective responsibility, taken as a statement about the authorship of the administration as a group, is a pure myth. The principle has certainly been attenuated, so that there is a huge difference between the central and extensive responsibility of the prime minister and the minimal amount borne by the most junior ministers. But the doctrine lends legitimacy to the dependence of the more responsible upon the less, and the fact of joint accountability is an inducement as well as an entitlement for cabinet ministers to inform themselves about, and comment on, the work of their colleagues —although it does not confer the time or the capacity to do so. Above all, collective ministerial responsibility still means that for their attempts and their failures to control the prime minister and their colleagues the cabinet must be responsible, in the authorship sense, as the administration as a whole must be responsible, in the same sense, for supporting or failing to support the cabinet.

The principle of collective responsibility thus limits the power of individual members, of the cabinet as a whole, and of the prime minister. It helps to channel the ambitions of politicians and make them less disruptive of the group cooperation that is essential to effective and responsible government. Even the most ruthless "lone wolf" must secure the cooperation of other party leaders if he is to reach the top and, once there, he cannot dispense with them. On the other hand, the principle has also

[25] Lord (R. A. B.) Butler has said in an interview, "In my time there have been periods when the Prime Minister has got together two or three Ministers, taken a decision, and the Cabinet has then just become a rubber stamp." But, he added later, "It depends really whether the Prime Minister is surrounded by a very powerful collection of Cabinet Ministers," *The Listener*, September 16, 1965, p. 407. Conspicuous among examples of the former situation were Neville Chamberlain's conduct of foreign policy in 1938–39, see Duff Cooper, *Old Men Forget* (New York: Dutton, 1953), pp. 189–242.

served to increase the power of the cabinet as a whole: against the monarch originally, thereby depriving him of the freedom to play off the leading statesmen against each other, and against the House of Commons, which is thereby constrained to judge and support governments as a whole rather than individual ministers.[26] By the same process, however, cabinets have become more directly dependent on and accountable to the electorate which, through the party and electoral systems, chooses the government and not, as, for example, in the Third and Fourth French Republics, simply the members of an assembly who then must bargain and compromise between themselves before providing a government.

The principle has other important effects. The coherence of the government exercises a strong pressure on the opposition to unite in the presentation of a clear alternative set of policies and ministers, for only thus can it make a serious claim to provide an alternative government. Both the government and opposition parties are thus led to seek internal compromises at deeper levels of agreement than might otherwise be the case. While "horse-trading" is probably an inescapable aspect of political life, it cannot form the only basis for cooperation when those concerned must be prepared publicly to defend both sides of any "deal." There is thus more chance that the parties will put forward programs embodying a coherent policy and not simply a compendium of miscellaneous responses to particular pressures. Any democratic government must probably do some things solely in response to such pressure. Yet when every major demand and all important policies must be accepted by a cabinet collectively answerable to a national electorate, then all demands and all policy proposals must at least be dressed up in terms of some potentially national interest. The result of this may, at times, only be to encourage hypocrisy and deception, but in general it must serve to limit the demands made on governments and the policies accepted or pursued by governments.

Vital and beneficial as the British system of collective cabinet

[26] But see the next section on Individual Ministerial Responsibility.

responsibility is, its continuance and well-being are not automatically ensured. In 1931 there took place a famous departure from the general rule in the form of an "agreement to differ" about tariffs among the members and supporters of the newly formed National Government. The Conservatives were convinced of the need for import duties to protect industry from the slump. The Liberals were equally convinced that any departure from free international trade would be disastrous. Compromise was clearly ruled out by the nature of the conflict, and ordinarily the result would have been for one or the other to resign from the government. Both sides, however, were still convinced that their continued participation in the government was necessary to combat the financial crisis that had called the coalition into being. They therefore agreed to differ and leave the decision to a free vote of the House of Commons. Tariffs were imposed. (In the following year an extension of the principle and the adoption of discriminatory tariffs in favor of Commonwealth producers—the system of imperial preference—was too much for some of the Liberals. They resigned; the rest continue their conservative alliance as Liberal Nationals until this day.)

Had the agreement to differ become a general practice, and had cabinets continued to stand for both sides of major disputes, it is easy to see that the whole system would have broken down. How, for example, could the government be judged on its tariff policy when it was both for and against it, and how was a supporter to know just what he was supporting when voting for the government? This experience suggests that the system works best when a cabinet rests upon some genuine agreement on principles, as may be expected only when it is formed from one group of party leaders or, as in wartime, when some single objective obviously transcends all other considerations and the principal means to its attainment are dictated by the objective itself. The cabinet and party systems are thus mutually dependent. In one other way, too, this is true. It is at least arguable that the "agreement to differ," like other unsatisfactory features of British politics in the nineteen thirties, escaped retribution largely because the opposition party was too small, too divided, and too unattractive to provide a genuine alternative government. Once again it must be stated that in Britain government is the product of the conflict and interplay between government and opposition.

INDIVIDUAL MINISTERIAL RESPONSIBILITY

It is not only collectively that ministers bear responsibility for the conduct of government. Each minister is also understood to be responsible individually for his own decisions and for all the actions of the government department or office under his control. The general formula to be found in statutes granting powers to the government is that "the minister may . . ." or "the minister will . . ." and not, "the department or ministry may or will. . . ." [27] One minor result of this is that letters from a department, even on very trivial matters, frequently begin with some such wording as "I am directed by the Secretary of State to inform you . . . ," a statement which is patently improbable. (It is, of course, possible.) Legally and constitutionally a government department is its minister's responsibility, and its civil-service staff is there simply to do the minister's bidding and carry out his policy.[28]

The actual "cash value" of the concept of individual responsibility is less easily discerned. Certainly it includes the notion that the minister should be the public spokesman and defender of that part of the administrative structure within his competence. It is he or, in his absence, his junior minister who will explain the policy of the department or of the government insofar as it concerns the department, in Parliament and elsewhere; and upon him falls the task of answering criticisms directed at his department. Anything for which he is technically responsible may be questioned or debated in Parliament. A minister does not feel bound to defend the actions of one of his officials, should that action have been taken in defiance of departmental policy or instructions

---

[27] On the other hand, certain powers are vested directly in the four Scottish departments, set up to administer certain services within Scotland in answer to strong nationalist pressure there. All are under the control of the Secretary of State for Scotland, who also has certain powers.

[28] See the discussion of the civil service in Chapter 6.

or have resulted from the purely personal incompetence of a junior official. But in all other circumstances the minister is bound to accept the burden of justifying a departmental action, although, quite obviously, he cannot hope even to be informed of all that is done in his name. Nevertheless, just as the cabinet may have the final word in all matters of general policy, so may the minister have the last word in his own department. Admittedly a minister may contribute little to the running of his department beyond his signature and the ability to say *yes* to the advice tendered by his officials. But even when this is known to be the case, it is still the minister who serves as the public target for praise and blame directed at the record of his department.

Historically, the minister was simply the man appointed by the monarch to run one sphere of the crown's governmental machinery. Once it had been accepted that the minister was chosen on the basis of the support vouchsafed him and/or his colleagues in Parliament, however, he became the means whereby the conduct of administration was made at least responsive to public opinion.[29] For it is through questions and discussion in Parliament that M.P.s may most surely inform themselves about and then criticize the conduct of administration. It is only through the minister that M.P.s may constitutionally attack the policy of a department and it is only over him that they have any direct power. Just as the monarch could and did dismiss his ministers when they ceased to be loyal, faithful, or efficient servants, so traditional constitutional doctrine states that a minister must resign not only if a whole government is defeated, but also if he or his department individually cease to satisfy the House of Commons. More recently, however, strong arguments have been put forward to suggest that this doctrine has no place, strictly speaking, in the twentieth-century constitution.[30]

There is no question but that a minister will resign in the case of a purely personal indiscretion or blunder, unless his departure

[29] This was as true in the nineteenth century as it is today, despite the different "publics" concerned.
[30] See, in particular, S. E. Finer, "The Individual Responsibility of Ministers," *Public Administration* (Winter 1956).

from office might undermine the strength of the government even more than his staying. Thus in 1948 a junior minister resigned when he was discovered to have accepted gifts from people under circumstances that might have appeared to involve a corrupt relationship, and in 1963 the Secretary of State for War, Mr. Profumo, resigned after confessing that he had misled Parliament about the nature of his relationship with a girl who had simultaneously been associated with a Russian diplomat. There is no doubt, either, that a minister will probably not resign, however unpopular his conduct, if he has merely been carrying out government policy and continues to have the support of his colleagues. These are the limiting cases. The resignation, in 1954, of Sir Thomas Dugdale, Minister of Agriculture, is an example of what may be called the middle ground. His action followed a report on the administrative mismanagement of a case about which the minister personally knew nothing until late in the episode, and connected with powers compulsorily to purchase land about which his party was not enthusiastic. Admitting responsibility for tolerating the procedures that made the case possible, Sir Thomas also outlined steps taken to end those procedures before resigning. Against this it may be permissible to cite Harold Macmillan's refusal to accept the resignation of the First Lord of the Admiralty in 1961 after an official report criticized naval security arrangements, or Mr. J. Amery's refusal, in 1964, to resign from Civil Aviation after it had been shown to have grossly overpaid a private contractor. On the other hand, it is certain that the departmental record of a minister will have an important effect upon his subsequent governmental career, even if, for example, his unpopularity or inefficiency are not cited as reasons for this subsequent departure from office.[31] The fact remains, however, that no modern prime minister has been forced to lose an individual minister merely because this has been demanded in the House of Commons.[32]

[31] Officially it may be "to make way for a younger man," for "private reasons," or for reasons of "health" or "business." These will, of course, in many cases be the true explanation.

[32] The resignation from the Foreign Secretaryship of Sir Samuel Hoare in 1935 after public anger over his Ethiopian policy was long thought to

Individual ministerial responsibility today therefore appears to be no more meaningful in Britain than in the United States, in that the House of Commons seems to have no more power over a minister's tenure of office than has Congress. (If any weight be attached to the Senate's power to withhold ratification of a cabinet appointment, then the Commons seems to have even less power than Congress.) In neither case, however, is the power negligible. Prime ministers and presidents will both, on occasion, remove the political heads of departments because their continuance in office is the cause of more political difficulties than they are willing to face. Despite these resemblances, however, the situations in the two countries are not identical. Congress's inability directly to force the resignation of a secretary is founded on the constitutional principle of the separation of powers, whose spirit Congress's indirect power may appear to violate. The inability of the House of Commons results rather from the extension of the shield of collective responsibility to protect individual ministers from a legitimate exercise of the House's powers. But one must not press this line of argument too far. The very existence of the concept of ministerial responsibility influences behavior. It helps to shape the attitudes of the House and the cabinet, and hence the determination with which they will attack and defend any individual; it provides legitimate grounds for a prime minister to dismiss a colleague, should he desire to, whether because of his record or as a sop to critics of the government; and it is impossible to assess how many mistakes would have been made, or bold ventures initiated, but for the belief that a minister's personal position would suffer therefrom.

At this stage in British constitutional development the accountability of individual ministers directly to Parliament may have been weakened, but that to his leader and colleagues has been

---

be such an example. It now appears that he resigned because he was not prepared to join with the cabinet in repudiating past policy. This case is therefore an example of collective rather than individual responsibility. See his autobiography, Lord Templewood, *Nine Troubled Years* (London: Collins, 1954).

strengthened at least as much. Indeed, it is probably correct to say that a minister's security today depends almost entirely on his relations with his party, his colleagues, and his leader. Since their attitude is likely to be influenced by the minister's showing in the House of Commons (of which they form the bulk), it is not clear that the change has relieved ministers of much anxiety or lessened their need for alertness. The individual minister can never be certain, should trouble arise, that the protection of collective responsibility will in fact be extended to shield him from the traditional obligation to resign.

CABINET AND COMMONS

Hitherto it has been stated that the cabinet can normally count on the continuing support of its majority in the House of Commons.[33] That statement must now be explained.

The rules of the constitution establish an apparent balance of power between the two bodies. Without the support of the Commons for its legislation and its financial requirements, no government could govern. Should a majority therefore express its lack of confidence in the government, either by passing a formal vote of censure or by failing to pass a measure demanded by the government, it must resign—or take the issue to the country by dissolving Parliament. Thus, as it used to be said, the power of the Commons to dismiss the government is balanced by the power of the government to dissolve the Commons, and it is this second power which, more than any other factor, prevents M.P.s from voting against a government that hitherto they have supported. This may well have been a correct statement of the facts at least until the late eighteenth century. A new election, at which the influence of the crown or the local magnates could be brought to bear upon the voters, would often result in returning a majority more sympathetic to the crown.

Nowadays party loyalty and discipline provide the principal ex-

[33] The House of Lords is unimportant so far as a government's tenure of office is concerned, as we will see in the following chapter.

planation of party cohesion. But constitutional writers sometimes talk of the power to dissolve the Commons as a "big stick" or even a "terrifying power." [34] This is, apparently, because of the suggestion that potentially dissident M.P.s are loath to expend effort and money on a premature election at which they may lose their seats. Despite the fact that some politicians still seem to share this view it must be rejected in modern conditions.

To appreciate the position, attention should initially be focused on the factors motivating those among a government's supporters who have decided, or might decide, to support it no longer. There have been many such defecting groups, usually small in number, but only twice in this century have their votes resulted in a change of government: late in 1924, when MacDonald lost an election held because the Liberals had withdrawn their support from his minority Labour government; and in May 1940, when the adverse votes of thirty-three of Chamberlain's supporters, and the abstention of another sixty, led him to resign, despite the fact that he still secured a majority of eighty-one votes. It is noteworthy that the only actual defeat occurred during a year when no single party had a majority in the House, when in fact a three-party system existed, and that Chamberlain's resignation took place at a period when national unity and a government with wide support were vitally necessary.[35] Neither government was saved by the existence of the power of dissolution.

It may be argued that it is only when the two-party system is functioning "normally" that the power is effective (when, one might suppose, it is least necessary). If so, there is nothing to indicate that it is effective for the reasons usually given. Few M.P.s now pay their own election expenses, which are borne largely by the parties. The financial argument, indeed, applies principally to the party organizations and leaders, and is almost always one *against* threatening an election for disciplinary or any other rea-

---

[34] The quotations are from Sir Ivor Jennings, op. cit., p. 474, and B. E. Carter, *The Office of Prime Minister* (London: Faber, 1956), p. 274.
[35] The debate took place just after the final withdrawal of British troops from Norway and the completion of the German occupation of that country.

sons. It is true that an election campaign is or may be exhausting for the individuals concerned, but not dramatically more so than the everyday work of a parliamentarian—except in the case of the prime minister and leader of the opposition, who feel impelled to undertake national speaking tours. Both these points, in other words, are reasons why a prime minister should attempt to conciliate potential defectors rather than threaten them with an election. In order to substantiate the third argument, that defectors are deterred by the possible loss of their seats, it would be necessary to show both that the great majority of rebels have had large majorities, while those in "marginal" constituencies are models of regularity, and that no other explanation can be found for this correlation.[36]

At best, however, the power to dissolve, as presented, can provide no more than a small part of the explanation of party voting, if only because the reasons put forward apply exclusively to members of the government majority, whereas party voting also characterizes the opposition, even if to a slightly lesser extent. Another approach is therefore indicated if one is to understand why it is that British M.P.s vote the party line so much more consistently than do, for example, their American counterparts.

Paradoxical as it may seem at first, it is the power to dismiss governments or, rather, the fact that governments nowadays consider that any adverse vote, unless immediately reversed, is tantamount to dismissal, that prevents M.P.s from defecting. To defect in numbers sufficient to abolish a government's majority may result in the other party's being put in power either immediately or after a new election. Party loyalty, the natural preference for a government drawn from one's own party, is therefore the principal sanction. Party rebels, accordingly, even when sufficiently incensed to vote against their party or abstain from voting, are normally careful to see that their numbers are small enough not to imperil the government's majority—which is why the smaller the

---

[36] Unpublished research by the author failed to uncover any correlation, and Robert I. Jackson, *Rebels and Whips* (London: Macmillan, 1968), p. 196, shows that, if anything, an inverse correlation has prevailed in the period 1945–66.

majority, the fewer the revolts. After the 1956 Suez invasion fifteen Conservative M.P.s refused to vote for their government's decision to withdraw from Port Said. They probably would not have done so had the Conservative majority been very small, since the Labour party, the only alternative governing party, would have been even "softer" toward Egypt, and thus, from their point of view, even less worthy of support. Only where all the other differences between the two parties are less important than the question at issue, or when two or more possible coalitions are almost equally desirable or undesirable, is one likely to see any group defecting under circumstances where this would involve dismissing a government.[37] Even then the likelihood of such a revolt will also depend upon the rebels' estimate of the effects of rebellion upon their own futures. These are likely to be adverse since, as we have already seen, third parties and small groups usually fare badly at British elections. (This would, of course, be true whether or not governments had the power to dissolve Parliament, so long as elections continued to take place at all.)

Other forces, internal to the party, reinforce loyalty in helping to maintain party solidarity in the House. The fact that M.P.s are elected in their capacity as party members and supporters, their feelings of community with at least some of their party colleagues, and their reluctance to break old ties and personal associations all play their part. So, too, does ambition. The politician with ambition for office will normally tread carefully, therefore, but not too carefully: there are instances of men receiving promotion because of as well as despite rebellion and a proper show of independence. There is, too, the ultimate possibility of expulsion from the party in Parliament, a sentence which is comparatively rarely passed, but which, if permanent, carries with it the certainty of personal defeat at the next election. None of these factors, and particularly expulsion, is trivial, but not even expulsion can effectively or too frequently be applied against a large group without

[37] Examples include, the defection of a large group of Liberals to the Conservatives over the question of Irish Home Rule in 1886, which led to the downfall of Gladstone's second administration, and the withdrawal of Liberal support from the first Labour government in 1924.

damaging the fortunes of the party, possibly irreparably. To the other reasons given for voting conformity on the part of M.P.s must therefore be added the continuous efforts of the party leadership to avoid putting too great and too constant a strain upon the loyalty of their supporters.

In contrast to the picture just given, it is often imagined that M.P.s are simply cowed or coerced into supporting the government with their votes. In one sense only is this view tenable. No government need resign except upon formal verdicts of censure and no-confidence or the rejection by the House of the basic principles of essential legislation. In recent decades, however, governments more and more have come to regard any vote, even upon questions of apparently minor detail, as votes of confidence. Indeed, unless it is formally announced beforehand that a question is being left to a so-called free vote, it is now assumed as a matter of course that any defeat in the House of Commons must be reversed or else lead to the government's resigning or dissolving Parliament. It is to this point, if anywhere, that criticism of the power of the government should principally be directed.

The common misconceptions of the nature of party regularity are further encouraged by reference to the activities of the whips, whose very name conjures up visions of a reign of terror within the party. The whips are, in fact, the M.P.s appointed to manage the affairs of the party in each House of Parliament, the government ones being paid a salary. Their duties are wide, and include much of the administrative work of arranging parliamentary business as well as purely intraparty work. Their primary functions, however, are to act as the intermediaries between the party leaders and their followers, keeping each in touch with the feelings and attitudes of the other. As such, they will advise the leaders on appointments, tactics, and policy, and will attempt, conversely, to persuade and cajole M.P.s to accord their full support to the party's leaders. In this latter task they have a number of powerful instruments: they have extensive direct powers of patronage, they advise the prime minister upon questions of promotion as well as on official action against rebels, and in innumerable relatively small ways they can make life easy or difficult for an M.P.[38] But their principal role is simply to keep the internal party machinery well oiled, so that the natural forces for loyalty may continue to do their work. One of their tasks, therefore, is to circulate information about forthcoming debates, indicating when votes are expected, how party members should vote (not always easy to appreciate, given the language of many motions), and, by the number of underlinings, how important each vote is. These printed instructions are also referred to as "whips"—a "three-line whip," for example, being one wherein a particular vote is trebly underlined as one of major importance that a member should attend if humanly possible. The printed "whips" are also used to summon members to party meetings of all kinds.[39] It is perhaps a fair summary to say that the main concern of the party whips is to help maintain party cohesion, occasionally by pressures and threats, often by persuasion, and mainly by pointing out to members how best to demonstrate the loyalty they naturally feel, and to the leaders how best to earn that loyalty.

The situation is a little different when a party is in opposition, since the object in view is to obtain rather than retain office. Defection then has less obviously and directly damaging results. But insofar as it makes the job of the government easier (a divided opposition is less dangerous), and the likelihood of attracting electoral support less, such signs of disunity are still kept in check. Nevertheless, M.P.s may usually indulge their personalities more freely when in opposition, without incurring disfavor, simply because less is at stake. At all times, too, the Labour party seems to experience open rebellion or the threat of it more frequently than do the Conservatives. It may be that this reflects the greater emphasis in the latter upon the need to stay in office if anything is to be accomplished and the presence in the former of more people who place "purity" above power, as well as the natural ten-

[38] See the invaluable discussion in Jackson, op. cit., especially on pp. 292–307.

[39] Hence the use of the phrase "to withdraw the whip" as a synonym for expulsion from the party in Parliament.

dency of reform parties to embrace a wider range of opinions than one more concerned with preservation. But of both parties it is true to say, in the words of a Conservative Chief Whip, that "politics is a matter of power, and any good government can always get its way. Paying attention to its own backbenchers is part of the technique of ensuring that it will get its way." [40]

To argue, as we have done, that the standard account of the power of dissolution is misleading (when applied to the contemporary situation) is not, however, to say that the power is unimportant. In at least two ways its existence may exert a strong influence upon behavior. In the first place, it means that within the limits of the present maximum period of five years between elections it is the government that decides[41] when to hold a general election, and that may thus choose the circumstances (or even create them) that appear most favorable to its own chances.[42] Others will be able to venture intelligent guesses about the probable date, but they can never *know*. This uncertainty may well have a "disciplining" effect. Potential rebels are less likely to defect if they think there will be an early election, because of the stronger pull of party loyalty and the greater desirability of party unity at such a time. The opposition, too, must always bear this possibility in mind. If at times the hint of an election may lead it to intensify its attacks upon the government, at others it will be restrained by the fear of having its bluff called at the polls, and at all times such a hint will encourage it to try to remain united and ready for battle at short notice.

In the second place, the power of dissolution may be important whenever a government depends for its parliamentary majority upon the votes of M.P.s who belong to no party or to a third party. Such members would probably be vulnerable to the traditional deterrent qualities of a dissolution to the extent that non-

---

[40] *The Listener,* December 26, 1963, p. 1057.

[41] Subject to what has been said above or will be said shortly about the monarch's prerogatives.

[42] The right is now apparently acknowledged to be the prime minister's. It is up to him to decide whether or not to consult the cabinet.

party or small-party members are likely to have small financial resources and uncertain electoral prospects.[43] On the other hand, in such circumstances the monarch would no longer be bound to grant a dissolution to a defeated prime minister. If, for example, the "floating" group were prepared to support an alternative government that could be formed from the existing House of Commons, then the monarch might well refuse to dissolve Parliament. Only, indeed, if all reasonable combinations of parties and groups had been tried would a dissolution almost certainly *be* granted.

To cite the most recent illustration, after the election held late in 1923 the Conservative party remained the largest single party in the House of Commons, but it had fewer seats than the Labour and Liberal parties combined. Mr. Baldwin, the Conservative prime minister, did not resign at once, but waited until the Liberals, who held the balance of power, had voted against him. Ramsay MacDonald was thereupon invited to form the first Labour government, sustained by the votes of the Liberals, whose leaders nevertheless did not join the government. Later in the same year (1924) a somewhat confused situation resulted in the Liberals' voting against the Labour government. The only two possible governments had thus been defeated in the life of the same Parliament and, for this reason, despite some doubts at the time, one must defend the king's decision to grant a dissolution to Mr. MacDonald.[44]

It is, indeed, in precisely such a situation that the power of dissolution is most valuable and effective—but not purely or necessarily as a deterrent.[45] Had there been no power of dissolution,

[43] Even in this case, however, the deterrent value of dissolution is conditional—the M.P.s concerned might conceivably have adequate finances and a strong electoral base.

[44] See the similar situation that arose in Canada in 1926 and the discussion thereof in E. A. Forsey, *The Royal Power of Dissolution of Parliament in the British Commonwealth* (London: Oxford University Press, 1943), pp. 131–250.

[45] The situation in 1924 was too confused, and Mr. MacDonald's actions too unpredictable, for this incident to be conclusive as to the deterrent value of dissolution or the threat to dissolve.

the House of Commons would have had to continue for a full term and the country would have had to suffer a succession of minority or coalition governments, none of which might have been any more long-lived or powerful than the Labour one. The Liberal party, furthermore, would have wielded inordinate power during this period and, such was its internal condition, might well have split under the strains involved in holding the balance, thus compounding the instability of the system. As it was, the election of 1924 gave the Conservative party a clear majority that enabled it to remain in office until after the election of 1929, when, it is worth recalling, a situation similar to that of 1923 resulted and the second Labour government was formed.[46] The power of dissolution, it might be concluded, thus rescued Britain from a longer period of governmental instability. What is more, the knowledge that it can do so must help to prevent dissatisfied groups of M.P.s from defecting in the hope that they could perform comparable balancing roles, or in order to put in the other side for a limited purpose, after which they could restore the former government to office.[47] The existence of the power of dissolution, this is to say, helps to ensure that M.P.s accept or reject governments as a whole and not merely on a single issue unless that issue is of supreme and overriding importance. But it is not dissolution alone that has this result. The dissolution of 1924, to revert to the example already cited, led to stable government because *the resulting election produced a clear majority* for a single party. On the other hand, as we have seen, the elections of 1923 and 1929 (exceptionally) did not produce such a majority. It is, therefore, only in conjunction with the existing electoral system and voting patterns, the voters' preference for strong government, and the other social and political forces that tend to produce a substantially two-party

[46] Although the Labour party in 1929 was the largest single party, whereas it was not in 1923–24, it had still to depend on Liberal support for office.

[47] As, for example, the left wing of the Conservative party might have wished to put Labour in office in 1956 to prevent, or end, the Suez invasion, and subsequently restore the Conservative government to pursue the rest of its policies.

system, that the power of dissolution may be relied upon to assist in stabilizing and strengthening governments.[48]

Finally, something must be said of another major problem: the capacity of political ministers to exercise their crucial constitutional responsibilities effectively. Neither the increased use of cabinet committees, the greater role of the prime minister (backed by an enlarged cabinet secretariat), the multiplication of ministerial posts, nor occasional experiments with "overlords" and "coordinating" ministers have yet succeeded in reducing the immense physical strain of office, creating time for long-term policy deliberation or enabling the politician to master the work of government. Suggestions for reform are legion, primarily of a structural kind.[49] In the late 1960s however, more and more attention began to be given to the techniques and instruments of decision-making.[50]

The risk cannot be entirely discounted, meantime, that cabinets will either govern largely in the light of the thinking carried out while in opposition, or will rapidly exhaust their inspiration and thereafter simply drift, or will become almost totally dependent upon advice from the civil service—than any of which, of course, many worse fates can be imagined.

The British cabinet system represents a fusion rather than a separation of powers. It also embodies a concentration both of power and of responsibility, most noticeably while it rests upon

[48] It follows from this analysis, I think, that the power of dissolution would have made little, if any, difference to the stability of governments in the Third or Fourth French Republics, or at least that the case for believing otherwise must rest upon stronger foundations than unqualified references to the strength of British cabinets.

[49] See the various opinions expressed in, for example, the *Report* of the Haldane Committee, cited in the first footnote to this chapter; L. S. Amery, *Thoughts on the Constitution* (London: Oxford University Press, 1947); H. J. Laski, *Reflections on the Constitution* (Manchester: Manchester University Press, 1951); B. Chapman, *British Government Observed* (London: Allen and Unwin, 1963); or H. Berkeley, *The Power of the Prime Minister* (London: Allen and Unwin, 1968).

[50] See, in particular, J. Bray, *Decisions in Government* (London: Gollancz, 1970). We will return to this issue in Chapter 6.

the two-party system. Even so, the cabinet is not all-powerful. It is losing power to the prime minister and, as we will see, it is subject to continuous influence from Parliament and ever more guidance from its senior civil-service advisers, not to mention the constant activities of pressure groups and the decisive power of the electorate. But it is at all times armed with sufficient constitutional power to function effectively as Her Majesty's Government and to serve as the focal point of all political endeavor. It is impossible to talk of government policy, or a government decision, unless that policy or decision has implicitly or explicitly been approved by the cabinet. At worst, a cabinet will therefore be like a dam, containing and channeling the political forces that produce national policy; while at best, it will be more like a generating-station, driven by the waters of national life, but transmuting their energy into new and more potent forms.

5

Parliament

SOVEREIGNTY

The sovereignty of Parliament is normally cited as a fundamental principle of the British constitution.[1] Parliament is sovereign, it is said, in that it can amend or abolish the constitution by the same legislative processes as it can, say, regulate betting on horse races. It can also override previous legislation at will, prolong its own life indefinitely, make criticism of the government a penal offense, and, in short, do anything except bind succeeding Parliaments, all without *legal* let or hindrance.

The situation is, of course, much less sinister than this might suggest. The principle does not, for one thing, imply any political power to do whatever Parliament feels like. It is simply a legal principle that is more accurately stated in other terms. What it amounts to is that the courts have adopted the practice of accepting validly made Acts of Parliament as being superior to other legal rules (for example, those of common law), including rules laid down by previous Acts. The sovereignty of Parliament is therefore itself an example of case law. It is also one on which there are remarkably few cases, so that some doubt exists as to its precise implications and, in particular, as to how closely judges

[1] See the classic statement of the principle in A. V. Dicey, *Introduction to the Study of the Law of the Constitution* (London: Macmillan; 10th ed. by E. C. S. Wade, 1960), Part I.

will examine an Act to ensure that it is in fact "validly made." [2] In principle, however, valid statutes must be assented to by the queen and both Houses of Parliament so that, for example, a resolution of the House of Commons alone will have no general legal force.[3] The main *political* effects of the doctrine are, first, that a government with the support of Parliament knows that it possesses or can acquire all the legal powers necessary to carry through its program and, second, that political disputes must be argued in political and not legal terms, in contrast to American experience, where the institution of judicial review sometimes has the opposite result.

THE HOUSE OF LORDS

In everyday discussion "Parliament" is normally used to denote the House of Commons only, or primarily. This usage reflects the legislative inaction of the monarchy and the subordinate position of the House of Lords. Convention progressively limited the powers of the House of Lords in the nineteenth century. For example, the rule came to be accepted that the Lords should automatically agree to financial legislation already passed by the Commons. After the second chamber rejected the budget of 1909, however, its powers were limited by the Parliament Act of 1911. As amended in 1949, it declares that an Act may legally be passed without the approval of the House of Lords if it is agreed to twice by the House of Commons in separate sessions, provided that a year should elapse between its acceptance in principle for the first time and its final acceptance after passing through all the procedural requirements for the second time. Legislation to extend the life of Parliament beyond its present maximum must, however, receive the assent of the House of Lords. Financial legislation, on the other hand, may become law within one month of its being

[2] See G. Marshall, "What Is Parliament? The Changing Concept of Parliamentary Sovereignty," *Political Studies,* vol. II (1954), pp. 193–209.

[3] See *Stockdale vs. Hansard* (1839). Account must also be taken of the limitations upon the powers of the House of Lords (see below).

passed by the Commons, regardless of the attitude of the Lords.[4] The first Parliament Act was violently opposed by the Lords, who passed it only when told that the king had agreed to create enough new peers to secure a favorable majority. The second Act, which established the one-year period of delay for ordinary legislation in place of a two-year one, was passed under the provisions of the first Act. They were introduced by, respectively, a Liberal and a Labour government against the opposition, in both cases, of the Conservative party which, in this century, has been able to count on a permanent majority in the House of Lords.

The House has over 1,000 members, about 800 of whom are hereditary English and United Kingdom peers of varying rank.[5] The remainder consists of royal princes (who take no part in governmental proceeding), the two archbishops and 24 senior bishops of the Church of England, nonhereditary life peers and peeresses (created under an act of 1958), and nine Justices appointed for life to discharge the House's duties as the supreme court in the country. Peerages are conferred by the monarch on the advice of the prime minister usually as a reward for some kind of public service, primarily in politics and in business.

The average attendance in the House is small, rarely exceeding two hundred, and is largely made up of those who are or have been ministers, supplemented by the first holders of titles and life peers. Procedure is highly informal, and most debates are not followed by a vote. This is to say that the House of Lords confines itself principally to discussion and to the minor revision of bills, about three-quarters of which have already been passed by the House of Commons. What changes it makes, moreover, are frequently requested by the government, which has decided further to modify legislation after, or even because of, the discussion in the House of Commons. Its most important function in this re-

---

[4] Financial legislation is officially defined as legislation certified to be such by the Speaker of the House of Commons. Speakers, to date, have been very cautious and have frequently refused to certify budget legislation because it contained matter not strictly financial.

[5] In descending order of precedence: duke, marquis, earl, viscount, baron.

spect, however, is often to discuss clauses in a bill that were passed by the Commons without any debate due to shortage of time. Frequently, too, the Lords will hold debates on general problems about which government action is either contemplated or desired. These debates, frequently of high standard, are on subjects ranging, for example, from deer poaching in the Scottish Highlands to foreign policy.

In all these ways the House now performs useful if ancillary functions. For the most part the Lords do not press their disagreements with the House of Commons, but acquiesce, sometimes under protest, in the decisions taken in the popular chamber. For these reasons one no longer hears much talk of abolishing the House of Lords. Nevertheless, in 1948 and 1968 there were all-party conferences that tried, without success, to secure agreement about reform; in 1958 the Conservatives passed legislation authorizing the creation of life peerages (the most revolutionary feature of which was the decision to include women among their recipients);[6] and in 1963 they passed legislation permitting individuals to refuse to inherit a peerage or to renounce an existing title (thereby allowing them to be M.P.s).

Without being the cause of strong political feelings, the House of Lords is criticized both from the left and the right. On the left dissatisfaction is voiced both on social and political grounds. Socially, the objection is against the system of titles in general [7] and, in particular, against the principle that membership of any governmental organ should rest on a hereditary claim. Politically, it is objected, above all, that the House of Lords is predominantly and apparently permanently conservative in character, and that no guarantee exists that it will always act with forbearance in the face of left-wing legislation and never obstruct the implementing of a

[6] But as Sir Alec Douglas-, then Lord, Home said on behalf of the government: "Taking women into a parliamentary embrace would seem to be only a modest extension of the normal functions and privileges of a peer." House of Lords, October 30, 1957.

[7] A system of titles and other honors, although not necessarily hereditary ones, may nevertheless be one of the less pernicious forms of political or official reward and patronage.

reform program. Conversely, no major measure actively supported by the Conservative party or government has been rejected in the past century. If one were rejected today, it would be a startling action by a House, only one-ninth of whose members admit to supporting either the Labour or Liberal parties.[8]

That there is any right-wing discontent with the present position of the House of Lords may seem surprising. It stems, however, from an uneasy feeling that it is difficult to justify even the present powers of the second chamber as it is now constituted. A reformed House, it is felt, would be more capable of acting as a brake on "radical legislation," if only because to impose delay might then seem more disinterested. Such a brake is desirable, the argument usually continues, because, at least toward the end of a five-year term of office, a radical government should do nothing radical without again consulting the people at an election. (This endorsement of the theory that a government is bound by its "mandate" from the electors to implement its electoral program and nothing else is not balanced by any suggested provisions whereby a reformed House of Lords would be able to make a government *act*, rather than do nothing, in the face of real or alleged public demand.)[9] Although critics abound, agreement on what to do about the House of Lords is elusive. The Labour government, with substantial acceptance from the Conservative front bench, introduced a scheme for reform which, in effect, would have largely eliminated the hereditary membership and produced a small House that consisted mostly of appointed members. But it was impossible to secure a back-bench consensus and, in 1969, the bill was withdrawn, a fact regretted (or indeed, noticed) by few.

There are severe limits to the type of reform desirable. To institute an elected House of Lords would either pose a threat to the

[8] Between them, these parties obtained 50 percent of the popular vote even in the 1970 election.

[9] The theory of a definite "mandate" to a government from the electorate has received little respectable backing outside this context. In practice it is cited primarily as a weapon whereby to attack the other side or to defend one's own actions. The electoral studies discussed in Chapter 3 lend little support to the doctrine. Nevertheless, the mere fact that the theory is bruited with reference to parties and governments

authority of the Commons or, if this threat were disposed of, lead to the election of relative nonentities. The second is obviously undesirable and would involve a significant regression from the existing state of affairs. On the other hand, to increase the real powers of the House in any way would be to upset the whole relationship between the government and Parliament to the extent that the government may be faced with conflicting majorities in the two Houses. Were this eventuality made impossible, moreover, then the point of having a more powerful second chamber becomes doubtful.[10] At present, as for the past century or more, the complexion of the government depends entirely upon the party strengths in the Commons, and its tenure of office is unaffected, constitutionally speaking, by the degree of support it obtains from the Lords. These facts both reflect and in part explain the relative weakness of the upper chamber. The remainder of our discussion of Parliament may therefore confine itself almost exclusively to the House of Commons and its place within the constitution.

THE HOUSE OF COMMONS

It has already been remarked that government in Britain proceeds by way of an organized confrontation of government and opposition. It has also been suggested that Parliament can in no way be said to govern the country itself. The principal function of the House of Commons, and therefore of Parliament, is rather to sustain the government and the official opposition and provide the principal "oratorical battleground" [11] for the conflict between them. It is, of course, easy to imagine a government's being able to survive and function without the continuing presence of the

in Britain tells one something important about British politics. To the author's knowledge there is no corresponding notion in French politics or, except possibly with reference to a president, in American.

[10] The objection against the existing House, with relatively few powers, is not so much that its majority may differ from that in the Commons as that it never changes.

[11] Sir Ivor Jennings, *Parliament,* 2d ed. (Cambridge: Cambridge University Press, 1957), p. 529.

Commons. It is necessary only to assume the grant of sufficiently wide legislative and discretionary powers. But for several reasons the existence and satisfactory functioning of the Commons are well-nigh indispensable to the effective operation of an opposition party and hence, except possibly in the very short run, to the maintenance of *good* government. It is in the House that the best opportunities exist for extracting the information about the government's plans and actions that is necessary properly to evaluate and criticize or even fully to understand them. It is there, too, that governments are not only expected to explain and defend their policies, but also to justify them in the face of critical cross-examination. Equally, of course, the opposition parties will be called upon to defend and justify the alternatives they propound. The extent to which the mere need to offer a public justification for an action serves to control and limit a party cannot be measured, but is obviously a vital constituent of free democratic government. Too often it is overlooked in assessments of the power of Parliament, which is therefore sometimes underestimated. At all times, finally, the House of Commons serves as an indispensable avenue for the expression of discontent and the airing of grievances (perhaps its most basic traditional function). Although the opposition parties play the most obvious role in these respects, thus to control the work of government is one of the principal concerns of government supporters as well.

In discussing and assessing the work of the House of Commons it is important to avoid passing judgments based on the mistaken notion that its purpose is to legislate or otherwise to govern rather than to criticize those who do govern. Nor should it be forgotten that throughout almost all its history the latter has been Parliament's essential role. If there exists any fundamental separation of powers in British government, it consists not of a separation between legislature and executive but of one between the doers and the controllers, between those who initiate policies and take action on the one hand and, on the other, those who criticize the actions and attempt to ensure that the policies adopted are broadly acceptable to the community. The methods whereby Parliament discharges its duties are continuously evolving as circumstances change and, with them, the demands placed on government. But the principal innovation of the modern constitution has been to superimpose the further task of providing and sustaining the government. Even this, however, was no sudden development. For centuries the House of Commons has been a training ground as well as a testing ground of ministers.

ORGANIZATION AND PROCEDURE

The physical layout of the House is itself informative. The chamber is rectangular in shape, with rows of benches banked along the longer sides of it, like the choir stalls in a cathedral. As in some cathedrals, the benches are divided into two groups facing each other across a floor. On one group sit the government and its supporters, and on the other sit the members of the opposition party or parties. Physically as well as politically the government and alternative government sit permanently confronted and divided. There are no cross-benches for independent or minor-party members who neither support nor oppose the government consistently; they, too, must sit either with the government or the opposition. At one end of the floor is the "bar" of the House through which members enter, and at which offenders against the privileges of the House may be arraigned or petitioners may attend. At the other end is a table for the clerks of the House, who, it may be said, handle the paper work of the Commons. The table extends some way along the central floor of the House and separates the front benches on which sit the leaders of the government and of the opposition. Customarily the leaders speak from this part of the table. All other members of the House speak from wherever they happen to have found room for themselves. Beyond the table, on a dais, sits the Speaker, wigged and gowned, facing the bar of the House, with the government to his right and the opposition to his left. The position of his chair, elevated and separated from both parties by the clerks' table, symbolizes both his authority over the conduct of the House and the tradition that he be impartial in applying and interpreting the rules and, indeed, in the discharge of all his duties as chairman of the House. Despite the fact that the Speaker is elected by the House from among its members, rarely is his impartiality impugned. Rarely, therefore, is the election contested and, once elected, the Speaker is normally re-elected automatically for as long as he wishes. Customarily the government, in whose gift the speakership lies, will consult with the opposition before nominating a member better known for his moderation and committee work than for his partisanship and debating prowess.[12]

The manner of selecting a Speaker is typical of the way in which all the business of the House is arranged. The rules of procedure consist in part of customary rules dating back to the seventeenth century or beyond and in part of standing orders formally adopted at later dates and comprehensible only with reference to the older rules that they modify or supersede. Most of the later rules have been adopted in the last one hundred years and are designed to expedite business or limit the scope for pure obstruction.

All the rules are applied by the Speaker, and round them there has now grown up a considerable body of "case law" in the shape of Speakers' rulings. Within the chamber the Speaker's decision about the meaning or application of any rule is final, but the power to decide what the rules should be lies with the majority, which is to say, with the government. If a government were so minded, it could, therefore, deny to the opposition or to its own supporters any opportunity to question or to criticize. But governments are not so minded. Conscious of the possibility that, after the next election, they may themselves be in opposition, and conscious, too, that by abusing their power they may contribute to this result, their members always try to take the other side with them in any proposed changes in procedure. They do not always succeed. Nor do they necessarily accept the proposals coming from the all-party select committees on procedure that normally precede any substantial change. But they usually feel it incumbent

---

[12] Exceptionally Speaker Morrison, who retired in 1959, had been a minister. His appointment was not, therefore, universally welcomed, but in fact he seems to have upheld the tradition with distinction.

upon themselves to produce respectable reasons for procedural innovations, and not to depart too far from what would be generally acceptable.

In arranging the order of business and the agenda for the House, governments again consult with the opposition (the "usual channels" for negotiation being the party whips) about the amount of time to devote to particular items as well as when to debate them, or even whether to debate them at all. Thus, for example, the government may agree to provide time for a debate on a recent government decision in the realm of foreign policy if, in exchange, the opposition will help to secure the speedy passage of legislation on building standards. It is understood that the government is there to govern and that the opposition should therefore not attempt continuously to obstruct its legislative program. In return, the government attempts to ensure that there will always be some opportunity for discussion and criticism, and respects certain traditional rights belonging to the opposition—for example, that the opposition decides which estimates of expenditure should be debated in full,[13] and that the opposition always is given time to move and support a formal vote of censure upon the government. In this manner a balance is maintained between the demands of government and the freedom to criticize.

This balance is constantly shifting and, at times, is severely strained by the expanding role of modern governments, but few would say categorically that this balance has yet been destroyed. Clearly, however, the whole system depends for its successful working upon the continuation of at least some mutual confidence between government and opposition and upon their both continuing to respect the parliamentary tradition itself. Both conditions have been undermined on occasion, and might, for example, have been totally submerged early in this century by the passions associated with Irish Home Rule, woman's suffrage, and developing trade unionism, had not the First World War occasioned a reemphasis upon national unity. Today, however, the prestige and satisfactory working of the House of Commons seem threatened

[13] It being impossible to discuss them all and still have time for any other business during the year.

more by the predominance of both front benches to the detriment of the ordinary back-bench member, and by the increasing tendency to take important decisions off the floor of the House entirely, than by militant party antagonisms.

MEMBERS AND THEIR POWERS

The ordinary back-bench member of Parliament, by comparison with a United States senator, or even congressman, seems unimportant and powerless. He is neither. Nevertheless, he is relatively limited both in his opportunities for initiative and in the effectiveness of his efforts.

It has been estimated that during the period 1950–59, about one-fifth of the average session was devoted to business initiated by Private Members (an official category that includes opposition front-benchers as well as all back-bench members). The 159 working days that made up the session were apportioned approximately as follows:

Government time	69.5 days	(43.7%)
Opposition time	32 days	(20.1%)
Private Members' time	35 days	(22.0%)
(formal bills and motions: 19 days)		
Other (mixed)	22.5 days	(14.2%)[14]

Private Members' time includes only the time devoted to bills, motions, and debates initiated by back-benchers. It does not include, for example, time devoted to questions, nor is account taken of the numerous small committees appointed by the House. In both these spheres ordinary members can make important contributions to the work of Parliament. All members, likewise, have the right to take part in debates and discussion initiated by either front bench. But in practice the priority traditionally granted to official

[14] See Sir Thomas Erskine May, *Treatise on the Law, Privileges, Proceedings and Usage of Parliament,* 17th ed. by Sir Barnett Cocks, 1964, pp. 299–310. This is the standard work on the procedure of Parliament and the bible for Speakers, members, and scholars throughout the Commonwealth. It is normally referred to simply as "Erskine May."

party spokesmen and privy councillors[15] may empty this right of much value—for all that members known to have distinctive views or to be particularly well informed may also find it comparatively easy to "catch the Speaker's eye."

Except in the official questioning of ministers, however, the back-bench member is made constantly aware that he must follow a long way behind the two front benches in determining what is to be discussed in the House. During the war and for several years after, for example, he was completely deprived of the times normally set aside for his bills and motions, which, since 1960, have received twenty days per session. Even within these times the back-bencher is aware that the outcome of any debate is largely preordained by the government's attitude, as the support and attitudes of the parties usually make all conclusions virtually foregone; but not entirely so. The Chamberlain government resigned in 1940 in large part because of the expressed and critical opinion of its back-bench supporters; governments frequently undertake to appoint committees of inquiry or royal commissions because of back-bench pressure; in 1969, to take but one example, the government withdrew the bill to reform the House of Lords in the face of back-bench resistance, and many bills may receive important amendments for the same reason. As Sir Alan Herbert showed before the war, and Mr. Roy Jenkins and others have shown since, it is also possible for a Private Member to secure the passage of a bill to which the government was initially hostile or indifferent.[16] It is, furthermore, impossible accurately to assess the

---

[15] The Privy Councillors are mainly ministers or ex-ministers. Membership of the Privy Council is now largely a formal matter, although attended by important legal consequences, including an oath of secrecy and a right of personal access to the monarch. Several committees of the Privy Council, however, may be important, as is the Judicial Committee, which is the supreme court of appeal for certain territories within the Commonwealth. Some modern departments, Education included, began life as committees of the Council.

[16] See A. P. Herbert, *The Ayes Have It* (London: Methuen, 1937), for an account of his Matrimonial Causes Act, and Roy Jenkins's account of the struggle for his Obscene Publications Act in "Obscenity, Censorship and the Law," *Encounter* (October 1959), pp. 62–66.

importance of "prenatal" back-bench influence that may prevent a government from introducing certain legislation at all. But the fact remains that governments get their way: of 133 government bills introduced in the Commons between 1962 and 1965, 130 were passed.[17] The position of the back-bencher is fundamentally a function of his political power and his relationship to the formal and informal channels of access to the government and administration. Without examining them, it is impossible to understand the nature and significance of the House of Commons today.

In addition to his rights as a member, chief among which are those to raise questions and air grievances on the floor of the House, the back-bencher has two principal sources of power: as a party member he is, in association with his colleagues, the ultimate arbiter of the party's leadership; and he is the elected representative of his constituency. Of these, the first is probably the most important, although, of course, it confers direct power over the government only upon the government's supporters. This power is limited by the need to agree on a successor and to obtain front-bench support as well as by anxiety not to injure the M.P.'s own position or the electoral chances of the party. Nevertheless, the led must be willing to follow, or the leaders will perish. Back-bench influence is continuous, if not always obvious.

Every M.P. "represents" his constituency in two main senses. He is there in their stead, formally assenting to legislation and taxation, and accepting responsibility for the nation's government on behalf of all the commons (i.e., the common people). In Britain bills are passed, in law, by the House of Commons, not by the members who happened to vote with the majority, so that all citizens are deemed to have concurred in and accepted the resulting obligations. The M.P. is a representative, secondly, in the sense that one of his duties is to make representations on behalf of his constituents, particularly with reference to purely local or individual interests and grievances. Once elected, it is customary for an M.P. to emphasize that he regards himself as

[17] R. M. Punnett, *British Government and Politics* (London: Heinemann, 1968), p. 231.

the representative of all the voters and not only of his own party followers. This claim is normally substantially justified. An M.P. is not, however, a representative in the sense of being a copy or mirror of the political divisions or ideas within his constituency. At most it can be said only that he will support or oppose the government on behalf of the party that won the largest number of votes, although he cannot be forced to resign should he change his allegiance after being elected. Nor is he necessarily a "representative" (i.e., typical) example of his constituents. It cannot even be claimed, as we shall see, that members of Parliament as a group are typical of the people they "represent." On the other hand, he must be *responsive* enough to the opinions and interests of his constituents to fill his two representative roles adequately and, above all, to maximize his chance of reelection.[18]

His principal concern today, however, is with his party, for it is the party that primarily decides whether he will be elected. It is the general standing of the party nationally and locally, along with the social composition of the constituency which, more than any other factors, will win or lose his seat. An M.P. can and must, of course, attend to the wishes of his local party and his constituents. He is chosen as candidate by the local party organization which, in a safe seat, may have fifty or more applicants or nominees (drawn from any part of the country) from whom to choose.[19] The national parties have the rarely used power to veto a particular selection, but they cannot ensure one, so that the local leadership retains the crucial power. Nor can the M.P., once elected to Parliament, count upon automatic reendorsement at subsequent elections. Only, therefore, if he can find another local party willing to select him as its candidate dare he ignore his local activists. The latter, furthermore, seem still to be essential helpers

---

[18] See the excellent discussion in H. F. Pitkin, *The Concept of Representation* (Berkeley: University of California Press, 1967), especially Chapter 10.

[19] On the process of selection see M. Rush, *The Selection of Parliamentary Candidates* (London: Nelson, 1969), and A. Ranney, *Pathways to Parliament* (Madison: University of Wisconsin Press, 1965).

in wooing the voters upon whom, obviously, the candidate depends for his election. He is thus controlled by these local groups to some degree. If this were not so, he could with less justice claim to speak for them in the House of Commons and in the wider circles of his party.

The essence of the back-bencher's position may therefore be said to consist of its being intermediate between the front benches and the voters. His relation to each, moreover, is in part determined by his relation to the other. The front bench cannot ignore him because he may air issues in the House, because he is in close touch with his constituency, and because he, with his fellows, has the ultimate power over the destiny of the leaders. For these reasons, too, he is guaranteed access to his leaders, directly or through the whips, and, regardless of his party, to the administrative departments. His constituents may depend upon him to intercede on their behalf with the government and administration in order to secure the redress of their grievances. But they wield power over him as voters. In virtue of this power inherent in representative government, the citizen is assured of a hearing from the M.P. and, through him, of at least one point of access to the government; indeed, in the case of the ordinary citizen, it will be the only assured point of access.

The back-bencher's influence is not necessarily confined to that derived in these ways (and from his own capabilities) any more than the voter is restricted to this one channel of access to government. Their relationships to pressure groups must also be taken into account.[20] It is through them that the variety of interests and opinions seek their primary expression, thus making good any failure of M.P.s to "represent" them. A back-bencher who is known to speak for an important interest or pressure group will gain in influence thereby, just as he will from any other special qualification or expertise that lends weight to his views. The

[20] The term "pressure group" is used here to cover any group, whatever its primary *raison d'être*, other than a political party, that attempts deliberately to influence the conduct of government in pursuit of some common aim.

services of a back-bencher, in turn, may be as useful to pressure groups as to constituents, and for the same reasons: his access to the administration, his right to air points in public, and his share in the policy-making processes of his party. But back-benchers are above all useful to groups that have not yet fully established their public position and therefore whose right automatically to be consulted on matters affecting them has not yet been conceded by the government and administration.

For established groups and for groups drawn from the major social interests (employers, trade unions, and the national churches, for example), direct parliamentary representation is less important than the close relations with the administration that accrue to them naturally because of their powerful positions in society.[21] The leaders of pressure groups know, better than most people, that the decisions important to them are taken not by the House of Commons, but by the administration. Conversely, the facts that back-benchers may hope only to *influence* the decisions taken by their leaders or by the civil service, and that they must normally work within the broad limits of their party's policy, help to confer immunity upon them from the worst types of political pressure. This is one possible reason why students of British politics long tended to deny that pressure groups existed at all. Another reason, probably, was that these groups are so built into the system that their operations need be less public and less strident than they are, for example, in the United States. It has simply been taken for granted that the major interests in the community should be represented in Parliament. For centuries they have in fact secured representation, directly by means of patronage, the sponsorship of candidates, or through the desire of men successful in one walk of life to embark upon a political career, and indirectly through the many formal and informal channels of access to members of

[21] For example, it has been said that "the Unions which have sponsored groups of M.P.s do not use them as their general spokesmen on the bigger issues of the day because they do not need them." See A. Barker and M. Rush, *The Member of Parliament and His Information* (London: Allen and Unwin, 1970), p. 270.

both Houses.[22] In this way, too, party leaders as well as back-benchers are linked to the complex of pressure groups, although the demands of their leadership role and the need to concern themselves with party policy and a national electorate normally prevent them from being direct or overt pressure-group spokesmen to the extent possible for a back-bench member.

Some indication of the groups and interests now particularly favored may be gathered from the available statistics relating to the occupational and educational backgrounds of members of the Commons and of the cabinet.[23]

Neither the House of Commons, nor the cabinet, provides a cross section of the public in terms of either education or occupation. This is explicable, probably, in terms of such factors as the attitudes of constituency selection committees (including deference to success or ability, as well as, and at times superseding the desire to be represented by someone like themselves); the inclination to enter politics of people already accustomed to making decisions and to influencing others verbally; and the filtering effect of financial necessity, that favors sponsored candidates and those who have skills or occupations that can still be used, after an M.P. is elected, to supplement the relatively low salary of a back-bencher. The result, it might be argued, is that the House primarily reflects and maintains the existing unequal distribution of prestige and power within British society. Certainly, access to government through Parliament, as in other ways, is more easily attained by "respectable" groups, organizations, and classes than by others. Not that it is denied to all others: securing representa-

---

[22] See Samuel H. Beer, "The Representation of Interests in British Government," *American Political Science Review,* September 1957, pp. 613–50, and, on the general topic, G. C. Moodie and G. Studdert-Kennedy, *Opinions, Publics and Pressure Groups* (London: Allen and Unwin, 1970), Chapters 4 and 5.

[23] The first two tables are adapted, by permission, from those given in D. E. Butler and A. King, *The British General Election of 1966* (London: Macmillan, 1966), pp. 208–9. The present author is responsible for supplying the third table and the percentages in the others.

OCCUPATIONAL BACKGROUND OF M.P.s ELECTED IN 1966

	Conservative	Labour	Total
Professions	117 (46.3%)	156 (43.0%)	273 (44.3%)
Law	70	54	
Armed forces	19	3	
Teaching	4	72	
Business	75 (29.6%)	32 (9.0%)	107 (17.7%)
Small	2	2	
Director	40	3	
Executive	12	11	
Miscellaneous	59 (23.3%)	66 (18.0%)	125 (20.2%)
Private means	5	0	
Politics	2	9	
Journalism	17	29	
Farmer	27	2	
Manual workers	2 (0.8%)	109 (30.0%)	111 (18.0%)
Skilled	2	47	
Miners	0	32	
TOTALS	253 (100%)	363* (100%)	616† (100%)

* Of the Labour total, 132 were sponsored by trade unions.
† Also elected were 12 Liberals and one other.

tion in the House, indeed, may be one way of increasing a group's prestige and power, as it has been for organized labor. No list of occupational and educational backgrounds, moreover, can provide a complete guide to the interests, attitudes, or affiliations of members, for all that it may be indicative thereof, nor do such factors necessarily outweigh the need to satisfy a very mixed electorate.

Whatever the ability, electoral backing, or pressure-group allegiance of a back-bencher, however, the fact remains that until and unless he is promoted to the front bench, he cannot hope to do more than influence the decisions taken by others. In his speeches, conversations, or otherwise, the back-bencher's purpose can therefore only be to persuade rather than decide. His targets within the House are the government, the leaders of the opposition, and his colleagues. Outside it, they are his constituents, his party, and the general public. In other words, his purpose is to persuade the actual or potential governmental decision-makers directly or through those with power over them. Only thus can he hope to further his aims and ambitions.

While the major decisions on policy may often be taken in areas remote from the back-bencher, there are other spheres of

EDUCATIONAL BACKGROUND OF M.P.s ELECTED IN 1966

	Conservative	Labour	Total
Elementary only / Secondary only	20 { 2 / 18 } (8.0%)	173* { 80 / 93 } (47.6%)	193 (31.3%)
Public school only	63 (24.9%)	4 (1.1%)	67 (10.9%)
Secondary and university	29 (11.4%)	124 (34.2%)	153 (24.9%)
Public school and university	141 (55.7%)	62 (17.1%)	203 (32.9%)
TOTAL	253 (100%)	363 (100%)	616 (100%)
Universities: Oxford and Cambridge	144 (56.9%)	83 (22.8%)	227 (36.8%)
All other	26 (10.3%)	103 (28.2%)	129 (20.9%)
Public schools: Eton	55 (21.7%)		
Harrow and Winchester	22 (8.7%)	5 (1.4%)	82 (13.3%)
All other	127 (50.2%)	61 (16.8%)	188 (30.5%)

* Includes 88 who acquired some adult or further education.

EDUCATIONAL AND OCCUPATIONAL BACKGROUNDS OF CABINET MINISTERS

	CONSERVATIVE		LABOUR	
	November 1959	*October 1964*	*October 1947*	*October 1969*
Occupation				
Professional	8 (4 lawyers)	13 (8 lawyers, 1 educator)	9 (2 lawyers, 7 educators)	19 (3 lawyers, 8 educators)
Business	7	3	1 (small)	1 (temporary)
Manual	0	0	5	1
Other	2	3	2	0
(Unknown)	(2)	(4)	(0)	(0)
TOTAL	19	23	17	21
Education				
Elementary only	0	0	7	0
State Secondary	1	2	2	13
Public Schools	16	21	6	6
Eton	7	11	1	0
Other fee-paying	2	0	1	0
(Unknown)	(0)	(0)	(1)	(2)
TOTAL	19	23	17	21
Education				
All	16	17 (plus 3 at Military Academy)	8	16
Oxford and Cambridge	15	17	6	11

SOURCE: Entries in the relevant volumes of *Who's Who?*

government in which the able and conscientious individual makes an important and useful contribution. He is constantly being called upon to intercede between the citizen and the official. Frequently, it is true, his work could be as well performed by anyone with some familiarity with legislation and some confidence in dealing with bureaucracy.

But, should it be a matter of rectifying an injustice or of bringing to light an abuse of power, then a member is in the unique position of being able to raise it in the House when all other means fail.[24] Members of Parliament may not always be able to secure a redress of grievances by these means alone, but about their effectiveness on occasion there can be no dispute. Although many a minister, or even government, has been harried into changes in administrative practice, or even legislation, as a result of back-bench persistence, where more is required than merely publicizing the government's actions in order to secure some change or redress or to set in motion the forces that could secure them, the back-bencher may well be powerless. Members of Parliament have been growing increasingly dissatisfied with this position, a feeling that seemed to acquire a greater sense of direction with the influx of a number of new and relatively young Labour members after the elections of 1964 and 1966.

Members of Parliament seem to agree that their role embraces three functions: "to sustain or oppose the government of the day, to scrutinize the activities of the government, and to represent their constituents." [25] By and large they are not disposed to challenge the doctrine that their central function is either to support or to oppose the government. Similarly, although there has been a growing feeling that the representation of constituents can take up an excessive amount of their time and needs reinforcement, it does not constitute a major problem. The focal point of parliamentary dissatisfaction, therefore, is the M.P.'s ability effectively to "scrutinize the activities of the Government."

The fundamental problem is, of course, the expanding role of government. The annual output of statutes, for example, increased from 202 pages in 1900 to 1,817 in 1965. Furthermore, most major pieces of legislation amount to skeleton acts in which the

[24] P. G. Richards, *Honourable Members,* 2d ed. (London: Faber, 1964), p. 170.
[25] Barker and Rush, op. cit., p. 22.

detail is left to the minister, and in which much of this "detail" may consist of the major decisions about the implementation of policy. The bulk of government business is not legislative, of course, and it too has increased immensely, but without corresponding changes in the procedures whereby members of Parliament can become informed about government action, let alone place themselves in a position effectively to assess or criticize it. In brief, the criticisms amount to a serious doubt whether the classic doctrine of individual ministerial responsibility with its stress on the "sanctity" and confidentiality of the minister's relations with his civil servants, and on the exclusiveness of the minister's relations to the whole House of Commons (rather than to any one part of it), now serves as an effective means of rendering government accountable.

There is only a limited number of ways in which any large assembly can improve the quality of its work: it can try to do less, to enable it to perform the remainder of its tasks more effectively (for example, by a radical devolution of some of its formal powers to independent agencies); it can attempt to introduce a more extensive, or different, division of labor among its own members; and it can seek to improve the ancillary staff and services on which it depends for information and advice. All three have had their advocates, but only the last two were pursued in the sixties.[26]

The principal changes made in House of Commons procedure constitute moves toward a new division of labor. At one level the main effect has been to cut down the number of decisions considered by the whole House and increase the number referred to its standing committees. Thus an increasing number of the formal stages of legislative procedure[27] are, or may be, taken in committee—not only the committee stage, but the prior second read-

---

[26] The first strategy, mainly associated with issues of "regionalism" and, in Scotland and Wales, of nationalist aspirations, is part of the remit of the Constitutional Commission, set up in 1969 under the chairmanship of Lord Crowther, to which we will return in the last chapter.

[27] See the Note on legislative procedure at the end of this chapter.

ing, and subsequent report stages, have been thus treated and, more radically in terms of parliamentary tradition, so has the examination of financial legislation. In this way, it is hoped, the time of the whole House will be reserved for major policy debates, discussions of principle, and ventilation of grievances or new ideas for which it is best suited. At the same time it is hoped that back-benchers may find, in committee, some of the scope denied them in the front-bench dominated House. Long before the sixties, of course, the legislative committees had become one of the principal means whereby back-benchers could make positive, if minor, changes in the content of legislation. The smaller and more intimate atmosphere, and the fact that committee decisions could be overturned in the whole House, meant that an individual M.P. had greater opportunity and more chance of success.

The major debate, nevertheless, may all too frequently be an occasion for only front-bench pronouncements, the exchange of partisan "pleasantries," and the exposure of ignorance.[28] The content must be improved if the benefits of a more rational division of time and labor are to be realized. One method of doing so is for the government to provide more information about its thinking and plans, especially before these have been made final within the departments and in negotiations with outside organizations. Thus the government, since 1966, has adopted the practice of issuing occasional so-called "Green Papers" on forthcoming major items of legislation and, late in 1969, created a new precedent with its White Paper,[29] which set out estimates of public expenditure from 1968–69 to 1973–74, and which was debated

[28] For an example of a largely unproductive confrontation on an important issue see the debates described in M. J. Barnett, *The Politics of Legislation: The Rent Act of 1957* (London: Weidenfeld and Nicolson, 1969), pp. 159–93. This excellent case study is an invaluable documentation of the weaknesses in the whole system of government that reformers are anxious to remedy. See the further discussion of this study in G. C. Moodie and G. Studdert-Kennedy, *Opinions, Publics and Pressure-Groups* (London: Allen and Unwin, 1970), final chapter.

[29] *Public Expenditure 1968–69 to 1973–74* (Cmnd. 4234 of 1969).

in January 1970. This was the first serious attempt by a British government to involve Parliament in discussing the major long-term problems of resource allocation.

The attempt to improve the value of debates is also one reason for the most important development, the extension of the division of labor by a greater, and in some respects novel, use of select committees. In the nineteenth century they were frequent means of studying and reporting upon particular problems, and certain established ones have been on the parliamentary scene continuously, most notably those on Public Accounts, Estimates, and, in the postwar period, Statutory Instruments and the Nationalised Industries. Nevertheless, in Reports of the Commons Select Committee on Procedure, as well as in unofficial publications, the demand for new committees designed regularly to scrutinize and report on the work of the departments or on particular policy areas grew steadily.[30]

Shortly after the 1966 general election, therefore, two such specialized Select Committees were set up, one on Science and Technology and the other on Agriculture. They were followed in the next three years by Committees on Education and Science, on the work of the Scottish Departments, on Race Relations and Immigration, and on Overseas Aid and Development as well as by the Committee on the Parliamentary Commissioner (to which we will return shortly). On the other hand, the Committee on Agriculture, which had had a succession of major disagreements with the department, was wound up at the end of 1968, and the government has made it clear that none of these specialized committees will even be as "permanent" as those on Estimates or Nationalised Industries. It seems likely, therefore, that progress will be slower than the reformist M.P.s would wish. But the trend is unlikely to dry up completely. Thus a survey carried out among a sample of M.P.s in 1967[31] found that only 8 percent thought that M.P.s as a whole feel adequately informed on gov-

[30] See both as an example and for further information, B. Crick, *The Reform of Parliament* (London: Weidenfeld and Nicolson, 1964).

[31] Barker and Rush, op. cit., pp. 150 and 410.

ernment administration and, furthermore, that some 73 percent of M.P.s were in favor of the principle of using the select committee device to strengthen parliamentary scrutiny of the work of government.

One advantage of using select committees as the way of developing greater expertise among back-bench M.P.s is that the tradition of having an official associated with their work had already been established by the committees on Public Accounts and Statutory Instruments (the Comptroller and Auditor General and the Speaker's Counsel, respectively). It was thus natural, to take the most notable example, to copy this relationship in 1967 when trying to improve the machinery investigating particular complaints against the civil service, and therefore simultaneously to appoint a Parliamentary Commissioner for Administration (the so-called "ombudsman") and a select committee to whom he reports. Here, too, it may be noted that the change is a cautious one. The commissioner's sole concern is with "mal-administration"; he has, for example, no power to comment on policy. He is also restricted, on the one hand, to those matters referred to him by individual M.P.s and, on the other, to the work of the central departments.[32] The other specialist select committees have not been permitted to appoint comparable servants. They have, however, made use of the enlarged and qualified staff of the House of Commons Library, of additional clerks, and of outside experts retained to advise on particular investigations.[33] To this extent, therefore, something has also been done to pursue the third strategy referred to above—improving the support given to members of Parliament.

If these reforming trends continue, however, they are likely to generate additional pressure to better the position of the M.P. as an individual and not merely as a committee member. It is unlikely, first of all, that the overdue but substantial increase in

[32] A local "ombudsman" was appointed in Northern Ireland in December 1969, however, and in February 1970, the government announced its desire to appoint one with jurisdiction in the Health Service.

[33] For details of this development see Barker and Rush, op. cit., pp. 335–37.

parliamentary salaries granted in 1964 will be considered adequate for long.[34] Secondly, despite some improvement in the situation, M.P.s will probably continue their pressure for office space and secretarial assistance. In the longer run, too, it is significant that the 1967 investigations to which we referred found that over one-third of the M.P.s interviewed expressed a desire for a personal assistant who could both carry out research and attend to constituency affairs.[35] At present few M.P.s, especially on the Labour side, can afford to pay a full-time secretary, let alone a personal assistant.

The final question that will be raised more acutely is whether the proportion of M.P.s who now give their services virtually full-time to Parliament is large enough. In 1967 not much more than one-third could be so labeled. It is significant that the proportion of Labour M.P.s who are full-time is close to two-thirds, compared with little more than one-tenth of the Conservatives.[36]

By 1970, therefore, Parliament had begun to equip itself for its enlarged responsibilities and thus, possibly, to arrest the decline in its prestige lamented by so many people in the 1950s and 1960s. In appraising these developments,[37] however, it is important to remember that they are unlikely to alter the balance of power between the cabinet and Commons fundamentally, just as it is important to remember that that balance had not tilted as overpoweringly in favor of the executive as some of the critics

[34] The salary, including a taxable allowance for expenses was then raised from £1,750 to £3,250. Certain other minor improvements in M.P.s' conditions, including pension provisions, were made at the same time.

[35] Barker and Rush, op. cit., pp. 326–32.

[36] Barker and Rush, op. cit., pp. 371–74. This fact, along with the difference between the parties in their access to secretarial help and in the extent to which their party headquarters are major sources of information (Barker and Rush found 80 percent Conservatives saying "yes," 74 percent Labour saying "no"—Barker and Rush, op. cit., p. 234) may help to explain the stronger Labour drive for reform and illustrate one of the links between social structure and a constitution.

[37] A brief and useful review of the main changes 1964–69 is to be found in C. J. Boulton, "Recent Developments in House of Commons' Procedure," *Parliamentary Affairs*, Winter 1969/70, pp. 61–71.

have suggested. The fact is that Parliament has always been, and still is, the most important forum of and focus for public political debate (the Lords as well as the Commons), that on occasion the House of Commons could safely be relied upon to speak loudly and clearly for the British people, and that to a citizen in trouble with the government the best advice has always been to "write to your M.P." The changes set in motion, even if they are carried much further than it is legitimate to expect,[38] would still leave intact that situation in which the primary functions of Parliament are to sustain the government, and, above all, to try to ensure that the work of government is broadly responsive to the wishes and needs of the public.

NOTES

LEGISLATIVE PROCEDURE IN THE HOUSE OF COMMONS

Bills fall into two categories: public and private. The latter are defined in Erskine May as "bills for the particular interest or benefit of any person or persons." In modern times they are primarily desired by local authorities seeking special powers additional to those granted by general legislation. They are considered under special procedures in which very small committees play the main part, while the right of the House to make the final decisions is reserved. Private bills should not be confused with Private Members' bills. The latter are "private" only in origin, being legislation proposed by a nonministerial M.P. They are in fact public bills subject to substantially the same procedure as ones introduced by the government. Public bills themselves are officially and simply defined as all bills that are not private ones. The terminology may be reminiscent of a Gilbert libretto, but the principles of classification are reasonably straightforward.

Public bills are considered and debated in a series of stages. These are normally: (1) first reading: the bill is introduced by title and the motion "that this bill be given a first reading" is usually carried without discussion. The full text is then ordered to

[38] The defeat of the Labour government in 1970 is, however, likely to slow down, or even reverse, this process of reform.

be printed. The function of the mover at this stage is primarily to give notice of pending legislation on a particular subject; (2) second reading: a full-scale debate takes place on the general principles of the bill as a whole. If they are accepted, possibly on the promise of some amendment, the bill proceeds to (3) committee stage: the bill is discussed clause by clause, detailed amendments to which are in order. This stage is now usually held in a standing committee or in the Committee of the Whole House (see below); (4) report stage: the committee reports back to the House, which may accept or reject the changes made and make new ones; (5) third reading: a final general debate at which further verbal amendments may be proposed, but none of substance. Thereafter the bill will be sent to the House of Lords for consideration in similar stages or, if the bill originated there (as do about one-quarter of all public bills, few of them of major political significance), for consideration of the Commons' amendments. If the Lords persevere in decisions differing from the Commons', the government must give way, allow the whole bill to lapse, or invoke the provisions of the Parliament Acts of 1911 and 1949 and thus override the wishes of the Upper House.

COMMITTEES OF THE HOUSE OF COMMONS

Committee of the Whole House. Sitting under special rules, the whole House of Commons will sometimes take the committee stage of urgent or very short bills, bills of constitutional or great political significance, and, indeed, any others so decided by the government. The whole House also used to discuss the estimates of expenditure as "the Committee of Supply," and directly authorize expenditure or discuss revenue proposals as "the Committee of Ways and Means."

Standing Committees. As many of these as necessary are appointed (usually eight). They are known simply by letters of the alphabet, *A, B, C,* and so on, with the exceptions to be mentioned shortly. They consist of between sixteen and fifty members appointed in proportion to the strengths of the parties in the House. They are purely legislative and, in principle, are nonspecialist—that is, they are intended to represent the whole House and, like it, to consider any bill put before them. In practice, however, the members may be chosen because of some special interest or experience. The minister in charge of a government bill is always a member of the appropriate standing committee. One of the exceptions referred to is the Scottish Standing Committee, drawn entirely from M.P.'s for the Scottish constituencies, which conducts the committee stage of purely Scottish legislation. It is not to be, but often is, confused with either the new Scottish Select Committee or the Scottish Grand Committee, consisting of all seventy-one Scottish members and twelve others, which may discuss the Scottish estimates, other purely Scottish affairs, and the second reading of Scottish bills. There also exist Welsh standing and grand committees. The chairmen of all committees are drawn from a panel of back-benchers appointed by the Speaker.

Select Committees. They are so called because the members are selected and named at the time each committee is established. They normally consist of between thirteen and thirty members. They are set up as required to investigate and report upon a specific problem or topic, which may be a question of privilege, or the management of the Palace of Westminster (the Houses of Parliament building), or some other problem that the House itself wishes to study. These committees have power to send for papers and persons. Certain select committees are regularly reestablished: those on public accounts, estimates, statutory instruments, the nationalized industries, the parliamentary commissioner, and procedure being the most well known.

In addition to what has been said in the body of the chapter it may be useful to say a little more about two of these committees. The Committee on Nationalized Industries was originally intended to confine itself to examination of the published annual reports and accounts of these industries, to refrain from investigating policy, and to confine itself to those things for which a minister was responsible. (The appropriate ministers are, broadly speaking, entitled by statute to issue general directions to the managing boards, which they appoint, but not to make decisions about the day-to-day running of the industries. They are responsible, naturally enough, only for those aspects of the industries about which they are able to make decisions.) Ministers and governments attempted to define these terms of reference strictly, but were slowly forced to retreat. The later reports of this committee have, as a result, been both far-ranging and, on occasion, profound. Its successful battles were part of the necessary groundwork for the new committees set up in 1966 and after.

The Select Committee on Estimates, designed to assist the House in examining the annual estimates of government expenditure, has been another icebreaker. Through effective use of subcommittees, interrogation of officials, and rigorous self-discipline about the range of items to be investigated, it has demonstrated both the potential value of such informed and concentrated scrutiny and the possibility of combining positive recommendations with an essentially bipartisan approach. There are many people who still see the way forward in terms of simply enlarging the scope of this committee. The recommendations of the Select Committee on Procedure, important and productive as they have been, would have had less impact but for the experience of these two committees.

6

Administration and Civil Service

ORGANIZATION

The most important units in the central governmental administration are the departments headed by political ministers who, with their ministerial colleagues,[1] are also in some degree responsible for the direction of the myriad other public offices and authorities.[2] Of these latter bodies, some are controlled directly by a nondepartmental minister or a ministerial department. Others, like the boards of the nationalized industries and the University Grants Committee, have been subjected only to a limited degree of ministerial control in order to insulate their work from direct or continuous political involvement.

It is in the departments that almost all of the 700,000-odd nonindustrial civil servants work.[3] Only a tiny fraction of these

[1] Ministers like the Law Officers or the Lord Privy Seal have offices, but not departments, under them.

[2] Although the number of departments changes frequently as new ones are created or existing ones merged, in early 1970 there were under twenty of them. This creation and reorganization rarely requires legislation, and is normally a matter of executive discretion.

[3] The standard definition of civil servants is "those servants of the Crown, other than holders of political or judicial offices, who are employed in a civil capacity, and whose remuneration is paid wholly and directly out of monies voted by Parliament." See W. J. M. Mackenzie and J. W. Grove, *Central Administration in Britain* (London: Longmans, 1957), pp. 11–13. This definition includes "industrial" civil servants who work in Admiralty dockyards or government arsenals, for example. The majority of public servants, e.g., those in nationalized indus-

are *politically* important. In 1967, for example, all but some 90,000 were concerned entirely with routine administrative, technical, or post-office work, or were employed as typists, messengers, cleaners, and porters.[4] Their work is, of course, administratively essential, and they are the people who have the most frequent face-to-face contact with the public. But for our present purposes they must largely be ignored.

The system of recruitment to the higher levels derives from two fundamental principles that were first clearly accepted in 1870: that the service be designed to offer a "career open to the talents" as they emerge from the educational system; and that a basic division of labor should be recognized within the service.[5] For the fifty years between 1920 and 1970, the most important division was the three-fold classification of general officials into administrative, executive, and clerical. The last was concerned with the detailed routine work of any large administrative machine and, in its work, was closely guided by instructions from the classes above it. At the top was the administrative class, whose duties may be described as the formation of policy and the general management of the administrative machine. The work of the executive class may be most conveniently defined as covering everything between the work of the other two classes—it performed responsible work, demanding good judgment, within the broad framework of policy decisions made elsewhere.[6] Certain specialist classes (professional, technical, and legal) exist separately and alongside the general ones.

---

tries, do not fall within this definition, in most cases because their remuneration is either not paid from "monies voted by Parliament" or is so only in part or indirectly.

[4] Since 1969 the post office has ceased to be a ministerial department, its status being like that of the nationalized industries.

[5] The modern civil service was largely inspired by the famous *Report on the Organisation of the Permanent Civil Service* by Stafford H. Northcote and C. E. Trevelyan, published in 1854. For an excellent brief discussion, see Wyn Griffith, *The British Civil Service 1854–1954* (London: HMSO, 1954); also K. C. Wheare, *The Civil Service in the Constitution* (London: Athlone Press, 1954). The text of the *Report* is reprinted in *Public Administration* (1954).

[6] See the definitions quoted in Mackenzie and Grove, op. cit., pp. 62–63.

Each class was further subdivided into grades, each with their appropriate levels of pay and responsibility. Following the recommendations of the Fulton Committee,[7] the division between the administrative and executive classes is to be replaced by an extended ladder of grades. But the distinction between kinds of work will be blurred rather than abolished (already some 30 percent of new entrants into the higher class consist of people promoted from below); and the broad features of recruitment, to which we will now turn, will not be substantially affected.

The essential features of the method of recruitment to the civil service are, firstly, that it be competitive and, secondly, that the different points of entry into the structure be designed to attract the ablest candidates at each stage in the educational system. Thus the highest "managerial" grades, like the old administrative class, and the higher professional and scientific ones recruit entrants on the basis of university degree level qualifications combined with an elaborate testing and interviewing system; the lowest levels are recruited on the basis of examinations and interviews geared to the minimum school-leaving age; and the old executive class by examinations for grammar school and the less highly qualified university graduates.

An important corollary of these features—not that it is universally accepted as such—is that candidates for the general classes need not have studied subjects with a real or assumed relevance to their future work. One reason for this is to try to ensure that no one of ability be barred from applying. This principle is further defended on the ground that general intelligence and the ability to take responsibility are more important to a high-level administrator than, say, a training in economics that may in any case be outdated by the time it is most useful. The only essential qualities, it is argued, are good judgment and the ability to use and evaluate the expertise of others.

Selection on the grounds of general rather than specialized qualifications has an additional justification. Both for the sake of the service and to offer the greatest possible career opportunities

[7] See *The Civil Service: Report of the Committee, 1966–68,* Cmnd. 3638 of 1968.

to civil servants, great emphasis is placed on the ideal of a unified civil service. Thus almost all of the three thousand administrative civil servants have been members of the one general administrative class. The sole exception is the corresponding group in the diplomatic service, which is separately recruited and trained to fill some of the top positions within the Foreign and Commonwealth Office and its overseas branches (embassies, United Nations delegations, etc.). More than half of the over eighty thousand executive civil servants have. similarly, been members of one general executive class. Members of the general classes are technically recruited to the civil service first, and only thereafter allocated to particular departments or offices. Throughout their subsequent careers they remain at least eligible for transfer between departments. The separate departmental classes are maintained partly from a sense of reverence for tradition but principally because special training and experience is required (for example, in the collection of taxes). The Fulton Committee has also urged that further attempts be made to extend the main grading system (defined in terms of pay, status, and degree of responsibility) even to the specialist classes in order to reemphasize the common qualities in civil service life.

Since 1968 responsibility for civil service organization and management has been vested in a new Civil Service Department, whose head is the prime minister, instead of, as formerly, the establishment division of the Treasury. Attached to it is the semi-autonomous Civil Service Commission, which is responsible for recruitment, and acts independently of departmental or ministerial supervision in the actual conduct of examinations and interviews. In this way, too, stress is laid on ability (and not, in this context, political patronage) as the fundamental and overriding qualification for employment in the civil service.

CONSTITUTIONAL STATUS OF MINISTERIAL DEPARTMENTS

The constitutional status of ministerial departments may be said to rest upon two basic principles, the first of which is that of ministerial responsibility.[8] From the point of view of the civil servant this means that it is the minister, the man at the top, who has to bear the brunt of criticism for any shortcoming within the department, and, as a necessary corollary, that the minister's decisions (which may in fact be taken by the cabinet) must be accepted and acted upon by the department. One of the primary duties of the civil servant, therefore, is to try to keep his minister out of trouble, especially, but not exclusively, where the "trouble" is accidental rather than the foreseeable outcome of conscious decisions on policy. Indications of the seriousness with which this duty is taken may be found in the care with which a department's officials will prepare answers to parliamentary questions and in the fact that their preparation takes absolute priority over any other work. Thus, through its minister, a department is kept more in touch with and responsive to Parliament and the electorate. But ministerial responsibility is more than a control mechanism. It is also, for the civil servant, a defense mechanism. The principle is so interpreted as to shield individual officials from public criticism and direct political involvement. Even in their appearance before select committees, for example, officials have tended to maintain the roles of their departments' spokesmen and servants, talking in terms of departmental, not personal, policy and practice. Through ministerial representation, too, officials are assured of the opportunity to defend their actions against inevitable criticism in Parliament and elsewhere, as well as to provide authoritative explanations of their intentions, without which their work might be seriously hampered by public ignorance or misunderstanding.[9]

The second basic principle governing the constitutional position of ministerial departments is that their officials be the civil *servants* of the crown. Legally, this means that they have no rights against their employer to be paid, pensioned, or retained in service, and that the conditions of their employment are governed

[8] See Chapter 4.
[9] Nineteenth-century experiments with independent boards administering controversial services (like the Poor Law) were not persevered with, partly because of the administrative inconveniences attending the lack of an authoritative parliamentary spokesman.

not by statute[10] but by regulations or Orders-in-Council. In fact, of course, for reasons intimately connected with the general standing of the government as well as in the interests of efficiency and recruitment, their positions are more secure and assured than any other outside the universities and the courts of law. The other implications of this principle are therefore of more importance. What they amount to, in brief, is that the political and administrative virtues of the ideal civil servant are much like those of the perfect butler or valet of tradition. He should be discreet, unobtrusive, loyal, tactful, and fully capable of running the entire household, including his master (so long as the last quality is not apparent outside the family). In particular, the civil servant is expected to refrain from personal comment on political questions or the affairs of his department and, in short, to do nothing in public (other than to resign) that might imply any personal, as opposed to departmental, opinion on public issues. At no time, either, must he disclose information about the internal operations of his department or its affairs without authorization. This rule is, clearly, a necessary corollary of the principle of strict ministerial responsibility and a condition of the official's being able to serve a succession of political masters with different personal and party policies.

Civil servants were, for many years, expected to confine their political activities exclusively to the ballot box. Since 1953, however, the prohibition has been greatly relaxed. Very broadly speaking, it was then agreed that political activity be denied only to the administrative and executive classes (and members of comparable specialist grades) and to "those who work in local offices and deal directly with the individual citizen in relation to his personal circumstances." [11] Even these groups may, at the discretion of their department, be allowed to take part in local politics. This

[10] Acts of Parliament are necessary to *enable* salaries and pensions to be paid, and others, e.g., the Official Secrets Act, apply specifically, if not exclusively, to civil servants; but appointments are, in law, made at the discretion of the crown.

[11] From the statement of government policy on *Political Activities of Civil Servants* (London: HMSO, Cmd. 8783 of 1953), p. 6.

permission is commonly granted, except to members of the "higher civil service." [12]

THE HIGHER CIVIL SERVICE

The phrase "the higher civil service" is frequently used to refer to the most important members of the civil service, but little agreement exists about its precise connotation.[13] Essentially, however, the higher civil service consists of the chief policy advisers to ministers and those in most regular personal contact with ministers. At its largest, the higher civil service will consist only of the administrative class and certain individual civil servants drawn from the most senior levels of the executive classes (possibly), of the inspectorates, and, increasingly, of the professional, legal, and scientific groups. At most, therefore, it will include something in the region of three thousand people. More realistically, from the point of view of policy-making, it will probably number about one thousand and will certainly include no more than fifteen hundred people, of whom the largest single group will be drawn from the administrative class, but with a growing proportion from the specialist groups.

The duties of the higher civil service range at least as widely as those of the government it serves and advises. Ministers—rela-

[12] All civil servants may belong to any political party, including the Fascist and Communist parties. But see the note on security provisions at the end of this chapter.

[13] For example, the *Report* of the Royal Commission on the Civil Service (London: HMSO, Cmd. 9613 of 1950), includes within its scope all civil servants above the salary level of a principal (nearly 3,000 people); R. K. Kelsall, in his *Higher Civil Servants in Britain* (London: Routledge and Kegan Paul, 1955), on the other hand, limits it to home administrative civil servants of and above the grade of assistant secretary (1,045 people in 1950). The administrative grades, in ascending order, have been assistant principal, principal, assistant secretary, under secretary, deputy secretary, and permanent secretary. Some 50 percent are in the two lowest grades. See also the excellent "insider's" account, H. E. Dale, *The Higher Civil Service* (London: Oxford University Press, 1941).

tively inexperienced and impermanent—are necessarily dependent on their permanent expert advisers for knowledge and guidance. As in all countries, too, one of the primary tasks of civil servants is to act as filters for their superiors, ensuring that only the most important matters (but all of them) should be placed before ministers. Inevitably, therefore, civil servants must make many decisions without reference to the minister—even on important matters of "policy." By all accounts they do so, insofar as they can, only in accordance with the known preferences and principles of the minister, just as they always consult the minister before deciding questions in which they know him to be especially interested. Moreover, because of the doctrine of ministerial responsibility, even the most senior members of the higher civil service in Britain will play a much less public and much less "political" role than many of their American counterparts.

It is not possible for an outsider accurately to measure the extent or nature of civil service influence on the conduct of government—and particularly upon the formation of policy, which is our principal concern—yet some general remarks can be made. Some ministers will be little or no more than the spokesmen for their permanent officials. But unless a minister is capable at least of stating his department's view in dealings with other ministers or the cabinet, and of seeing that his department works within the confines of government policy, he is unlikely to remain in office for long. Others will make a decisive impact upon the whole work of their departments. Even the strongest minister, however, must leave all but the most important decisions to his officials. These considerations apart, the extent to which departmental policy is made by its higher civil servants or by its political head will depend on the personalities involved and the degree to which the minister and the cabinet are dependent on those officials for their knowledge and ideas. This dependence will tend to increase with the complexity and technicality of the issues, their remoteness from ordinary experience, and the shortage of time and facilities available to those other than the official. On all these grounds it may be surmised that the influence of the civil service will continue to increase.

If the role of the civil service raises certain doubts about the sufficiency of ministerial responsibility as a control mechanism, the principle itself nevertheless remains intact and unchallenged. Civil servants in fact take pains to keep their ministers out of trouble by careful and responsible work, by attempting to forestall and to meet criticism, and, it must also be noted, by resort to "the pathological secretiveness of British government." [14] Ample testimony also exists to the integrity of civil servants and their ability to serve successive political masters and policies.[15] The principle is also invoked to help the civil servant resist particular pressures. He is the one who normally conducts the extensive and continuous negotiations and discussions with other departments and with outside interests and organizations, but he can always fall back on the defense that the final decision must rest with the minister.

Anxiety is often voiced about the power vested in the civil service.[16] As we have suggested, there exist solid grounds for it. But it may be possible to quiet the doubts without fundamental reorganization. If, for example, the developments in the House of Commons committee system continue, and if ministers were to be given larger and better equipped personal staffs (drawn from within or without the civil service) to extend their capacity for effective and informed guidance, the problem might swiftly be transformed.[17]

It is difficult to assess the nature of civil service influence, but there are grounds for thinking that the most important problems lie in its nature rather than in its extent. It must be granted that the civil service has saved many a minister from error (and thereby established some ministerial reputations for efficiency and

[14] The phrase is quoted from Brian Chapman, *The Profession of Government* (London: Allen and Unwin, 1959), p. 321.

[15] See, for example, that of Lord Attlee in his "Civil Servants, Ministers, Parliament and the Public," *Political Quarterly,* XXV (1954), pp. 308–15.

[16] See Chapters 5 and 7 of this text.

[17] These changes, which are mentioned merely to illustrate the magnitude of the problem, are discussed in the previous chapter and the works cited there, and in B. Chapman, op. cit., pp. 275–81.

vision) for as the repository of governmental experience and of the principles of administrative "rationality" it is able to resist the claims of political pressures. The beneficial influence of its discretion, ability, and remarkable incorruptibility is also undeniable. But there are other grounds for disquiet.

The conditions and nature of the work of the civil servant must encourage the feeling that he is part of a governmental, as well as administrative, elite and that he possesses superior wisdom as well as experience; intimate contact with a rapidly changing set of ministers of varied accomplishment does not necessarily provide evidence for the view that "self-government is preferable to good government." [18] This feeling is likely to be further encouraged by his social origins and educational background. Despite an appreciable widening of the social range of entrants since 1939 and before,[19] a study of the civil service carried out in 1967 revealed that 67 percent of the administrative class were the children of fathers in the two top groups in the Registrar-General's classification of occupations (the professional and managerial, which amounted to little over 18 percent of the population in 1961); that 37 percent had attended fee-paying schools; that, of university graduates (almost nine-tenths of the class), 64 percent had degrees from Oxford or Cambridge; and—a fact that must lend greater weight to the impact of education—that 65 percent had had no employment previous to their joining the service.[20] When interpreting such figures it should be emphasized that they carry no necessary partisan implications (the three best-known higher civil service Soviet agents, Burgess, Maclean, and Philby, all had this social background) nor provide any evidence of conspiracy, for recruitment by ability cannot escape the effects of the social

[18] To quote an old Liberal maxim. For figures on the rapidly changing set of ministers see A. King, "Britain's Ministerial Turnover," *New Society,* August 18, 1966, pp. 257–58.

[19] Documented in R. K. Kelsall, op. cit.

[20] The study was conducted for the Fulton Committee by A. H. Halsey and I. M. Crewe. It is published as *The Civil Service, Vol. 3 (1): Social Survey of the Civil Service* (London: HMSO, 1969). The information quoted is from pp. 19, 26, and 27; but also see pp. 34–111 and 397–419.

and educational systems. But the figures are politically significant to the extent that the social composition of the service helps define those with the readiest *informal* access to the administrative machine and, by the same token, indicates the problems and way of life (of the majority) of which the service has least immediate sympathy and understanding.

The 1967 study also showed that over 70 percent of the graduate members of the administrative class had taken their degrees in the humanities, especially history and the classics, the rest being broadly divided between the natural and social sciences.[21] This was, presumably, part of the evidence for the Fulton Committee's criticism of the civil service as "amateur" and its recommendations for greater specialization, of qualifications as well as in service, and more intensive post entry training. The last of these has been accepted: a new Civil Service College was established in 1969. But the Civil Service Department is unconvinced by the case for much greater specialization. It is clear that the higher civil service must continue to recruit the ablest people it can find. It is equally clear that more and recurrent training is required if the service is to be able properly to employ (but not to be dominated by) the expertise of others, effectively to apply modern managerial and decision-making techniques, and to acquire and assimilate all relevant information.[22] There is much force in the view that "what is required today is more and better 'generalists' and 'all-rounders' in administration, and *not* more specialists," [23] and that to produce these generalists should be the object of further training.

The defects of the British higher civil service are not, therefore, as profound as some have alleged. They are, however, compounded by the inadequacy of the pure doctrine of ministerial

[21] Halsey and Crewe, op. cit., p. 400.

[22] See the slightly different kinds of shortcoming depicted in M. J. Barnett, *The Politics of Legislation: The Rent Act of 1957* (London: Weidenfeld and Nicolson, 1969), especially pp. 40–89, and J. Bray, *Decision in Government* (London: Gollancz, 1970).

[23] Eric Hobsbaum, in the course of an incisive critique of "cloudy thinking" in the Fulton Report, *The Listener,* July 18, 1968, p. 68 (emphasis in the original).

responsibility as a means of securing that continuous and extensive dialogue between elected politicians and permanent officials on which both responsible and responsive government depend. But if parliamentary reform and the Fulton Committee recommendation for less civil service anonymity can together secure more open government, as certain select committees have discovered to be possible, then the specter of bureaucracy may well be exorcised comparatively quickly. In the British context the last word can perhaps be given to Sir Kenneth Wheare, who once said that "if Civil Servants appear . . . at times to act as Ministers in disguise, does not the remedy lie in stronger Ministers and a more independent and vigilant House of Commons rather than in weaker Civil Servants?" [24]

NOTES

"SECURITY"

By the terms of the Official Secrets Act and various Treasury and departmental regulations, civil servants are under the strictest obligations not to disclose information pertaining to their work. Since March 1948, steps have also been taken to try to prevent unauthorized disclosures by removing from "sensitive" posts individuals believed to be politically or (since 1956) personally unreliable. They must be transferred to nonsensitive posts, or allowed to resign without official discredit, or (only as a last resort) dismissed. Appeal lies to an independent committee of two retired civil servants and a trade-union official. Procedures are informal, not judicial. The accused person, but not the committee, may be denied complete access to the evidence.[25]

[24] K. C. Wheare, op. cit., p. 30.
[25] See Mackenzie and Grove, op. cit., pp. 152–55; H. H. Wilson and Harvey Glickman, *The Problem of Internal Security in Great Britain, 1948–53* (Garden City, N.Y.: Doubleday, 1954); the *Statement on the Findings of the Conference of Privy Councillors on Security* (London: HMSO, Cmd. 9715 of 1956); *Security Procedures in the Public Service* (London: HMSO, Cmnd. 1681 of 1962).

THE UNIVERSITY GRANTS COMMITTEE

The University Grants Committee (UGC) is an exceptional body, and one that has attracted a great deal of attention and even envy elsewhere.[26] Although it is appointed by the government to allocate public money to the universities, most of its members are drawn from those who work or have worked in those institutions. The chairman and secretary (the only full-time members) are both civil servants, but even the former has always been appointed from the academic world. Since 1964 the UGC has been a committee of the Department of Education and Science, and not of the Treasury (as formerly), but the basic relationship is the same: the Ministry determines the total sum of money to be granted to the universities, doing so within limits imposed by the Chancellor of the Exchequer and upon the basis of requests from the UGC; but exactly how the money shall be distributed to particular universities and for what purposes, is decided by the UGC in consultation with the universities. Inevitably, as the cost of higher and other forms of tertiary education mount,[27] the government has taken an increasing interest in how the money is spent. The Department of Education is clearly disposed to exert its influence on the strategy of higher education to a greater extent than did the Treasury. Since 1968, furthermore, the accounts of the UGC and the universities have been open to inspection by the Comptroller and Auditor-General, and thus to comment by the Public Accounts Committee of the House of Commons. But all concerned proclaim their aversion to any governmental or political interference with the decisions traditionally regarded as falling within the bounds of academic freedom and, despite numerous expressions of alarm, the UGC seems both to be developing a more positive role in the long-term allocation of resources and still to be preserving

[26] It has, for example, been copied in India. See an invaluable American study: H. W. Dodds and others, *Government Assistance to Universities in Great Britain* (London: Oxford University Press, 1952). See also R. O. Berdahl, *British Universities and the State* (Berkeley: University of California Press, 1959).

[27] See Chapter 2.

its status as an influential intermediary and thus as a defender of university autonomy. How long it can continue to do so, or whether some new set of procedures must be devised,[28] is debatable. So too is the question of its "exportability."

It has worked well in Britain where the Treasury civil servants have similar social backgrounds to a substantial proportion of M.P.s and to the members of both the UGC and the principal governing bodies of the universities, where the university world is fairly small and not notoriously radical in outlook, and where the political tradition readily permits much of the business of the UGC (in its own words) to be "dealt with informally between persons well known to each other." It might not work as well where these conditions were absent.

[28] See, for example, the proposals of the Select Committee on Education and Science in its *Student Relations, I: Report* (London: HMSO, 1969).

7

Law and Order

The British people have become accustomed to a reasonably high standard of honesty and competence among their public servants.[1] The latter, in turn, seem to rely on a reasonably high standard of law-abidingness among the British people. Key figures in the day-to-day interaction of the public and authority are the members of the police. In all societies public attitudes toward policemen are likely to be ambivalent. In Britain, it may be said, feelings of respect, even affection, generally outweigh more negative attitudes. In the early 1960s only motorists and young people showed antagonism toward the police, while in 1969 a sample survey found that 86 percent of the population respected the police and over 90 percent found them honest, fair, friendly, and helpful—and this despite several publicized cases, in the preceding decade, of violent behavior on the part of an overworked and undermanned force.[2] Nevertheless, police relations with the public continue to be predominantly peaceful and relatively amicable; the police have never become closely identified with any political movement, and at no stage have they been a privileged (or alien) group set apart from the rest of society. For this state of affairs the

[1] See G. Almond and S. Verba, *The Civic Culture* (Princeton: Princeton University Press, 1963), pp. 108–9.

[2] See the *Report* of the Royal Commission on the Police (London: HMSO, Cmnd. 1728 of 1962); *The Sunday Times,* December 21, 1969; and G. Marshall, *Police and Government* (London: Methuen, 1965), pp. 105–9.

institutional context in which the police work is largely responsible.

There are almost fifty regular civilian police forces in England and Wales.[3] The Metropolitan Police in London is under the control of the Home Secretary, acting through a Commissioner appointed by and responsible to him. Elsewhere the forces are under the supervision of local police authorities: committees composed of local magistrates and councillors from the various local authorities in the area. These forces are financed by the local authorities, but half of the cost is covered by a grant from the central government. With the grant goes control by the Home Secretary, who must be satisfied as to the proper and efficient use of the money. The Home Secretary must also approve the appointment or dismissal of the Chief Constable, who assumes primary responsibility for recruiting and running the force in each area and for ensuring that it meets the minimum standards prescribed by the Home Office. All forces are subject to periodic inspection by Her Majesty's Inspectors of Constabulary (appointed by the Home Secretary).

The precise legal relationships between police, central, and local government are not entirely clear.[4] On the one hand, as we have seen, the central government bears a general responsibility for the maintenance of efficient police forces throughout the country.[5] On the other hand, the Chief Constable (subject to being dismissed) exercises a degree of original authority and wide discretion about decisions to investigate particular cases and, subject to consultation with and guidance from the national Director of Public Prosecutions, about whether or not to prosecute. Uncertainty is involved in such policy questions as the methods of controlling demonstrations, action taken on real or alleged offenses

[3] This is less than half the number that there were when the Royal Commission recommended amalgamations to produce more effective policing. The following account does not, unless specifically stated, apply to the similar organization in Scotland.

[4] See the discussion in G. Marshall, op. cit., from which most of this account is derived.

[5] The case for a fully national force is argued in Lord Goodhart's dissent to the *Report* of the Royal Commission of 1959–62.

by motorists, and laws pertaining to obscenity, to name only those fields that regularly give rise to controversy or protest. From time to time, too, this local discretion has led to prosecutions, under the Official Secrets Act or ancient statutes, which have not obviously been free from ideological considerations.[6] The uncertainty relates to the extent, if any, to which Chief Constables are subject to central regulation or command, or to questioning (let alone instruction) from the local police authority.

For the most part, however, Britain has succeeded in containing any tendencies for the police to become either the mere agents of any political government or too independently powerful. The second of these dangers is guarded against by public opinion itself (the police being the first to acknowledge their dependence on public cooperation), strongly reinforced by the law and the courts. Thus, by law, the police must whenever possible obtain a warrant from a local magistrate before entering any premises without the occupier's permission; must lay specific charges against any arrested person before a magistrate within (usually) twenty-four hours of arrest, and produce some good reason for his continued detention, or else release him; must bring the accused person to trial within a further limited period; and must adhere to strict rules, imposed and enforced by the courts, about the manner of obtaining and producing evidence (including "confessions" and statements from the accused). Once trial commences, they appear only as witnesses, subject to no special privileges or immunities.[7]

The power of the police is further contained by the established criminal-law principle that any person accused shall be deemed innocent until proved guilty beyond reasonable doubt. The practice of leaving questions of fact to be determined by a jury in all serious criminal trials may also, if less confidently, be seen as a safeguard against arbitrary police power. The opportunities for injustice to result from police incompetence or excessive zeal are

---

[6] These are, obviously, partial explanations for the antagonisms to the police, noted at the beginning of this chapter, on the part of motorists and the young.

[7] Occasionally in an English Court of Summary Jurisdiction a police officer will conduct the prosecution personally, but it is more usual for this work to be done by a lawyer retained for the purpose.

thus severely restricted, if not yet reduced to the human minimum so far as the ordinary police and the criminal law are concerned.[8]

At first sight British practice seems to violate the principle of the separation of judicial and executive power. The head of the judiciary, the Lord Chancellor, is a member of the cabinet and presides over the House of Lords. All judges and magistrates are appointed by or on his advice.[9] There might thus seem to be close political supervision of the judiciary. In fact, it is completely independent of political pressure or interference. It was so even in the nineteenth century when, according to Professor Laski's studies, the great majority of senior judgeships were conferred as a political reward.[10]

All superior judges are appointed "during good behaviour subject to a power of removal by His Majesty on an address presented to His Majesty by both Houses of Parliament"—to quote the phrase used in the Judicature (Consolidation) Act, 1925, and derived from the Act of Settlement, 1701. The security of tenure thus granted (for the removal procedure has never been used in Britain) provides the first explanation of judicial independence. Another lies in English history and tradition: in the facts that the courts and Parliament were allies during the seventeenth-century struggles against royal power, and that those struggles seemed, to both of them, to be on behalf of the common-law rights of which the judges provided the surest defense. Parliamentary and public opinion continue to be highly sensitive to any suggestion of "political" (which means, in this context, executive) interference with the work of the courts. For the most part, indeed, to vest the appointment power in ministers who are accountable to Parliament is regarded as a safeguard against possible abuses of irresponsible power.

[8] For a critical account of police procedure in one case, see Ludovic Kennedy, *10 Rillington Place* (London: Gollancz, 1961).

[9] Except in the old royal possession of the Duchy of Lancaster, whose Chancellor appoints magistrates and county-court judges, and in Scotland, where appointments are the responsibility of the Secretary of State in all cases. Both these men are ministers.

[10] H. J. Laski, *Studies in Law and Politics* (London: Allen and Unwin, 1932), pp. 168–73.

English Courts of Law

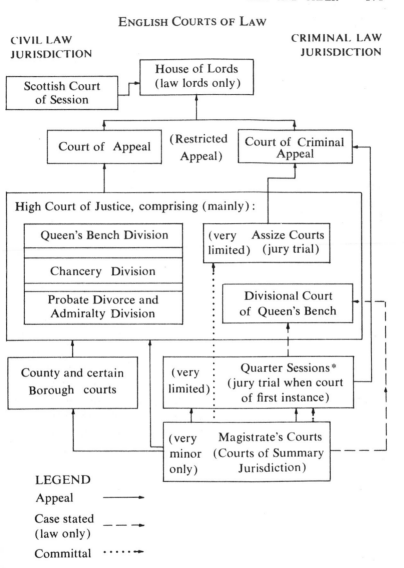

CIVIL LAW
JURISDICTION

CRIMINAL LAW
JURISDICTION

Scottish Court of Session

House of Lords (law lords only)

Court of Appeal

(Restricted Appeal)

Court of Criminal Appeal

High Court of Justice, comprising (mainly):

Queen's Bench Division

Chancery Division

Probate Divorce and Admiralty Division

(very limited) Assize Courts (jury trial)

Divisional Court of Queen's Bench

County and certain Borough courts

(very limited)

Quarter Sessions* (jury trial when court of first instance)

(very minor only) Magistrate's Courts (Courts of Summary Jurisdiction)

LEGEND

Appeal ⟶

Case stated (law only) – – ⟶

Committal · · · · · ⟶

* *The Royal Commission on Assizes and Quarter Sessions, 1966/69* (London: HMSO Cmnd. 4153 of 1969), has proposed, in its report published in December 1969, that, among other changes designed to speed the administration of justice, the assizes, quarter sessions and certain other, more local, criminal courts should be replaced by a single Crown Court.

The fact that the courts accept the supremacy of Parliament in the law-making field is also an important bastion against political pressures. It means that an unpopular decision results in pressure upon Parliament for legislation and not upon the courts directly or through those who appoint the judges. Thus the decision of the House of Lords in the famous Taff Vale case,[11] which destroyed well-established beliefs about the legal rights and status of trade unions, and which seemed to imperil their very existence as effective organizations, resulted in a political campaign by the unions for the return of sympathetic M.P.s and not, as might have happened, in lasting hostility to or defiance of the courts.[12]

Possibly the single most important factor in any explanation of the position of the judiciary in Britain is the organization of the legal profession itself. The profession comprises two distinct branches—barristers and solicitors. The former have the exclusive right to plead in the higher courts and, in fact, specialize in advocacy. The latter, who form by far the greater part of the profession, are responsible for most other types of legal work, including the interviewing of clients and, possibly, appearing for them in magistrates' and county courts. But it comprises only two branches; for, by law or custom, the judiciary and the legal ministers (except for the Secretary of State for Scotland—and in judicial matters he is advised by the Lord Advocate, who is a lawyer) are all appointed from barristers of some years' standing. What is even more important, perhaps, is that they continue to be members of the Inns of Court, the ancient bodies responsible for organizing, disciplining, admitting, and in part educating members of the bar.[13] The legal minister and the judiciary are thus members

[11] *Taff Vale Railway Co. v. Amalgamated Society of Railway Servants* (1901), A.C. 426.

[12] The result was the passage of the Trades Disputes Act, 1906, by the newly elected Liberal government. The Taff Vale campaign also undoubtedly helped secure the election in 1906 of the thirty independent Labour M.P.s who formed the Parliamentary Labour party.

[13] For a brief, informative, and very readable account of the profession, see R. M. Jackson, *The Machinery of Justice in England*, 2d ed. (Cambridge: Cambridge University Press, 1953), pp. 203–21. This book should be consulted on all the points, other than the police, discussed in this chapter.

of a tightly organized and largely self-governing profession, jealous of its traditions and with a strong vested interest in the maintenance of its independence.[14]

The rule of law is a concept that is difficult to define with precision. Nevertheless, it is sometimes listed among the basic principles of the British constitution.[15] If by this phrase is broadly meant an absence of arbitrary and unregulated public power, it is clearly safeguarded in Britain by the nature and powers both of the police and of the judiciary. More specifically, too, it is maintained by certain well-established principles of British law, among them: that the citizen may not be punished except for a specific breach of a definite rule of law; that, while officials or public persons and organizations may be granted special powers, they do not escape judicial scrutiny to ensure that they act only within those powers; that, in their individual capacities, officials do not escape from the general obligations imposed on ordinary citizens; and that, in general, so far as judicial rules and procedures can ensure it, there exists equality before the law. This is not to say, however, that there are no grounds for anxiety.

In Britain, judges rightly have a high reputation for impartiality and the ability to weigh evidence.[16] It is less certain, however, that the system has been able to eliminate a social bias rooted both in the individualism and conservatism inherent in the common law and in the finances of justice in Britain. Money is important in two different ways. To become a lawyer, and particularly a barrister, is difficult if not impossible for anyone without at least a small private income. For the most part, therefore, the legal profession is composed of, and mixes socially with, people from the higher so-

[14] In Scotland the position is similar. There is a twofold division also, into advocates and solicitors, the former being organized in the Faculty of Advocates, which performs functions comparable with those of the Inns of Court. In both countries, too, the solicitors are largely self-governing, if less tightly organized.

[15] See A. V. Dicey, *Introduction to the Study of the Law of the Constitution,* 10th ed., Part II (London: Wade, 1960).

[16] As is indicated, for example, by the heavy demands upon them and, to a slightly lesser extent, upon barristers, for service upon arbitration boards, royal commissions, and other committees of inquiry, usually as chairmen.

cial classes. As Lord Justice Scrutton has said: "It is very difficult sometimes to be sure that you have put yourself into a thoroughly impartial position between two disputants, one of your own class and one not of your class." [17]

Money matters also to the extent that for a client to obtain justice is a costly affair in terms of court and lawyers' fees. In a big case, these may easily run into tens of thousands of pounds. The government has assumed some responsibility for helping those in need. Under the Poor Prisoner's Defense Act of 1930 the courts are empowered to ensure that a poor prisoner obtains a solicitor and, if necessary, a barrister to undertake his defense in criminal cases. A fairly strict means test is applied, but the vast majority of applications are granted.[18] The Legal Aid and Advice Act of 1949 provided that public assistance also be available in some, and eventually all, civil actions (for plaintiff as well as defendant), the scheme being administered, under the direction of the Lord Chancellor, by the Law Society.[19] As general economic conditions have improved, the Act has progressively been implemented—the latest section to be brought into force being the provisions establishing a system of free oral legal advice. The result is that legal aid may be obtained, subject to a means test, to bring any but the more trivial civil actions, or to defend any action outside the magistrates' courts and except for certain specified categories of proceedings—among them defamation and breach of promise of marriage—in the county courts and above. The principle has thus been accepted that money should not bar access to the courts even if, perhaps, the level of the means test is still low enough to hinder the full application of that principle. Both in the sphere of legal aid and, particularly, of legal advice as a prelude to or substitute for litigation, these provisions only go some of the way to meeting the full requirements of equal access to justice; but even so, the growth of legal aid was cited by the 1969

[17] 1 *Cambridge Law Journal*, p. 8, cited in Jackson, op. cit., p. 234.
[18] See Jackson, op. cit., p. 129, for a table of applications and refusals.
[19] That is, by the professional association to which most solicitors belong.

Royal Commission as one reason for the overloading of the criminal courts.[20]

It is partly because of this social bias in the legal system that there has been a proliferation of special administrative tribunals appointed by ministers to decide, originally or on appeal, cases arising out of the application of social policy to particular persons, places, or circumstances.[21] Other reasons have included the desire for speedier and more informal procedures than are normally obtainable in the courts, and the claim that many of the issues which present themselves involve too many questions of "policy" to be suitable subjects for judicial determination. The existence of these tribunals, their powers, their procedures, and above all the lack, in many cases, of statutory provision for appeal to the courts and the difficulties of judicial review, have given rise to almost continuous disquiet, particularly, but not exclusively, among judges and lawyers. They have, accordingly, been the subject of two major inquiries.[22] The report of the second of these, the Franks Committee, was quickly followed by the Tribunals and Inquiries Act, 1958, which established the general principle of judicial review on points of law as well as providing for numerous procedural

[20] See the *Report* of the (Widgery) Committee on Legal Aid and Criminal Proceedings, Cmnd. 2934 of 1966, and the *Report* cited above at p. (149). For a further discussion of the social problems involved, see *Justice for All* (London: Fabian Society, 1968), a report of the Society of Labour Lawyers.

[21] Examples of such tribunals, which vary widely in their power, procedure, and composition, include: the Licensing Authority for Public Service Vehicles; the Special Commissioners of Income Tax; rent tribunals; and appeal tribunals to deal with pensions, special benefits, and other aspects of the social services.

There also exist many private tribunals exercising statutory functions: for example, the disciplinary committees established by, and with jurisdiction over, members of the legal, medical, and other professions. From their decisions appeal lies, on points of law, to the Judicial Committee of the Privy Council.

[22] See the *Reports* of the Committee on Ministers' Powers, Cmd. 4060 of 1932, and of the Committee on Administrative Tribunals and Inquiries, Cmd. 218 of 1957.

reforms on lines suggested by the committee. By this Act, too, a council was set up to keep the working of some thirty named tribunals under constant review and to make reports thereon. The controversy about executive quasi-judicial powers, which raged so loud in the thirties, forties, and fifties, has been muted since that time except in the politically highly sensitive areas of land purchase and town planning—but, even there, there is no serious suggestion that the regular judiciary should assume full responsibility.

8

Local Government

Local-government authorities are very closely linked to the central administration in their operations, but organizationally they retain their independence. By a "local authority" in Britain is meant, broadly speaking, a local-government unit whose powers are vested in a council elected by, and politically responsible to, a local electorate, but which is legally subordinate to, and indeed the creation of, the central organs of government.

The Times has said that "Local Government as initiator, partner, or agent makes most of the public arrangements for the difficult business of living together in a technically complex, mobile and populous society." [1] In fulfilling these responsibilities the local authorities collectively employ about two million people, of whom a quarter of a million are administrators. By 1968, furthermore, local authorities were wholly or partially responsible for something like one-third of total public expenditure. It has been all the more significant, therefore, that the structure of local government, as opposed to its precise powers and functions, has remained virtually unchanged since the end of the nineteenth century. The need for reform had long been recognized, particularly by those outside local government, but not until 1966 did it lead to the setting up of a royal commission that reported in 1969.[2] In February 1970, the government stated that it would accept the broad proposals of

---

[1] In a leading article, February 5, 1970.
[2] *Report* of the Royal (Maud) Commission on Local Government in England, Cmnd. 4040 of 1969.

the commission. However, because the government also stated that it might take five years before the new organization recommended by the commission would take effect, we must begin this chapter by looking at the structure to be reformed.

Essentially, local government has been organized into what is known as the "dual system," that is to say, into two sets of authorities that are quite independent of each other. On the one hand are the largest cities in England and Wales (the county boroughs) which are self-contained and independent of the system in the administrative counties. On the other hand are the county councils that are responsible for some local government services throughout the whole of their areas, but separately elected councils are responsible for other services in the urban and rural districts into which the counties are subdivided. All in all something like 1,200 separate authorities exist in England and Wales.[3]

Two other principles must be noted. The first is that each local council, if one excepts the two-tier county system, is the only local-government body within its area, and is thus a multi-purpose authority responsible for *all* the powers limited to its area.[4] The second principle is that of a correlation between range of function and type of authority—each category of authority having its distinctive set of powers. Unfortunately, the operation of this principle is vitiated by a substantial adherence to the historic boundaries of counties and boroughs. The result is that, for example, the counties are widely different in area, population, and financial resources (and the same can be said of every other category), so that it is unrealistic to expect them to discharge the same functions with comparable efficiency. Local rivalry and pride have also made it very difficult to alter the status of particular areas to keep pace with population and other changes. Numerous Private Acts

---

[3] The system in Scotland is different in a number of relatively minor ways, including some of the nomenclature. The broad principles, however, have been assimilated to those operating in England and Wales. London has its own structure, which was reformed in 1966.

[4] There are not, and have not been since the nineteenth century, any independent *ad hoc* bodies like elected school boards in the field of local government.

of Parliament conferring greater powers on particular authorities, and the recommendations of successive boundary commissions (aimed at rationalizing the structure to some extent), have not fundamentally altered the position hence, in large measure, the need for reform.

The failure to reform the structure of local government has had unhealthy results. None of the existing areas is large enough to administer certain modern services, with the result that the central government has absorbed such formerly local responsibilities as hospital management, gas and electricity supply and distribution, and, in places, public transport.[5] In allocating powers to different types of authority it has been necessary either to accept inadequate performance by the smaller authorities within any category or else to deny those powers to the larger ones that could cope with them perfectly well. Increasingly local-government structure has ceased to reflect the actual units of social existence, particularly in the major conurbations, with deleterious effects upon the level of public interest,[6] as well as upon the performance of functions. (Town and country planning is perhaps the most obvious sufferer.)[7] Above all, structural shortcomings must accept some of the blame for the growth of central control over the day-to-day work of local authorities. Local authorities still have fairly wide discretion over such matters as recreational and cultural facilities,

[5] It is often said that the parish was the area appropriate to a time when walking was the principal means of transport, and the county, when the horse came into general use, but that neither is obviously the best area in an era in which all forms of communication have advanced somewhat beyond these means.

[6] Rarely do more than 40 percent of the local electorate go to the polls, and frequently very much less. No one can yet be certain why nonvoting is so prevalent, but this divorce of the administrative from the social pattern seems likely to form part of the explanation.

[7] The manifest failures adequately to plan and develop land are not wholly the result of such local causes as the separation of town and country or the multiplicity of weak local authorities. The absence of national legislation to deal with real-estate speculation, or of a more definite national policy on such issues as suburban sprawl, the conservation of agricultural land, and the development of city centers have tended to frustrate the good intentions of many local authorities.

child welfare, sanitation, street lighting, and other minor matters, but over their most important, dramatic, and expensive functions, among which are education (except universities) and low-rent housing, their discretion has been progressively narrowed by control from above.

The 40,000 councillors themselves are elected for three-year terms of office—together or one-third each year, according to the type of authority—by those local inhabitants qualified to vote in parliamentary elections.[8] In England and Wales the councils also appoint additional members, the aldermen, for a six-year term[9]—but in Scotland all councillors are elected. In all but some counties and the smallest authorities, the strong tendency is to conduct elections and all council business on strict party lines, and most usually on two-party lines: Labour versus anti-Labour (the names under which the latter rally vary considerably, but their support is principally Conservative). In those few councils that remain free of party organization the councillor possibly has more scope for personal initiative, but contested elections are fewer and power tends to lie with a local established oligarchy of landowners and farmers in rural, and of shopkeepers and merchants in urban areas, along with housewives and the retired.[10]

In all but the smallest councils the actual work of administration is carried on by committees and subcommittees of the council, the most influential members of which are usually the chairmen, or conveners, who act in particularly close conjunction with the council's officials. By statute, certain committees, for example, those on finance and (where appropriate) police, health, and education, must be established and must be consulted. In fact, it is rare for a council to overturn a committee recommendation or decision, although it may remit some matters for further consideration. Officials are the servants of the particular council that employs them

---

[8] Until after World War II the suffrage was restricted to those who paid local rates (the principal form of local taxation, which will be discussed below).

[9] Up to one-quarter of the total council may be aldermen.

[10] See L. J. Sharpe, "Elected Representatives in Local Government," *British Journal of Sociology,* vol. 13 (1962), pp. 189–208.

and, broadly, occupy the same constitutional position in relation to it as do civil servants to ministers and the cabinet. Increasingly, too, thanks largely to the energetic work of the National Association of Local Government Officers, their conditions of work are approximating those of the civil service—at least in the largest authorities. Elsewhere, it is more difficult to organize regular procedures for recruitment and promotion. Being a local-government officer is thus coming more and more to be regarded as a worthwhile career, offering considerable scope for initiative and providing a salary, if not yet prestige, comparable to all but the most lucrative positions in other professions.

Membership of a local council, however, is widely believed to attract fewer men of real vision and ability than formerly. Such an historical comparison is difficult to substantiate, but local government clearly attracts fewer such men than is desirable. Were it not that local-government service is one of the more useful stepping-stones to, and training grounds for, a parliamentary career, the position might be much worse. Many explanations of this state of affairs are commonly put forward. They include the structural weaknesses already mentioned, the general decline in local community life that seems to characterize modern industrial society, the dependence upon unpaid councillors,[11] and the combined effects of increased work and diminished opportunities for the exercise of initiative.

The principal independent source of local-authority revenue consists of the rates levied on land and buildings.[12] As such they have many shortcomings. In the modern world rates are a highly regressive and inadequate form of levy. They contribute less than one-third of local-authority income—a similar proportion comes from miscellaneous receipts, rents, and payment for services. What

---

[11] Councillors receive certain allowances for expenses and for loss of earnings while actually engaged on council work. Since neither amount to adequate compensation, the result is to restrict the number of people prepared to serve.

[12] Real property, after valuation, is given an assessed annual rental. The rates are levied in the form of a poundage—i.e., a demand is made upon the occupier for x shillings for each pound of assessed rental.

is more, rates tend to be least productive where the need is greatest: for example, in counties with small and thinly scattered populations that have to maintain a huge road mileage, or in poor industrial areas where slum property is inadequate to support the necessary expenditure on public health, housing, and schools. Government grants-in-aid are thus required to make good both the inadequacies and the inequities of the rating system, and with financial help must come control over expenditure. Since 1966 government aid has taken the form, primarily, of general rate support grants that allocate the product of a nominal addition to the poorer areas' total ratable value (the amount varying according to a general formula that takes account of need), with only a few grants specifically allocated to particular services.

The power of the central government to withhold part or all of a grant and to insist that grants be used only for "approved" expenditure clearly amounts to an important form of control exercised, in fact, by central departments. But it is not the only type of control. Local authorities are, of course, governed by parliamentary legislation. Their actions may be challenged in the courts as being *ultra vires* or otherwise illegal. And they are subject to various forms of nonfinancial administrative control. The relevant department must approve local-authority proposals in most spheres, including education, highway construction and maintenance, town planning, smoke abatement, fire services, and the police. Sanction must be obtained for raising loans for capital expenditure (and this in addition to approval of the actual scheme on which the loan is to be expended), and new by-laws must be confirmed. The appointment or dismissal of certain officials (the medical officer of health, for example) must also be approved. Local authorities are governed by departmental directions and regulations on many subjects; and in practice it may be hard to distinguish between regulations contained in statutory instruments —directions issued by a minister under his statutory powers—and suggestions or recommendations contained in circulars and memoranda.

To this list of controlling agencies must be added two important groups: inspectors and district auditors. Departmental control, financial or other, frequently operates on the basis of reports from itinerant inspectors.[13] They are experienced, qualified, and often specially trained officials who, in addition to their controlling functions, perform invaluable services as transmitters of knowledge and opinion among local authorities as well as between them and the departments. The district auditors examine the accounts relating to most local-authority expenditure for the purpose, mainly, of detecting illegal and unreasonable expenditure or misappropriation of grants; they have the power to disallow such items and to surcharge those responsible, subject to appeal to the Minister or the High Court. Their functions are thus semi-judicial and, despite their being civil servants, they in fact operate independently of ministerial control.

Even were local authorities financially independent, they would not be entirely free agents. Fundamentally, this is because the public would not tolerate marked local differences in the standards of education and other essentially national services. Financial weakness, allied to structural deficiencies, only provides a supplementary reason for central supervision. In many respects local authorities thus come close to being mere agents of the central administration; but they are unlikely ever to be that alone. The fact is that local councils, with all their weaknesses, are still the centers of more or less independent political interest and avenues for the politically ambitious. As such, the councils constitute what are probably the most effective spokesmen and defenders of purely local interests that could be devised, and ones which in fact government departments treat with considerable respect.

NOTE ON REFORM PROPOSALS

The main reforms endorsed by the Labour government may now be outlined.[14] The most radical proposal is to consolidate the ef-

---

[13] Those of education, constabulary, and housing and planning being perhaps the best known.

[14] See *Reform of Local Government in England,* Cmd. 4276 of 1970. The new Conservative government stated, very soon after entering office, that it did not necessarily approve the endorsement.

fective executive powers of local government in the councils of eighty-four main authorities to be directly elected by the voters in their areas; of the eighty-four, six will be metropolitan areas in the main conurbations outside London, and each of these will be sub-divided into a number of metropolitan districts. Outside these areas fifty-one so-called "unitary" authorities will be established, also with directly elected councils, which will perform all the major local government functions, including transport, planning, and education.

It is hoped, by these reforms, to establish a set of major authorities that are more rationally conceived in terms of the relation between area and function. In turn, this may lead to some relaxation in the severity of central control, the attraction of more able and imaginative people into local government service, and the provision of local centers of more interesting decision-making than now exist. If these hopes are realized, they should have beneficial effect both upon the level of participation by the local citizens and upon their confidence in the system of government.

At a lower level, within the unitary areas, many existing local authorities will continue to exist, if somewhat disguised as so-called local councils. As such they will have very few executive powers but they will have an important function as spokesmen for their inhabitants. It is also envisaged that, at some stage, eight indirectly elected provincial councils may also be established in England and Wales, evolving out of the regional economic planning councils.[15]

[15] See Chapter 9.

9

Government and the General Welfare

All politics and government are about, in some sense, "the general welfare" or "the public interest." But people's conceptions and perceptions of welfare and the public interest vary, as do they vary on the government's role in pursuing them. Recently, the notion of welfare has acquired a narrow usage in, for example, phrases like "the welfare state" or "welfare capitalism." In these contexts the term welfare is restricted either to the problem of taking care of remediable human hardship imposed by things like poverty, sickness, old age, infancy, and unemployment, or to employers' concern for what they think to be their workers' well-being, and the policy of seeking industrial peace by supplying canteens and pensions. In this chapter we will neither restrict "welfare" to these narrow senses, nor will we discuss the "general welfare" or "public interest" in their widest meanings. More usefully, we hope, we will focus on the expectations now prevailing in British society about the government's responsibilities, on the relevant areas of controversy, and on some of the organizations and methods adopted by British governments since 1945.

In the United Kingdom there seems to be a greater preparedness than in the United States to turn to government for the remedy of social deficiencies and abuses. This is especially true (for obvious constitutional and geographical reasons) because of the established role of the central government. This contrast also reflects the greater confidence Britons feel in their government and officials.[1] Thus the central government not only looks after such things as education and the provision of rented houses, it is also generally agreed that radio, television, and the arts constitute proper spheres for government aid. But only in the former two cases is aid associated with supervision and the prescription of standards.

Government activity is probably more extensive today than ever before; but in Britain, the principle of the government's general responsibility is not new. So-called "laissez faire" policies in the nineteenth century were a reaction against far-ranging, but outdated and restrictive laws passed in previous ages. And laissez faire policies themselves were never pursued to the extent that is often popularly imagined. Thus, for example, pioneer legislation about public health, hours and conditions of work, and urban amenity was enacted in the nineteenth century, and the foundations of the present system of national insurance were laid by the Liberal government of 1906–14. Such examples could be multiplied almost indefinitely. This is to say that the roots of government intervention lie deep in Britain's political tradition. There is now little or no dispute between the two major parties about the right of government to act as the supreme rule-maker in society if and when the need clearly arises. Dispute centers on the nature and the urgency of particular needs and on the best means of meeting them. It should also be remembered that the differences in governmental behavior tend to be narrower than those in party rhetoric. Both parties need to carry the bulk of the population with them, in order both to win office at an election, and successfully to implement their policies within the limits imposed by the acceptable procedures.

The lives of governments have probably never been entirely independent of the state of the economy. In this century certainly, and particularly between the wars, increasing demands have been directed at governments to deal with unemployment and economic depression. These demands were not fully articulated, nor was the responsibility for meeting them fully accepted, until the end of

[1] G. Almond and S. Verba, *The Civic Culture* (Princeton: Princeton University Press, 1963), pp. 108–10.

World War II. During the war, British society had been mobilized and directed by the government to a degree that seems to have been unequaled by any other participants except, possibly, the Soviet Union. In the light of this experience it was impossible to argue convincingly that governments were unable to control the general level of economic activity. In its White Paper on *Employment Policy* issued in 1944,[2] the wartime coalition government had pledged itself to maintain a policy of high postwar employment. After the 1945 election the Labour government committed itself still further to maintain full employment. By this they meant that the level of unemployment should stay below 3 percent of the labor force. The coalition government had also accepted, in principle, the comprehensive proposals of Sir William (later Lord) Beveridge's 1942 report on social security. Thus, by the end of the war, the government had assumed responsibility for both the general state of the economy and a minimum and well-nigh universal level of social security.

Since 1945 economic policy has never been far from the center of the political arena. The immediate problem was to secure the recovery and reconstruction of peacetime industry, without the high levels of unemployment that marred the corresponding period at the end of the First World War, and in the face of dependence upon the import of materials and goods of all kinds for which it could not pay. (This dependence served as a significant brake on recovery until the introduction of the European Recovery Program [the Marshall Plan] in 1947.)[3] At the same time, moreover, the government was electorally committed to extensive social reforms, including the nationalization of certain industries and the introduction of, as it then seemed, a radical scheme for welfare. Much of the success that attended Labour's efforts was attributable to the apparatus of planning and controls that it inherited from the war effort.

When the Conservative party won the 1951 election there was no immediate and drastic policy reversal. Admittedly, the Conservatives accelerated the "bonfire of controls" that Labour had

[2] Cmnd. 6527 of 1944.
[3] See Chapter 10.

begun and they carried it much further than Labour probably would have. But the Conservatives fully accepted the basic obligations in the realms of employment and welfare and, for the most part, the structural innovations of their predecessors (the sole exceptions being to sell off the nationalized iron and steel industry and part of the long distance road haulage industry). Full employment ceased to be a central political issue after the 1955 election, for by that time the Conservatives had demonstrated their capacity to maintain it. This is not to say that the voters no longer cared about employment; there was a clear public reaction to increases in unemployment in the early sixties.[4] But the absence of mass unemployment is now taken for granted.

After 1955, economic attention shifted to the more positive aims of affluence and growth. This shift was not always apparent; the foreground was too often filled by the expedients adopted in attempts to overcome the obstacles that constantly thwarted both parties in the pursuit of these aims. The most conspicuous obstacles were internal inflation and recurrent international financial crises. The diagnosis of the underlying causes varied, at least in emphasis, according to the political attitudes and perceptions of the observer. Even if one leaves out of account the extreme left-wing view that to abolish capitalism was the only solution, and the extreme right-wing view that all of Britain's economic troubles were the result of high taxation and the lack of freedom for private industry, one finds substantial differences in approach between the two parties. Labour increasingly tended to emphasize the lack of modernization and inefficiency in British industry— a managerial responsibility—while the Conservatives emphasized the increase in wages—which by implication was a union responsibility. Labour, in opposition, stressed economic growth and increased production as the solution, while the Conservatives stressed the importance of preserving the pound. Labour emphasized the need for public effort (for both social and economic reasons), while the Conservatives emphasized the need for private initiative and discipline. But all postwar governments have

[4] See D. Butler and D. Stokes, *Political Change in Britain* (London: Macmillan, 1969), p. 418.

had remarkably little room to maneuver in the face of the real economic situation and of the electorate's concern with immediate results (in terms of prices, income, and housing) rather than long-term strategy and the means to implement it. Nevertheless both in the economic policies pursued and in the administrative machinery adopted, the differences between the parties form part of the story of the government's attempt to safeguard public welfare.

Common to both parties has been what may be called the "standard" fiscal and monetary means of controlling the level and direction of economic activity; the manipulation of interest rates; the use of taxation to absorb purchasing power and to encourage or discourage particular kinds of expenditure or industrial effort; credit restrictions applied directly to the nationalized industries and indirectly to others through the Bank of England; and variations in the conditions under which hire purchase agreements may legally be concluded. Both parties have used these methods, but in the 1950s at least, an influential group within the Conservative party seemed to believe that these methods were sufficient to overcome Britain's economic problems—the primary objective was to ensure, as quickly as possible, that the market could operate freely.

By the early 1960s, however, these methods and aims no longer seemed adequate. The Macmillan government applied to join the European Economic Community partly in the hope that access to a new large consumer market, and increased competition from other producers, would constitute an economic wind of change. But the decision to apply for membership, and the protracted negotiations that preceded the French veto, constituted a powerful incentive to the government to look again at its own economic institutions and policies and to compare them, somewhat unfavorably, with the German "economic miracle" and the almost equally impressive recovery of the French economy. Inevitably, too, attention was directed to longer-term objectives than had been habitual in the crisis-ridden postwar period. This switch of attention not only brought government thinking more in line with the time-span of decision required by advanced technology and industrial investment, but in any case seemed to be required by other domestic problems and pressures. The unevenness of Britain's economic progress, the consequent necessity to alternate restrictive with expansionist policies, and the growing concentration of industry, prosperity, and population in an already over-crowded southeastern England were among the factors that suggested that insufficient attention was being paid to long-term economic policy.

From 1947, when Sir Stafford Cripps became Chancellor of the Exchequer, the department primarily responsible for economic policy had been the Treasury. The Treasury had always been the finance ministry and not unnaturally, given the central position of taxation, credit, and the international exchange, it had been drawn into the role of economic planner. One important mark of a new departure in policy, therefore, was the internal Treasury reorganization carried out in 1962, partly as a result of criticisms voiced by the House of Commons Select Committee on Estimates in 1957–58, and partly inspired by the report of the Plowden Committee published in 1961.[5] The main effects of reorganization were to set up two new economic groups within the financial and economic policy side of the Treasury, one concerned with the public sector, the other, called the National Economy Group, concerned primarily with long-term economic problems. Purely monetary and financial questions remained with the finance group.[6] By this means, it was hoped, the economic planning functions of the Treasury might be less dominated than they had been by the annual budgetary exercise and by the need to maintain that detailed control of departmental expenditure that had long been the core of Treasury control.[7] The establishment of the public sector group was also highly significant. It constituted a belated and

[5] Plowden Committee, *The Control of Public Expenditure,* Cmnd. 1432 of 1961.

[6] See A. Shonfield, *Modern Capitalism: The Changing Balance of Public and Private Power* (London: Oxford University Press, 1965), pp. 103–7; Chapters VI and VIII have been drawn upon extensively in the present discussion.

[7] See S. H. Beer, *Treasury Control* (London: Oxford University Press, 1957).

possibly unwilling recognition of the potential base for regulating the whole economy provided by those industries and economic activities for which the government was directly responsible.[8] Accompanying these Treasury changes other ministries, even before 1964, began to exercise a more positive influence on those sectors of the economy with which they dealt. One conspicuous example was the pressure exerted by the Ministry of Housing and Public Works on the building and construction industry in order to persuade them, if possible, more speedily to adopt modern and efficient construction techniques.

Simultaneously a new body was set up outside Whitehall in an attempt to put more steam into the notion of national planning. The National Economic Development Council (known as Neddy) is chaired by the Chancellor of the Exchequer, and draws its members from industrialists, trade union leaders, and initially somewhat in third place, civil servants from the economic ministries. As important as its establishment, perhaps, was the fact that it was armed with a permanent organization of officials and experts whose sole job was to brief the Council. This was shortly followed by "little neddies," six of them by 1964, concerned with the development of particular industries. Neddy, it was hoped, would be able to formulate long-term economic strategy, even to draw up a plan, and at the same time secure the advance commitment of the major economic interests to its implementation. It did lay public emphasis on economic development and the need for a more closely guided and controlled economy. But in both the National Council and the smaller industrial ones there was too much emphasis on the attempt to strike bargains between the two major interests and not enough pressure to assert the government's role as national planner. In their operations, therefore, it is not unfair to detect the working out of the corporatist theme within Conservative ideology.[9]

[8] See Chapter 2 for some figures on the significance of the nationalized industries. They cannot, of course, be rationally used for short-term economic manipulation.

[9] A. Shonfield, loc. cit.; see N. Harris, *Beliefs in Society: The Problem of Ideology* (London: Watts, 1965), Chapter 4.

Two other Conservative new departures deserve brief mention. The first was an attempt directly to influence wage levels, partly achieved by declaring a "pay-pause" for government employees. The more lasting step was to establish the three man National Incomes Commission which, operating in a semijudicial manner, examined wage claims referred to it by the government and pronounced upon their compatibility with government guidelines. This move was unpopular, but probably had some effect on wage levels. The other departure was to give official recognition to the need to divert growth and development toward those regions that not only were less developed but seemed to be declining steadily. Both approaches were carried further after Labour returned to office in 1964, and in the direction one would expect from a government less reluctant to use public power. To these points we will return shortly.

At the macroeconomic level the first innovation of the new government was immediately to set up the Department of Economic Affairs (DEA), constructed around the nucleus of the National Economic Development Organization and the National Economy Group from the Treasury, and charged with responsibility for long-term economic policy. The hope seemed to be that a separate "growth" department would provide a salutory counterbalance to the caution and financial preoccupations of the Treasury. The experiment, to judge by the policies actually pursued, was not a total success. Personal and general political factors played their part, as did the lack of sufficient experience of sophisticated economic analysis. But, essentially, its impact was limited by the decision to give overriding weight to the defense of the international value of sterling. Nevertheless, the DEA built up the staff and expertise used by the Ministry of Technology (with which it merged in 1969), and it prepared the first serious essay in long-term economic forecasting (although it mistakenly referred to the projections as a "plan"). Its most significant achievement, however, may turn out to be the regional economic councils and boards it has set up in eight English regions, in Scotland, and in Wales. Their purpose is to stimulate regional economic development by helping to coordinate the steps taken by various government departments, and by identifying what is needed in order to achieve balanced regional development. The councils have purely advisory powers and are composed of representatives of the major economic interests and associations and of other individuals within the region. They are assisted by the boards that consist of civil servants from the regional offices of various departments. By 1970 each board had a long-term development plan for its region that served as a guidline for all relevant bodies. They also, as importantly, serve as essential links between the regions and the central departments, a link without which overall central planning would be weaker and the regions would have less hope that their peculiar needs and problems would be catered to.

A second immediate organizational innovation in 1964 was the establishment of the Ministry of Technology (Mintech), marking the new government's intention to play an increasingly active role in the microeconomic sphere.[10] Mintech has helped to staff and service, as well as to increase the number of little Neddies; it has taken over from the old Ministry of Civil Aviation the task of subsidizing research and supervising the organization of the aircraft industry (one of its most costly enterprises); starting with machine tools and computers, it has tried to strengthen the weaknesses in what ought to be the growth points of British industry. Among its initiatives, for example, was the establishment, in 1966, of the Industrial Reorganization Corporation whose task it is to help finance and stimulate reorganization and mergers in British industries. But the Conservatives have abolished it too in this drive to prune government intervention.

Since it absorbed the DEA and Board of Trade at the end of 1969, the Ministry of Technology has shared with the Treasury primary responsibility for the government's economic commitments at all levels from the general level of activity to the development of the regions and particular industries. A variety of subsidiary organizations are responsible for special fields, among

[10] The Conservative's ambition to dismantle Mintech may mark a contrary intention.

them guaranteeing export credit, intervention in road and transport services, and the provision of a wide range of services to industry. The Monopolies Commission, to take but one example, examines and issues reports on proposals for industrial mergers and take-overs when requested to do so by Mintech. The commission, incidentally, should not be confused with the Restrictive Practices Court which is a special division of the High Court of Justice, sitting with lay assessors, empowered to make rulings on the legality of pricing, information, and other trading policies pursued by a particular industry or trade association.

The most controversial area of increased government intervention has been that of prices and incomes. Building on the foundations laid by the Conservatives (in the incomes field), Labour has laid immense stress on the need to include the level of prices and incomes within the scope of government supervision. To assist them in this the government established the National Board for Prices and Incomes to which it may refer most price increases and demands for increased wages, salaries, or dividends. The aim was to relate incomes to price levels and, above all, to increases in productivity. It was also hoped that the incomes policy would do something to mitigate the effects of what might be called "the free market" in wages on the poorly paid, the unorganized, and those whose productivity is difficult to measure. These groups have tended to fall below the wage levels established by formal collective bargaining between union and management and the less formal agreements and practices that jointly add up to the "wages drift." It has not, to put it mildly, been a conspicuous success either with employers or with trade unions. That it has had some effect is probably undeniable, but that it has had progressively less influence on incomes is also apparent. Significantly, in January 1970 the government stated its intention to merge the prices and incomes board with the monopolies commission to form a new commission for industry and manpower.

Partly in an attempt to forestall Conservative demands for reform of trade union law, and partly as another approach to the problem of wage increase and inflation, the government appointed the Royal Commission on Industrial Relations which reported in 1968.[11] The consequent draft legislation included proposals for penal sanctions against unofficial strikers and certain other "disciplinary" clauses, none recommended by the commission. This bill, as we have seen, was withdrawn in the face of opposition within Parliament, the Labour party, and the trade unions.[12] Meantime, however, the Industrial Relations Commission has been established to assist in the work of industrial conciliation and to help rationalize industrial relations. On assuming office in 1970 the Conservative government began immediately to prepare new legislative proposals in this area and made clear its determination to resist large wage demands.[13] Nothing was said, however, of the Donovan Report's recommendation that action be taken to encourage union reorganization and a more responsible attitude toward industrial relations on the part of management.

By 1970, therefore, the range of organizations and techniques for government economic intervention had been significantly enlarged. It does not follow from this, however, that Britain now has a planned economy, least of all in the sense in which this term is used with reference to the Soviet Union and other communist countries. Nor, on the other hand, has intervention by a Labour government been fundamentally hostile to the business community. Admittedly, while trying to make the present system work, the government has also tried to extend the power base for future reforms in pursuit of what Labour spokesmen call the "compassionate society." Loans, grants, subsidies, and tax incentives for the private sector, it must also be said, have in many cases been tied to guided investment, regional development, or the encouragement of exports and modernization. But, by these means the private sector, including agriculture, benefited from public expenditure to the tune of some £2,000 million in 1968,

[11] *Report* of the Royal (Donovan) Commission on Trade Union and Employers Associations, Cmnd. 3623 of 1968.

[12] See Chapter 5.

[13] But not by means of an "incomes policy" as this was hitherto understood. The Prices and Incomes Board was therefore abolished.

a sum that is almost equal to the much more commonly denounced expenditure on social security.

Apart from the consolidation of all the ministries concerned with social security into a single Ministry of Social Security in 1969, there have been no major structural changes in the social services during the sixties. This situation, however, is unlikely to endure. On the one hand, it is clear that there are still serious gaps in the welfare provisions.[14] The continued shortage of housing imposes immense suffering on large numbers of people in the worst urban areas; the aged and the families of the poor in many cases live in dire need; and to realize all the potential benefits from the National Health Service still requires heavy investment for equipment, hospitals, and health centers. At the same time, as critics of the system point out, it is possible, for example, to find families with substantial incomes living in subsidized local authority housing, and the total cost of the social services has increased by some 137 percent between 1959 and 1969.[15] In the seventies, therefore, the country will have to decide what proportion of the national income it can devote to social security and, within that sum, whether to subsidize people in need or, as now, to subsidize the services needed by them.

This account of government and welfare has been almost exclusively about those policies whose success or failure is potentially quantifiable and which have also been the primary concerns both of the government and of the public. But it is also important to note the growing attention to the quality of modern life as well as to the quantity of material goods available. One may reasonably expect the government to devote an increasing amount of time and energy to such problems as town planning, conservation, and both rural and urban amenity. To cope with these problems more effectively, for example, is at least one purpose underlying

[14] As one indication, it may be noted that in 1965 over £250 million was paid out in the form of special benefits to meet the grave and tightly defined need of those for whom the "ordinary" benefits were inadequate or inapplicable.

[15] See R. H. S. Crossman, *Paying for the Social Services* (London: Fabian Society, 1969).

the schemes for local government reform mentioned earlier. It also was one reason for consolidating the Ministry of Housing and parts of other ministries into the new Ministry of Local Government and Regional Planning in October 1969.

It is possible that the achievement in 1969–70 of a positive balance of payments marks another convenient watershed in the history of positive government. Already, new problems press hard on the heels of what may soon be the old problem of the balance of payments. On the organizational side the chief problem is the more adequate coordination of the multifarious social and economic agencies and activities of government. As we have already noted, one possible step forward has been taken with the consolidation of ministries. There are also signs, of which the most public was the 1969 White Paper on *Expenditure* discussed in Chapter 5, that the government and its civil servants are striving continuously to develop more complex techniques of forecasting, analysis, and decision-making. The problem is worsened, however, by the lack, or weakening, of the traditional focal points of integrated decision-making. As we have seen, the cabinet is no longer the effective supreme coordinating body it once was and the existing pattern of multipurpose local authorities is overdue for reconstruction. What this amounts to is that at the lowest level, as at the highest, there is no strong all-purpose authority, no point at which different strands of policy come together and have to be decided in relationship to one another. One of the questions that may be answered in the seventies is whether ministerial consolidation and the strengthened office of prime minister at the top, combined with local government reform and the development of regional authorities, will in fact reintegrate the present proliferation of *ad hoc* authorities and decisions.

In the final chapter we will return to certain other fundamental, and more political, problems facing British governments. At this point, therefore, we will end by suggesting that success in meeting these organizational problems of governing a modern economy would make parliamentary reform even more important. For only by strengthening the capacity of Parliament to scrutinize, by opening administration to the politician, is there any hope of bridging the gap between the technical and sophisticated decision-making techniques of civil servants, industrialists, and political leaders and the cruder economic preoccupations of the voter. Only thus, too, might the popular pressure for results lead to a more articulate and informed debate and, then, to more consistent and effective policies.

10

Foreign Relations

Britain's international position has changed fundamentally since 1914, when Britain could reasonably claim the status of a major world power, and even since 1939 when the increasing hollowness of that claim was not yet generally apparent. The economic, political, and military changes in the nature of international relations since World War II are too well known to require a review here. For Britain, in particular, the twenty-five years since the end of World War II have witnessed a steady whittling away of its international power and status. This was for some time concealed in the immediate postwar era by the glamor of victory and, as Marx said in explanation of John Stuart Mill's eminence, the flatness of the surrounding countryside. But by 1947, Britain, in common with the rest of Western Europe, had to turn to the United States for economic aid. Under the imaginative and generous European Recovery Program Britain and other Western European countries received massive assistance on the condition that they cooperated in its distribution and allocation. Thus began the interweaving of proposals for European unity with American policy that has remained a major theme in European history.

By 1970 Britain's new position was symbolized by, among other things, the virtual "end of Empire";[1] its failure significantly to influence either the conduct or the termination of the war in Vietnam; foreign debts of over £4,000 million, many of them

[1] Some forty former colonies or dependencies achieved independence, within or without the Commonwealth, between 1945 and 1970.

incurred to meet recurrent financial crises; the fact that Britain' "independent nuclear deterrent" was credible only because th United States made rocket warheads available; and Britain's re luctant decision to end its military presence east of Suez by th early 1970s. For such a real decline, talk by heads of state of new "special relationship" with the United States are neither real nor apparent compensation, let alone a substitute.

In the nineteenth century British policy had been largely de termined by the clear national interest in keeping the sea route open for reasons of trade and empire and, more locally, in ensur ing that the English Channel ports remained in unhostile hands In terms of relations with the major powers, which was to say with other European countries for the most part, two of the cen tral themes of British policy can be summarized in the concept of "diplomacy by conference" and the "balance of power." Th former has continued to be important and perhaps has never bee more important for British survival. It is often suggested that th latter has also continued to be important. Thus, as recently a 1958, an official booklet quoted with approval the followin passage:[2]

> The equilibrium established by such a grouping of [equal rival] forces is technically known as the balance of power, and it has become almost an historical truism to identify England's secular policy with the maintenance of this balance by throwing her weight now in this scale, and now in that, but ever on the side opposed to political dictatorship of the strongest single State or group at a given time (Sir Eyre Crowe, 1907).

Despite yearnings for such a role, most frequently voiced i support of arguments for the formation of some kind of third force, and despite occasional official rhetoric couched in these traditional terms, in fact the balance of power policy has had to be seriously modified. Britain did indeed join one of the two major postwar world groupings, but not only or even primarily

[2] As quoted in *Britain in Brief,* 2d ed. (London: HMSO, 1958), p. 47.

or traditional balance of power reasons. Rather it was the case that ideological sympathy, historic ties, geographic factors, military weakness, and the urgent need for economic assistance led Britain to choose the United States as its ally and protector. In some respects, even, it would be truer to say that Britain chose America as its international successor.[3] The formal cement of this alliance consists of the North Atlantic Treaty and the Southeast Asia Collective Defense Treaty (both of which, it is worth pointing out, contain many more members than merely the United States and Britain), and of a limited exchange of information about nuclear and biochemical weapons.

But even in the earlier postwar years when the American alliance formed its cornerstone, British foreign policy has suffered not only from lack of room to maneuver but also, it would seem, from uncertainty of purpose and of diagnosis.[4] In the past twenty-five years there has been a failure both at government and popular levels seriously to come to terms with Britain's new position. As a result, it is easier to talk about the variety of responses and attitudes to foreign affairs than it is clearly to delineate a consistent British foreign policy. Among the variety of responses two have predominated. The first has been the desire for a "little England" policy, a return, that is to say, to a position of "splendid isolation" as it was referred to in the late nineteenth century. This basic attitude has taken many forms ranging from a disinterest in foreign affairs, an attempt (not usually successful) to act as a broker between the great powers, a yearning for an international role confined to the fulfillment of United Nations obligations, a search for a third force in which the policy of isolation would be pursued not by Britain alone but by Britain in association with others, and most recently by signs that for many,

[3] It will be remembered that the 1947 Truman Doctrine was prompted at least partially by Britain's declared inability to continue as "defender" of Greece and the Eastern Mediterranean against foreign pressures. This may help explain the occasional patronizing touch in Anglo-American relations as Britain tries to "teach the new dog old tricks."

[4] See, for example, D. C. Watt, "Future Aims of British Foreign Policy," *The Political Quarterly,* vol. 41 (1970), pp. 95–105.

future foreign policy should consist simply of trade. The second predominant set of attitudes has been embodied in the continuing talk of "greatness." This too has taken more than one form. It has appeared, especially among Conservatives, as an assertion that Britain is still a great power and that, in association with the United States, Britain can still act as world policeman and champion of western values. Alongside this, more particularly in left-wing circles, the search for greatness has stressed the notion of Britain's giving "a moral lead" by acting as an international "conscience." This line was most intensively preached by some of the active supporters of, and spokesmen for, the Campaign for Nuclear Disarmament,[5] but it was not confined to them. At a more popular level and particularly among some of the younger generation, the 1960s have seen a new internationalism develop thriving on foreign travel and voluntary service overseas, but symbolized also by demonstrations about Vietnam or the civil war in Nigeria. None of these sets of attitudes constitute a realistic foreign policy; but they may have made it more difficult to formulate one, as well as reflecting the lack of a clear lead from Britain's rulers.

Insofar as one can detect a positive thread in British foreign policy it consists of the search for some wider grouping through which Britain can hope to influence world events. Reference has already been made to the alliance with the United States. It has become clear, however, that it does not in itself constitute foreign policy, and rhetoric about the "special relationship" has rung increasingly false as the inequality of the partnership has become more apparent and as certain conflicts of attitude and interest have become more obvious with the relaxation of the cold war. The United States and Britain continue to share important interests stemming from America's growing and Britain's traditional world role, and from the fact that the dollar and the pound sterling are the two major world trading currencies, not to mention their common language and political tradition, but in terms of power, the alliance is an uncomfortable one between a giant and

[5] See F. Parkin, *Middle Class Radicalism* (Manchester: Manchester University Press, 1968), especially pp. 93–109.

a relative midget each with its own perspectives. Significantly, Britain's decision to withdraw her troops east of Suez came at a time when the United States was being increasingly absorbed in the politics of the Far East rather than of Europe.

Even at its height the American alliance was not Britain's only important association. Alongside it, and to some extent in conflict with it, was Britain's link with the Commonwealth. The Commonwealth in the postwar period has never been a political or military alliance nor has it involved any treaty obligations. It is better described as a loose and largely informal association of independent states, linked by a history of colonial rule, by the practice of mutual consultation, and by the existence of certain common political traditions and aspirations. Crucial, too, were the members' mutual military and economic dependence, with Britain's now eroded strength and wealth as the focal point. As the postwar period progressed, moreover, it became increasingly clear that Britain could not defend the other members in a situation where even for its own defense it was increasingly dependent on the United States. Economically, too, as we have seen earlier, trade within the Commonwealth has declined, and, as the level of tariffs has been lowered by international agreement, so the significance of the special preference Britain has given to imports from Commonwealth countries has lost its significance. By 1970, although many traces of this historic association remain, the Commonwealth lacked the cohesion or strength for effective common action in world affairs.

These two international associations (with the United States and with the Commonwealth) had, however, helped to prevent Britain from developing its role as a European power. It is true that Britain had taken the lead in forming the Organization for Economic Cooperation and Development set up to implement the Marshall Plan. It is also true that in the immediate postwar period, European countries looked to Britain for help and guidance in reestablishing Europe in the international community. But Britain was only associated with the European Coal and Steel Community, and its refusal to join the proposed European Defense Community played a crucial part in the failure of that initiative in 1954. Consistently with this record, Britain took no part in the negotiations that led to the establishment of the European Economic Community (EEC or the Common Market) in 1959 and at first would not countenance anything approaching full membership. Admittedly, Britain then initiated the European Free Trade Association, the so-called "outer seven" (as opposed to the Common Market's "inner six"), but this was not so much an alternative search for a close international union as an attempt to increase the bargaining strength of those European countries which, while remaining outside the EEC, could expect to have their economic destinies vitally affected by it. By the early 1960s, however, not only did the Common Market member countries appear to be thriving economically, but Britain's own economic position continued to be precarious and the alleged restraints imposed upon it by the Commonwealth and the Anglo-American alliance seemed less relevant. On the one hand the United States was anxious for Britain to become a member of the Common Market and, on the other, the Conference of Commonwealth Prime Ministers in 1962, while expressing anxiety about the possibility of British membership, could produce no alternative solution to Britain's economic problem. It is ironic, perhaps, that these two associations were cited by President Charles de Gaulle in 1963 as reasons for his veto on Britain's first application to join. Undeterred by this rebuff the United Kingdom applied again in 1967, with certain other members of EFTA, only to be turned down once more by President de Gaulle. By late 1969 the departure of de Gaulle from the French government and the victory of the Social Democrats in Germany created a situation in which it seemed that Britain might be given a third chance to join the EEC. By then, however, British political leaders had not yet enunciated any clear objective (other than highly debatable economic ones) to be furthered by membership, nor had they demonstrated a clear grasp of the implications of the Community's stated purpose of eventual political union. It was still not possible to discern the essential structure of Britain's foreign policy.

For this state of affairs the explanation seems to lie in the peculiar vulnerability of the political system in this sphere. In the

United Kingdom the press devotes less space to international affairs than one would expect of a country that traditionally has seen itself as a great power on a world scale. The informed public on foreign affairs is comparatively small as a result not only of this deficiency in the mass media, but also of that lack of information and opportunities for discussion at the parliamentary level which we have already noted. There are, furthermore, few pressure groups operative in foreign affairs and most of them are either narrow in focus or see foreign policy as a mere incident to domestic concerns of an economic or social kind. At a time when new principles are required, the traditional secretiveness of decision-makers, the remaining weaknesses of Parliament, and the special dependence in international affairs of the general public upon its leaders have all contributed to Britain's inability to create a convincing new role for itself.

NOTE: THE COMMONWEALTH

All the members of the Commonwealth were once governed by or from the United Kingdom. This historical experience they share with the United States, the Union of South Africa, Eire, and Burma. But, unlike these four countries, they have maintained an association with the United Kingdom. The association is peculiar, however, in that it does not derive from any treaty or formal agreement enforceable at law, and in that its members are independent sovereign states in all the senses recognized by international law. Their freedom embraces even the right to secede—a right exercised in fact by South Africa, Eire, and Burma.

Until 1949 the chief external badge of association was that the members were "united by a common allegiance to the Crown." [6] The British king was also king of each member state, with the same constitutional function in each (although in what were formerly called "the Dominions" his functions were in fact exercised by governors-general, appointed as his personal representatives by

[6] To quote from the definition of the Commonwealth approved by the Imperial Conference of 1926 and generally known as the Balfour Declaration.

the monarch acting on the advice of the appropriate national government).

In British law the British colonies are colonies of *the crown,* and not of the nation or the government. The development of a nonpolitical monarchy at home was therefore a prerequisite to, and in fact encouraged the development of, self-government abroad in a way that did not destroy every link with Britain. Thus the road to colonial independence may be said to consist of the replacement of legal subjection to the powers of the British crown, exercised through or on the advice of the government in the United Kingdom, by a formal allegiance to the *person* of a nonpolitical monarch whose governmental powers are exercised by or on the advice of separate independent national governments. On the eve of the War of Independence Benjamin Franklin asserted that "America is not part of the dominions of Great Britain, but of the King's Dominions." Fortunately or unfortunately this distinction was then constitutionally unacceptable to Britain and so there existed no alternative to British rule except complete political and legal independence. Today he could have obtained self-government for America while continuing to be, as he acknowledged himself to be, "a subject of the British Crown." But not until the early twentieth century, in fact, did His Majesty's Government in each of the self-governing Dominions[7] become substantially equal in political status to the U.K. government—and even then the Statute of Westminster, 1931, was still necessary before the last legal inequalities could be removed.

After World War II Burma and Eire preferred to leave the Commonwealth rather than retain even this formal link with the crown which, to them, was still a symbol of past alien rule. India's later decision also to banish the royal symbol and become a republic presented a more serious challenge. The result, on this occasion, was a further loosening of the Commonwealth bond. A declaration issued by the Commonwealth prime ministers in 1949 agreed that the Republic of India could continue to belong to the Commonwealth of Nations "freely cooperating in the pursuit of

[7] In 1926, the year of the Balfour Declaration, they were Australia, Canada, Eire, Newfoundland, New Zealand, and the Union of South Africa.

peace, liberty and progress," and would accept "the King as the symbol of the free association of its independent member nations, and as such the Head of the Commonwealth." [8] The queen today is thus queen of some member countries, but in fifteen out of the twenty-seven members in 1969 she is recognized only as the head of the Commonwealth, to which status, as Mr. Nehru once stated, there is "no function attached."

The only other legal characteristic common to all members today is that they recognize each other's citizens either as British subjects or as Commonwealth citizens, both categories being distinguished from those of aliens or foreigners. However, this is of as little practical significance as the position of the crown. What rights accompany either status in each country is a matter for its own government to decide. The rights vary widely: Australia and India, for example, place severe restrictions on the entry and/or rights of certain Commonwealth citizens; in 1962 even the United Kingdom placed restrictions upon Commonwealth immigration and in early 1970 the Conservative party proposed that no distinction be made between Commonwealth citizens and other aliens.

Three other badges of membership deserve notice even in a short discussion: the prime ministers of all the Commonwealth countries meet periodically in special conferences; the member countries exchange high commissioners and not ambassadors; and, since 1965, there has existed a Commonwealth secretariat to assist the twin processes of consultation and cooperation which have lent day-to-day meaning to the concept of the Commonwealth.[9]

Mr. (later Lord) Attlee, speaking as prime minister in the House of Commons in April 1946, stated that "it is our practice and our duty, as members of the British Commonwealth, to keep other members of the Commonwealth fully and continuously informed of all matters that we are called upon to decide, but

[8] The full text may be found in N. Mansergh, *Documents and Speeches on British Commonwealth Affairs 1931–1952* (London: Oxford University Press, 1953), pp. 846–47.

[9] See H. J. Harvey, *Consultation and Cooperation in the Commonwealth* (London: Oxford University Press, 1952).

that may affect Commonwealth interests." Prime ministers, high commissioners (those in London meet together regularly with British ministers), finance and other ministers, civil servants, military leaders, and others all play their part in the exchange of information and opinion among the Commonwealth countries. The objects and extent of this must not be exaggerated or misunderstood. The purpose of consultation is to facilitate cooperation, should the members wish it, on any particular point, but there is no duty to agree or to concert policies, nor may any government shift the burden of responsibility for its own policies on to other Commonwealth shoulders. The United Kingdom, furthermore, apparently initiates more consultation and transmits more information than any other member, while communication between the other members is very limited. But even the United Kingdom has departed from its "practice and duty" on occasion: for example, it seems that Britain issued its ultimatum to Egypt in 1956 and subsequently invaded the Suez Canal area without even informing the other members of the Commonwealth of its intentions, let alone consulting them about the wisdom of its policy. Nevertheless, it is probably correct to say, with a Lord Chancellor addressing the House of Lords in 1948, that "the great benefit the Commonwealth brings is the joint consultation, alike in matters civil and military, the sharing of information, and the resulting solution of common difficulties." [10] Consultation and cooperation, however, must be about something of common interest and must be based on some shared values or aims if they are not to be empty rituals. But merely to mention the traditional bonds—the crown, economic interest, defense, foreign policy, "British type constitutions," and common political ideals—is to list points of increasing divergence. Moreover, while some of these traditional bonds are weakened by autonomous developments within the member countries or by the continuing divisions and friction in the field of race relations, those interests that the Commonwealth countries continue to share are hardly distinctive. Not even the withdrawal of South Africa in 1961, or Britain's reluctance to go

[10] Lord Jowett, quoted in Harvey, op. cit., p. 30.

all the way with Rhodesia, have led to greater coherence and consensus among the remaining members. Both Britain and the other independent members seem increasingly to be seeking their salvation in other groupings than the Commonwealth. We cannot here go into the question of whether this was inevitable, or whether different policies by Britain might have overcome the division between old and new members or have led to a new kind of economic relationship. The fact remains that by 1970 it would take a wild optimist, even given the Commonwealth's history of adaptability and flexibility, to expect recent trends quickly to reverse themselves.

11

The British
Political System:
An Overview

The concentration of constitutional authority and power at the cabinet level means that there can be no doubt as to who or what composes the government in Britain. The prime minister and his closest ministerial colleagues, i.e., the political core of the cabinet, usually (and justifiably) receive the blame or praise for anything within their jurisdiction that goes wrong or right. The very fact that the cabinet must accept or endorse any proposal for it to become effective policy not only makes it the focal point for all important political pressures and influences; it also reinforces the cabinet's party-derived ability significantly to resist or shape the influences that bear upon it and thus uphold the policies or principles to which it may be committed. Any surrender to blatant sectional pressure is taken to be a manifestation of weakness on the part of the government. Such a concentration of power and responsibility is not to be found in all democratic countries, however conducive it may be to strong and healthy government.

This system is democratic and not simply another example of autocracy at least in the sense that it is possible constitutionally to reward and punish as well as to praise or blame, and because this power ultimately belongs to the electorate. The electoral system may not be entirely "just," the parties may deprive their ordinary members of full freedom of political maneuver, and the House of Commons may be less powerful than the U.S. Senate, but the system has the corresponding merit that it is the electorate that directly *decides* who shall form the government and, to a significant if debatable extent, what policies shall be followed. It is, indeed, sometimes suggested that the resulting government obtains a "mandate" from the people to do certain things that it may neither ignore nor exceed in any important respect.[1]

The notion of a mandate from the electors is open to objection: no government faced with changing circumstances can be expected to act entirely in terms of its previous election program; it is not possible to decide which issues were the important ones and, even if it were, which were reasons why a party won and which were proposals despite which it won; and the electorate, in any event, appears to attach much less importance to programs and issues than do politicians or publicists. On these grounds alone it is clear that a government's electoral program is and should be neither a straitjacket nor even a complete blueprint, and that the idea of a mandate is vague at best and must be handled with extreme caution. It is nonetheless significant. The doctrine reflects a widespread belief that a party program should be reasonably full and that for the successful party subsequently to depart radically from its spirit and intentions is dishonorable. The mere existence of the doctrine, moreover, suggests that, for much of the time, these expectations are satisfied, and emphasizes that the parties normally possess distinctive general approaches of which the parties' programs and behavior are interconnected manifestations. The doctrine of the mandate does not mean that governments do the things they do simply *because* they committed themselves in their programs any more than it means their programs will stop them from doing things that appear to them, as Conservative or Labour leaders, to be necessitated by the demands of office. But it reflects the fact and expectation that, to an important degree, the general policies and approach of a government may be predicted solely on the basis of the election results and of the party programs offered at the previous election. Significantly, neither in France nor in the United States, for exam-

[1] See Chapter 5, and the discussion in, for example, Sir Ivor Jennings, *Cabinet Government,* 3d ed. (Cambridge: Cambridge University Press, 1959), pp. 503–9.

ple, does the concept of the mandate play the same part in constitutional or political debate.

The power, stability, and accountability of governments clearly are vitally dependent upon the existence and nature of the predominantly two-party system. So, too, is the power of the electorate to decide the general composition and approach of governments. On the other hand, a critic might say, the character of the two-party system, without even primary elections to supplement the interparty contest, severely restricts the voters' choice. A system wherein the voter is free only to choose between disciplined parties, in the selection of whose leaders and representatives he has no direct control—the critic might continue—hardly deserves to be called government by consent.[2] That the effective choice of the electorate is limited in this way must be granted. But it does not necessarily follow that the resulting system is not one of government by assent. (*Assent* preferably, since government by *consent,* strictly speaking, would involve something like government by continuous referendum and would probably be unworkable. In any case, it has never been tried.)

The introduction either of a multiparty system, as in the French Third and Fourth Republics, or of a more flexible and loosely knit two-party system, as in the United States, would perhaps extend the range of choice open to voters and to ordinary M.P.s— but at a price.[3] Such a change would inevitably lessen the direct control of the electorate over the personnel and policies of government: the electors would directly decide who should represent them, and might make their decision in the light of a wider selection of individuals and viewpoints, but their decision would less directly determine the behavior of government. And the resulting greater diffusion of power (among members of the legislature, or between them and the executive) would almost certainly blur the lines of accountability. This alternative is not clearly more democratic than the existing British system. The latter, moreover, has

---

[2] Rousseau and Marx made somewhat similar criticisms in previous centuries.

[3] In practice it is not obvious that important minority viewpoints have been ignored any less frequently in these countries than in Britain.

the advantage that the two-party system on the whole makes it more likely that the electorate, and its representatives, will be confronted with real and not utopian alternatives, and that there will be some genuine difference of approach between the contenders for office. Both are conducive to stable and mature government.

The critic's case would be more acceptable if the party struggle existed in a political vacuum. Through Parliament, the press, books, radio, television, public meetings, and demonstrations the political debate in Britain is continuous. By-elections are liable to take place at any time. Pressure groups of all kinds do not hibernate between elections. By all these means governments and parties are made aware of public reactions to their policies and actions. The process of selecting party leaders and formulating party policies reflects these influences at all times. Indeed, the parties are themselves the continual battlegrounds for almost every conceivable kind of ideological, tactical, group, and personal conflict. General elections are thus the occasion for a choice between alternatives that have already been shaped by the complicated interaction that helps to make up "public opinion."

Elections are, probably, the most important components of the democratic process, in that the possibility of losing an election is the most effective constitutional sanction upon governments and the main spur to opposition parties to heed public opinion. But in Britain account must also be taken of the continuous and direct confrontation of the two major parties that ensures that governments shall receive both organized support and organized opposition, and that Parliament and the electorate shall be presented with the continuous choice between *this* existing government and *that* alternative government. Such a system is democratic both in the sense that it reserves to the electors the ultimate power to accept and reject governments and in the sense that each party is forced by the competing attractions of the other party to heed the wishes of the governed.

There are dangers inherent in the British system, but the possibility that freedom and choice will be obliterated or emasculated by a two-party "dictatorship" is not among the more serious ones:

or, at least, not in the sense that the parties will ignore any important stream of public opinion. A more serious danger is that both may fail to raise awkward problems for fear that the other will make electoral capital therefrom—as, it may be argued, both major parties long failed to grasp the nettle of Britain's relations with the rest of Europe or to insist that consumption rather than investment bear the brunt of temporary economic sacrifice. It may be that the great weakness, as well as the great strength, of the system resides in the fact that the quality of government and its responsiveness to public attitudes depend upon the nature and existence of an alternative government at any given time. The weakness of the Labour party after 1931 (qualitatively as well as quantitatively) and, indeed, the divisions and weaknesses among the parties opposed to Conservative rule throughout the interwar period, must bear much of the responsibility for the failings of British governments in those years.

The British system, broadly speaking, is also an adaptable system, as was demonstrated by its capacity to meet the different but equally testing requirements both of waging World War II and, after 1945, of simultaneously reconverting the economy to more peaceful purposes and carrying through Labour's extensive program of social reform. In the 1960s, too, began a process of further adaptation within both Parliament and the administration, as we have seen. Characteristically, too, the process has been tentative, slow enough to be most easily discernible in retrospect, and founded on existing structures and procedures.

There is no reason to think that the process will be very different in the future despite the establishment, in 1969, of the (Crowther) Commission on the Constitution with the primary task of examining "the present functions of the central legislature and government in relation to the several countries nations and regions of the United Kingdom" (to quote from its terms of reference)—the Welsh and Scottish offices and the regional planning machinery have already laid foundations for even a fairly radical devolution of central power and an extension of the electoral principle to the regional or provincial levels. The system is likely to continue to be stable without being static.

An important element making for its stability is, of course, the existence of the numerous formal, semiformal, and informal links between government and the principal established groups within the economy and society as a whole. The importance of these links is widely appreciated, or possibly exaggerated, in popular references to "The Establishment," or in questions about who really governs the country,[4] neither of which are the monopoly of any particular political viewpoint. In a relatively compact and integrated society like the British, it is comparatively easy for people in the world of government, or education, or trade unions, or any other particular "world," to know about each other and even to become acquainted. It is also comparatively easy for the "top people" in all the worlds important for politics to become similarly related, assisted in many cases by a common background and education, but often brought together merely by their concern with government and administration.

Even where the common background is lacking, moreover, the weight of tradition and contact with others (particularly with the civil service, it may be surmised) appears to educate newcomers to ruling circles in established ways of doing business. Through the existence of these ruling circles—and this is what matters in our present context—the opinions and desires of government and of the major social interests become known to each other naturally, as it were, with obvious gains both to the government and to the interests and with a consequent strengthening of the whole political system. Moreover, for the most part this aspect of the system seems to be acceptable to the British people today. As one percipient American observer has put it: "by long tradition, England (sic) is a country that is 'run' and expects to be run, unlike America which 'goes.' "[5]

It is tempting, and not uncommon, to conclude that Britain is

[4] See, for example, the very interesting special number of *The Twentieth Century* (October 1957), entitled "Who Governs Britain?" for a series of different answers to this question, and A. Sampson, *The Anatomy of Britain Today* (London: Hodder and Stoughton, 1965).

[5] Marjorie Bremner, "Noblesse Oblige," in the special number of *The Twentieth Century* cited above, pp. 391–400. The emphasis is in the original.

ruled by an oligarchy of powerful men. It is certainly true that the doors into the corridors of power open most readily to those with wealth, or with the proper social and educational backgrounds, and that many of the adjacent rooms communicate with one another. But to change the metaphor, the ruling circles are by no means closed to all but rich public-school boys of middle- or upper-class origin. For this and other reasons it is misleading to talk without qualification of a "ruling class," which may imply that all rulers are drawn from the one social class.

Clearly, however, there are some who normally, and even without holding formal political office, have a much greater say in ruling than do others. When attention is focused on this fact in conjunction with the confidential style of consultation and decision-making that accompanies office both inside and outside government, it is not to be wondered at that up to two-thirds of respondents to an opinion poll felt they had "not enough say in the way the Government runs the country," or in which other national institutions behave, or that most working-class voters are dissatisfied with the degree of influence they feel they possess over the decisions of government (particularly in comparison with business and trade unions).[6] Among the younger age groups, and especially among "unrestful" students, such feelings are the most marked and, on occasion, the most violent, as well as leading, in the case of a small but vocal minority, to the most complete rejection of "the system." [7]

[6] See the results of a Gallup Poll, 1968, quoted in A. Barker and M. Rush, *The Member of Parliament and His Information* (London: Allen and Unwin, 1970), p. 171; and E. A. Nordlinger, *The Working Class Tories* (London: MacGibbon and Kee, 1967), Chapter 4. But cf D. Butler and D. Stokes, *Political Change in Britain* (London: Macmillan, 1969), p. 32, for a more ambivalent response.

[7] This minority has not been as violent (or as violently treated) as in e.g. France and the United States, but it is clearly only the local manifestation of an international phenomenon. Its nature and beliefs were clearly foreshadowed by the actions and attitudes of many members of the campaign for nuclear disarmament in the period 1958–62; see the fascinating study, F. Parkin, *Middle Class Radicalism* (Manchester: Manchester University Press, 1968), especially pp. 33–59 and 140–74.

POLITICAL PARTICIPATION

	United Kingdom	*United States*
Electorate	35,900,000 ⎫1964	c. 120,000,000 ⎫1968
Voted	77.1% ⎭	61% ⎭
Followed course of campaign	92%[1]	—
Not much or at all interested in politics	men 33%[1] women 60%	30%[3]
Identify with a political party	90%[1]	75%[3]
Regularly read political section of newspapers	56%[4]	44%(1960)
Member of at least one association (including trade unions)	47%[2]	57%[2]
Attended election meetings	8%[1]	7%[2]
Active in election campaign	3%[1]	13%[3]
Individual party member	c. 9%	—
Can name four or more party leaders	42%[2]	65%[2]
Could not name even one leader or ministry	13%[2]	13%[2]
Never talk politics with other people	29%[2]	24%[2]
Capable of using simplest programmatic concepts (right/left; conservative/liberal in United States)	16%[1]	15%[3]
"Ideologues" (have *system* of political beliefs)	2%[1]	c. 3%[3]

POLITICAL PARTICIPATION (*cont.*)

	United Kingdom	*United States*
Leaders (in government, civil service, industry, trade unions and other major pressure groups)	c. 5,000[5]	
Almost completely non-participating (est.)	20–30%	30+%

SOURCES: [1] D. Butler and D. Stokes, *Political Change in Britain* (data for 1964).
[2] G. Almond and S. Verba, *The Civic Culture* (data for 1959/60).
[3] A. Campbell and others, *The American Voter* (data for 1956).
[4] R. S. Milne and H. C. Mackenzie, *Marginal Seat* (data for 1955).
[5] W. L. Guttsman, *The British Political Elite*.

The fact of adaptation must therefore be appraised in association with the growth, during the late sixties, of more disaffection than has been observable since the unemployment marches of the thirties or the turbulence of the years immediately preceding World War I. It remains to be seen whether this disaffection will grow, whether and to what extent it will continue to provoke a "reaction" in favor of "discipline, law, and order" (the common conservative cry in defense of a threatened *status quo*), or to what extent radical protest can be canalized through the Labour party or some other political structure.

The substance of the radical critique also deserves brief comment. Like almost all British protest movements, this one attracts upper-class supporters and spokesmen, just as most established leaders and spokesmen have staunch lower-class followers. Neither power nor protest is the monopoly of a single class. More important, perhaps, is the fact, illustrated in the accompanying table of participation, that there is no single sharp cutoff point between politically active rulers and politically passive ruled. Finally, it remains true that the British political stage contains a plurality of actors, including the electorate, political parties, pressure groups, informed or special publics, and bureaucrats; that debate remains legally and politically free to a remarkable extent; and that there is a continuing tension between the democratic forces pressing for extended opportunities in a system of open politics and the fact of unequal power. As a result the "oligarchy" is not a single class, united in policy and tightly circumscribed, and its influence is not unchallenged. From this situation, as we have suggested before, comes much of the flavor of British politics.

Since the eighteenth century the British constitution has been an object of particular interest both to students and practitioners of government. One reason has been simply that during this time the policies of British governments have been of great importance to the world. More important, probably, has been the fact that to many people abroad, the institutional arrangements of British government seemed to contain some special recipe for combining freedom and order, either or both of which had too often been absent in their own countries. To this day it is not impossible to find overseas students of the constitution whose writings betray envy as well as intellectual curiosity.[8] At the same time British writers have not allowed undue national modesty to inhibit their own expressions of praise and approval. But is there any reason that a modern student of politics should pay particular heed to the British system? [9]

Government in Britain, it may be argued, has certain points of inherent interest to any student of politics. They have already been described and discussed in this and earlier chapters, but some of the main ones may be listed again. They include: the particularly vital relationship between constitutional law and the

[8] As two examples from many, ancient and modern, one might cite two books by French authors: Montesquieu's classic *Esprit des Lois,* first published in 1748, and a more recent laudatory account, A. Mathiot, *The British Political System* (Stanford, Calif.: Stanford University Press, 1958).

[9] Someone who has just devoted a good deal of time to writing about the system, particularly if he is British, is perhaps the last person to give a disinterested answer to this question. Nevertheless, one must be suggested.

conventions, and their continuing mutual influence as the constitutional structure is adapted to changing circumstances;[10] the essential role of the party system in determining the evolution and working of the constitution; the development, closely related to the party system, of the concept of a governmental dialogue between the government and the loyal opposition; the combination of a concentration of governing authority with a wide diffusion of political freedom and the right to participate; the combination of stable government with the right of a mass electorate to pass effective judgment upon the government; the association of strong party government with a permanent professional administration and an independent judiciary; the comparative security of individual liberties despite the absence of any "bill of rights"; and the way in which all these have reflected and sustained the continuing tensions between political democracy and social oligarchy (or at least hierarchy). These characteristics of the system all represent distinctive answers to perennial problems. They may not be the only answers, nor ones acceptable to all people, nor are they necessarily unique—but they are answers that have demonstrated a notable capacity to survive and to satisfy.

Another major point of interest about the British system is that many of these answers have been exported or copied, and therefore have been tested or are in process of being tested in widely differing conditions. In some degree the British system of government has inspired many constitutions in Europe throughout the nineteenth (particularly) and twentieth centuries—many of which have long since perished; it has been transplanted to the older, European-ruled, independent members of the Commonwealth, to unitary states like New Zealand as well as to federations in Australia and Canada; and it has provided at least the initial constitutional means whereby independent power has been wielded in the other formerly dependent territories of Britain's colonial empire.

Above all, perhaps, Britain presents one of the relatively few

[10] For a fuller discussion of this point see G. Marshall and G. C. Moodie, *Some Problems of the Constitution* (London: Hutchinson, 1959), Chapter 2, and the references cited there.

examples of a country that has played an important role in world affairs, and has done so, moreover, under a system of free representative government that has shown a rare capacity for survival without resort to domestic repression or violence on any significant scale. As such it is of interest to any theorist of stable and democratic politics, and its future developments are likely still to furnish relevant material. To conclude this survey, therefore, let us look briefly at some of the enduring problems or questions that seem likely continually to be posed by and about government in Britain.

Attention has already been called to the plurality of actors on the political stage. Simply to label the system "pluralist" is, however, to miss the plot of the story. For what exists in Britain is a *structured* pluralism, not a random collection of interacting characters, and one whose shape derives, speaking very broadly, from three elements.

The first element is the social and economic structure. This structure describes the important political resources (sources of power) in society, who controls them, and what informal channels of access exist between them and the formal decision-makers. Of particular significance are the major interests in society, using "interests" in the same, slightly old-fashioned sense that participants in the British and American nineteenth-century debates on suffrage, or the American founding fathers at Philadelphia, talked of the landed, or commercial, interests and, for example, insisted that government must represent these different interests and not mere numbers. Such interests lend structure to political life in that, even if unorganized, they cannot safely be ignored by any government. Even more than that, they form bases for the formation and cooperation of the most powerful pressure groups and, since pressure-group action alone is sufficient only for some purposes, for the formation and nourishment of the significant political parties.[11]

---

[11] A major part of the story of the decline of the Liberal party was its steady loss of an interest base distinct from the Conservatives—from the late nineteenth century on, the Conservatives gained increasing support from the industrial and commercial interests who hitherto had been almost exclusively Liberal—and its failure to retain or fully

By 1970 no other interest had risen, not even the technocrats or the "salariat," to rival the dual hegemony of organized capital and organized labor.

The second major structuring element is the political culture, the predominant beliefs and attitudes that underlie people's perceptions and evaluations of political issues, events, and actors. Among those which seem particularly important in British life are mutual trust, confidence in the fairness of officials, a significant faith in the citizen's own political effectiveness, an awareness and partial acceptance of stratification, a fairly widespread pride in the country's political arrangements, and an orientation toward authority that combines, to use Nordlinger's terminology, both directive and acquiescent attitudes.[12] By 1970 there were, as we have already suggested, signs of lessening acquiescence toward authority (particularly, but by no means only, among the younger generations), and a greater tendency to judge authority by results, i.e., to adopt an instrumental approach rather than to feel either deferential to, or a sense of solidarity with, those in authority. But it had by no means reached the point of incipient revolt or large-scale disaffection—partly, it may be, because of the sense of change in progress at the governmental level, and perhaps also because of the changes in the more personal branches of the law. (These last relationships are highly speculative, but it seems unlikely that the relaxation in the sixties of the laws on homosexuality, divorce, abortion, and obscenity that has alarmed some at the spread of "permissiveness" has not done something to reconcile others.) Most important, however, is the fact that although certain clusterings of attitudes, deviant and otherwise, may be found in particular groups or subsections of society, the cleavages

to gain the support of the expanding trade union and industrial labor interest.

[12] See the survey results reported in, among others, Butler and Stokes, op. cit.; Almond and Verba, op. cit.; E. A. Nordlinger, op. cit.; R. T. McKenzie and A. Silver, *Angels in Marble: Working Class Conservatives in Urban England* (London: Heinemann, 1968); F. Parkin, op. cit.; and J. H. Goldthorpe and others, *The Affluent Worker: Political Attitudes and Behaviour* (Cambridge: Cambridge University Press, 1968).

are not fully cumulative.[13] The political culture lends structure to political life not only to the extent that it embodies many of the standards of judgment and criteria of legitimacy, but also, for example, in that it helps define the ways in which members of the major interests see themselves and their role in society as well as the ways in which they are seen.

The last major structuring element is, of course, the formal system of government itself, the constitution in its widest sense. The way all political actors behave is inevitably shaped by the official decision-making procedures of any working constitution, if only because these procedures help to define who is to take part, and how; which are the useful "pressure-points" within the system, and to whom they are most accessible; what broadly, are the permissible and effective political strategies; and how competent will the government be.

These elements are not independent of one another or of the particular cast of actors at any given time; nor are they reducible to any one of these factors. One cannot explain or understand British, or any other, politics or history solely in terms of its beliefs, its socio-economic organization, its constitution, or the groups and individuals involved; one can only do so in terms of the continuing and shifting interactions between them. Only thus can one even begin to answer the basic question to be asked of any political system: "Under what set(s) of circumstances does who have the power to do what, and how?" [14] The most important and interesting problems and issues facing Britain, it follows, are those affecting the terms and nature of these continuing interactions.

"The crucial issue in modern capitalist planning, which is the relationship between public power and private enterprise, remains open and undecided in the British case." This was written in 1965,[15] but remained true five years later. It will probably con-

[13] See Chapter 3.

[14] This general political stance can only be stated dogmatically—this is not the place in which to argue it at the length that would be required.

[15] By Andrew Shonfield in his *Modern Capitalism: The Changing Balance of Public and Private Power* (London: Oxford University Press, 1965), p. 173.

tinue both to be undecided and to be an issue, if only because it is not a difficult technical, economic, and organizational problem alone, but also one vitally intertwined with all three of our structural elements. This is even more obviously so if one includes the trade union movement on the "private" side of the relationship and the general public on the other side.[16] In one form or another this will, indeed, be the central problem of domestic politics. What remains unpredictable is whether the shifting attitude toward established authority will spread, thus shifting the whole balance of the political culture; whether, then, it will breed increasing disorder and a victorious reaction thereto or, instead, will find constructive outlet in an intensified move further to adjust the balance between government and private power; whether the response of those in power to such phenomena as unofficial strikes, student unrest, and disruptive demonstrations will be a combination of more competent management with more open and shared decision-making, in government and in the other major social and economic institutions, or (possibly aided by the general intolerance associated with racial politics) a move toward tougher and more disciplinary government. These are the major domestic questions of the seventies.

How they are answered will not be purely a domestic matter, however. The outcome will depend as much on the state of the world economy, the policies and development of the European Economic Community (only slightly more if Britain is a member than if it is not), and the avoidance of a major war as it will on the results of British elections, of the national dialogue between government and opposition (both official and unofficial), and the tension between oligarchy and democracy.

The problems facing Britain are unique only in their specific context and presentation; otherwise they are widely familiar. In tackling them, however, Britain has certain strengths in its history

[16] We are not overlooking the fact that both the managers of private enterprises and the unions are members of the general public, nor that on some questions they may be allies against the consuming public; such interlacing "opponents" and such ambiguities are both the bane and the glory of self-government.

of relatively peaceful change and in its apparently well-rooted system of representative government. That the system falls far short of any democratic ideal and is vulnerable in its operations is undeniable,[17] but it nevertheless contains echoes of that ideal. Its attempts to deal with the new and conflicting pressures and demands may fail—although the chance of success seems as good as they are elsewhere. But a Briton may be pardoned for believing (still) that not only by way of awful example will his country continue to interest seekers after social and political sanity as well as knowledge.

[17] This theme is developed further and in a different context in G. C. Moodie and G. Studdert-Kennedy, *Opinions, Publics and Pressure Groups* (London: Allen and Unwin, 1970).

Bibliographical Guide

This guide is designed to indicate some general sources in which the principal topics discussed in this book may be followed up. It is highly selective, the emphasis being placed on more recent publications and on those books that offer ideas and perspectives as well as information. The list that follows does not, therefore, entirely duplicate the sources already cited in footnotes. Note that HMSO is used throughout as the standard abbreviation for Her Majesty's Stationery Office.

REFERENCE

Britain: An Official Handbook (London: HMSO, published annually).

Butler, D., and J. Freeman, *British Political Facts 1900–1968* (London: Macmillan, 1969).

The Political Companion (Glasgow: Political Reference Publications, quarterly since October 1969).

Whitaker's Almanack (London: Joseph Whitaker, published annually).

HISTORY

Chrimes, S. B., *English Constitutional History* (London: Oxford University Press, 1965).

Costin, W. C., and J. S. Watson, *The Law and Working of the Constitution: Documents 1660–1914,* 2 vols. (London: A. & C. Black, 1961–64).

Keir, D. L., *The Constitutional History of Modern Britain* (London: A. & C. Black, 1964).

Le May, G. H., *British Government 1914–53: Select Documents* (London: Methuen, 1954).

Marsh, D. C., *The Changing Social Structure of England and Wales 1871–1961* (London: Routledge and Kegan Paul, 1965).

Parris, H., *Constitutional Bureaucracy* (London: Allen and Unwin, 1969).

Taylor, A. J. P., *English History 1914–45* (London: Oxford University Press, 1965).

Youngson, A. J., *The British Economy 1920–57* (London: Allen and Unwin, 1960).

THE CONSTITUTION AND SYSTEM OF GOVERNMENT

GENERAL

Bagehot, W., *The English Constitution* (London: Fontana, 1963).

Bassett, R., *The Essentials of Parliamentary Democracy* (London: Cass, 1964).

Birch, A. H., *Representative and Responsible Government* (London: Allen and Unwin, 1964).

Jennings, Sir I., *The Law and the Constitution* (London: London University Press, 1959).

Marshall, G., and G. C. Moodie, *Some Problems of the Constitution*, 4th ed. (London: Hutchinson, 1967).

Mitchell, J. D. B., *Constitutional Law* (Edinburgh: Green, 1964).

PARLIAMENT

Barker, A., and M. Rush, *The Member of Parliament and His Information* (London: Allen and Unwin, 1970).

Bromhead, P. A., *The House of Lords in Contemporary Politics* (London: Routledge and Kegan Paul, 1958).

Butt, R., *The Power of Parliament* (London: Constable, 1967).

Coombes, D., *The MP and the Administration* (London: Allen and Unwin, 1966).

Crick, B., *The Reform of Parliament* (London: Weidenfeld and Nicolson, 1964).

Hanson, A. H., *Parliament and Public Ownership* (London: Cassell, 1962).

————, and B. Crick, *The Commons in Transition* (London: Fontana/Collins, 1970).

————, and H. V. Wiseman, *Parliament at Work* (London: Stevens, 1962).

Jackson, R. J., *Rebels and Whips* (London: Macmillan, 1968).

Johnson, N., *Parliament and Administration* (London: Allen and Unwin, 1966).

Reid, G., *The Politics of Financial Control* (London: Hutchinson, 1967).

Richards, P. G., *Honourable Members,* 2d ed. (London: Faber, 1964).

Walkland, S. A., *The Legislative Process in Great Britain* (London: Allen and Unwin, 1968).

Wiseman, H. V., ed., *Parliament and the Executive* (London: Routledge and Kegan Paul, 1966).

CABINET AND PRIME MINISTER

Carter, B. E., *The Office of Prime Minister* (London: Faber, 1956).

Daalder, H., *Cabinet Reform in Britain 1914–63* (London: Oxford University Press, 1964).

Jennings, Sir I., *Cabinet Government,* 3d ed. (Cambridge: Cambridge University Press, 1959).

King, A., ed., *The British Prime Minister* (London: Macmillan, 1969).

Mackintosh, J. P., *The British Cabinet,* 2d ed. (London: Stevens and Methuen, 1968).

CIVIL SERVICE AND ADMINISTRATION

Bray, J., *Decision in Government* (London: Gollancz, 1970).

Chapman, B., *The Profession of Government* (London: Allen and Unwin, 1959).

Chester, D. N., and F. M. G. Willson, *The Organisation of British Central Government 1914–64* (London: Allen and Unwin, 1968).

Finer, S. E., *A Primer of Public Administration* (London: Muller, 1961).

Grove, J. W., *Government and Industry* (London: Longman, 1962).

Hanson, A. H., ed., *Nationalisation: A Book of Readings* (London: Allen and Unwin, 1963).

Jackson, W. E., *Local Government in England and Wales* (Harmondsworth: Penguin Books, 1959).

Mackintosh, J. P., *The Devolution of Power: Local Democracy, Regionalism and Nationalism* (Harmondsworth: Penguin Books, 1968).

Ridley, F. F., *Specialists and Generalists* (London: Allen and Unwin, 1968).

Robson, W. A., *Local Government in Crisis* (London: Allen and Unwin, 1966).

Sisson, C. H., *The Spirit of Public Administration and some European Comparisons* (London: Faber, 1966).

THE LAW

Allen, Sir C. K., *Law in the Making* (London: Oxford University Press, 1951).

———, *Law and Orders* (London: Stevens, 1965).

Griffith, J. H. G., and H. Street, *Principles of Administrative Law*, 3d ed. (London: Pitman, 1967).

Hamson, C. J., *Executive Discretion and Judicial Control* (London: Stevens, 1954).

Jackson, R. M., *The Machinery of Justice in England* (Cambridge: Cambridge University Press, 1960).

Marshall, G., *Police and Government* (London: Methuen, 1965).

POLITICAL ACTION

PARTIES AND ELECTIONS

Beer, S. H., *Modern British Politics* (London: Faber, 1965).

Butler, D. E., *The British Electoral System Since 1918* (London: Oxford University Press, 1963).

Harrison, M., *Trade Unions and the Labour Party Since 1945* (London: Allen and Unwin, 1960).

Hoffman, J. D., *The Conservative Party in Opposition 1945–51* (London: MacGibbon and Kee, 1964).

McKenzie, R. T., *British Political Parties*, 2d ed. (London: Heinemann, 1963).

Rasmusson, J., *The Liberal Party: A Study of Retrenchment and Revival* (London: Constable, 1965).

Rush, M., *The Selection of Parliamentary Candidates* (London: Nelson, 1969).

VOTING

Blumler, J. G., and D. McQuail, *Television in Politics: Its Uses and Influence* (London: Faber, 1968).

Butler, D. E., and D. Stokes, *Political Change in Britain: Forces Shaping Electoral Choice* (London: Macmillan, 1969).

McKenzie, R. T., and A. Silver, *Angels in Marble: Working Class Conservatives in Urban England* (London: Heinemann, 1968)

Milne, R. S., and H. C. Mackenzie, *Marginal Seat* (London: Hansard Society, 1958).

Nordlinger, E. A., *Working Class Tories* (London: MacGibbon and Kee, 1967).

Pulzer, P. G. J., *Political Representation and Elections in Britain* (London: Allen and Unwin, 1967).

PRESSURE GROUPS

Finer, S. E., *Anonymous Empire*, 2d ed. (London: Pall Mall, 1965).

———, *Private Industry and Political Power* (London: Pall Mall, 1958).

Stewart, J. P. D., *British Pressure Groups* (London: Oxford University Press, 1958).

CASE STUDIES

Barnett, M. J., *The Politics of Legislation: The Rent Act of 1957* (London: Weidenfeld and Nicolson, 1969).

Eckstein, H., *Pressure Group Politics: The Case of the British Medical Association* (London: Allen and Unwin, 1960).

Parkin, F., *Middle Class Radicalism* (Manchester: Manchester University Press, 1968).

Rhodes, G., *Administrators in Action* (London: Allen and Unwin, 1965).

Rose, R., ed., *Policy Making in Britain* (London: Macmillan, 1969).

Wilson, H. H., *Pressure Group: The Campaign for Commercial Television* (London: Secker and Warburg, 1961).

Memoirs, Biographies, and Autobiographies of Monarchs and Politicians

ECONOMIC POLICY

Brittan, S., *The Treasury under the Tories 1951–64* (Harmondsworth: Penguin Books, 1964).

Caves, R., *Britain's Economic Prospects* (London: Allen and Unwin, 1968).

Hutchinson, T. W., *Economics and Economic Policy in Britain 1946–66* (London: Allen and Unwin, 1968).

Rogow, A. A., *The Labour Government and Private Industry 1945–51* (Oxford: Basil Blackwell, 1955).

Shonfield, A., *Modern Capitalism: The Changing Balance of Public and Private Power* (London: Oxford University Press, 1965).

FOREIGN POLICY

Northedge, F. S., *British Foreign Policy: The Process of Readjustment 1945–61* (London: Allen and Unwin, 1962).

Vital, D., *The Making of British Foreign Policy* (London: Allen and Unwin, 1968).

POLITICS AND SOCIETY

Guttsman, W. L., *The British Political Elite* (London: MacGibbon and Kee, 1963).

Milliband, R., *The State in Capitalist Society: An Analysis of the Western System of Power* (London: Weidenfeld and Nicolson, 1969).

Moodie, G. C., and G. Studdert-Kennedy, *Opinions, Publics, and Pressure Groups* (London: Allen and Unwin, 1970).

Rose, R., ed., *Studies in British Politics* (London: Macmillan, 1966).

Runciman, W. G., *Relative Deprivation and Social Justice: A Study of Attitudes to Social Inequality in Twentieth Century England* (London: Routledge and Kegan Paul, 1966).

OTHER SOURCES

The principal British periodicals dealing with government and politics are:

The British Journal of Political Science

The British Journal of Sociology

Government and Opposition

Parliamentary Affairs (journal of the Hansard Society)

The Political Quarterly

Political Studies (journal of the Political Studies Association of the United Kingdom)

Public Administration (journal of the Royal Institute for Public Administration)

Public Law

The more serious British monthly and weekly journals and national newspapers also carry much relevant descriptive and analytical material.

For information about, comment on, and proposals for action about current problems and issues, the following are virtually indispensable:

The annual *Reports* to Parliament of ministries, nationalized industries, Parliamentary committees, etc. (London: HMSO).

Reports of royal commissions and other government committees (London: HMSO).

The monthly pamphlets of the Fabian Society, London.

All the books listed include additional references.

Index